Launching Our Black Children for Success

Joyce A. Ladner, Ph.D., with
Theresa Foy DiGeronimo, M.Ed.

Foreword by Alvin F. Poussaint, M.D.

Launching Our Black Children for Success

A Guide for Parents of Kids
from Three to Eighteen

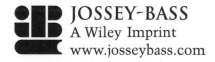

JOSSEY-BASS
A Wiley Imprint
www.josseybass.com

Published by Jossey-Bass
A Wiley Imprint
989 Market Street, San Francisco, CA 94103-1741   www.josseybass.com

Jossey-Bass books and products are available through most bookstores. To contact Jossey-
Bass directly call our Customer Care Department within the U.S. at 800-956-7739, outside
the U.S. at 317-572-3986, or fax 317-572-4002.

Jossey-Bass also publishes its books in a variety of electronic formats. Some content that
appears in print may not be available in electronic books.

Readers should be aware that Internet Web sites offered as citations and/or sources for further information may have changed or disappeared between when this book was written
and when it is read.

Excerpt in Chapter Five from *Teach Your Child to Behave* reprinted with permission. © 1990
Charles Schaefer and Theresa DiGeronimo.

Web site material in Chapter Six used with permission of National Crime Prevention
Council.

Excerpt in Chapter Eight from *Is Youth Violence Just Another Fact of Life?* © 2003 by the
American Psychological Association. Reprinted with permission.

Library of Congress Cataloging-in-Publication Data

Ladner, Joyce A.
    Launching our Black children for success : a guide for parents of kids from three to
eighteen / Joyce A. Ladner with Theresa Foy DiGeronimo ; foreword by Alvin F. Poussaint.
        p. cm.
    Includes bibliographical references and index.
    ISBN 0-7879-6488-3 (alk. paper)
    1. Success in children. 2. Success in adolescence. 3. African American children—
Psychology. 4. African American teenagers—Psychology. 5. Child rearing.
I. DiGeronimo, Theresa Foy. II. Title.
BF723.S77 L33 2003
649'.15796073—dc21   2003000400

Printed in the United States of America
FIRST EDITION
PB Printing   10 9 8 7 6 5 4 3 2 1

Contents

Foreword   ix
   Alvin F. Poussaint, M.D.

Acknowledgments   xv

Introduction   1

 1. Know Thyself   5

 2. How Well Do You Know Your Child?   27

 3. Building Strong Identity and
    Positive Self-Esteem   43

 4. Family Values   59

 5. The Power of Discipline: Its Use and Abuse   87

 6. Countering Negative Media and Peer Groups   107

 7. Education: They Can't Take It Away from You   123

 8. Drugs and Violence: No Place to Hide   147

 9. Raising Sons and Daughters: Gender
    Differences   175

10. Role Models: How to Find and Use Them   195

11. College Preparation, Application,
    and Selection   215

12. Coping Skills: The Key to Survival   243

Helpful Resources 257

Notes 263

Further Reading 269

About the Authors 271

Index 273

Foreword

As an African American parent of a twenty-four-year-old son and a young daughter, I have had the opportunity to reflect over more than a twenty-year span on the unique responsibilities of being a black parent. In the past half century, significant improvements have occurred in race relations, but conditions have not yet progressed to the point that white racism is irrelevant.

In *Launching Our Black Children for Success,* Dr. Joyce Ladner provides invaluable guidance on raising healthy and productive children within the context of the black experience in the United States. The author balances her discussion of the hurtful legacies of slavery and discrimination with common sense: "Hammering children over the head with the horrors of racism does not help them cope, yet hiding the facts of racism does not help them either. I believe the best approach is somewhere in the middle."

Dr. Ladner wisely emphasizes the key role that good parenting plays in rearing strong and resilient black children. In this illuminating book, she discusses parenting and child development issues in the framework of the real world. Given their social and economic circumstances, most black parents do an excellent job of child rearing.

A number of crucial elements are necessary for children's healthy psychological development; parental action or inaction in these areas determines how a youngster will mature.

From the beginning growing children require love, protective care, and emotional support from all members of their immediate family. Children's first ideas of themselves as persons depend upon the responses of others. They will feel they are good people when relationships with important people—parents, caregivers, grandparents, and relatives—around them are substantial. Early positive feelings help children learn and master tasks. Each success makes it easier to continue learning and exploring despite occasional setbacks. In time the child develops an inner sense that affirms: *I am an able person. I am a good person.*

This volume details how a parental emphasis on the development of both physical and intellectual skills in their children is vitally important. A positive sense of self is very closely linked with feelings of competence. Children who are taught to master their environment have a greater sense of empowerment. Those who feel in control of their fate are less susceptible to feelings of inferiority. Many black children have survived the hardships of poor environments because their parents raised them to be independent and self-reliant. Teaching children mastery of knowledge and skills also involves teaching them control and discipline in a balanced fashion without relying on the destructive use of corporal punishment.

Dr. Ladner emphasizes that the consequences of being part of an oppressed racial group can be offset by a strong feeling of self-worth established in the home. Later, racial pride (but not chauvinism) is an important aspect of a child's self-concept, accompanied by self-respect. In order for black children to develop a healthy image, their caregivers must display both self-respect and racial pride in their own lives. In addition, African American parents must be vigilant in protecting their children against racism from teachers, law enforcers, store owners, neighbors, and other children. A prime example is the racial profiling that occurs far too often, particularly in the criminal justice system. Wherever possible, parents should strive to eliminate racism in institutions outside the home that affect their youngsters.

Schools, for instance, have a profound influence on a child's perception of self. Teachers play an important role in the formation of student confidence. Studies have suggested that children's belief about their capabilities in school are related to their perception of teacher expectations. Social scientists have found that when teachers believe black students are inferior, they may behave as if these students cannot learn. African American children overwhelmed by such negative expectations frequently lose the motivation to succeed.

Dr. Ladner also describes how a child's sense of self is influenced by how he or she views the surrounding environment—both directly and through various media outlets. The powerful influence of television and films often requires parental guidance. Even a child in a strong family may develop self-doubt as a result of living in the midst of poverty and social disorganization. A poor child watching television may not see wholesome representations of his or her community and may develop the notion that he or she does not count in our society. Such a child may look around at deteriorated housing, roaches, and rodents and decide that the people who really count live in the upper-class homes shown on television.

As this book emphatically states, black parents must expose their little ones to their inspiring heritage. Black children should be given a sense of history, of how black people began as slaves in this country and have steadily improved and raised their social status despite overwhelming discrimination and oppression. Many black youngsters know very little about the civil rights movement and the black leaders, many now dead, who led it. A strong racial identity will lapse if children are not taught about their heritage and given positive examples of strength and success among African American people.

Black children have achieved despite the twin evils of racism and poverty. Some black youngsters, unfortunately, succumb to feelings of inferiority and behave in self-destructive and self-defeating ways. African American parents, besides helping children develop positive attitudes, must teach them to constructively assert themselves when the odds seem stacked against them.

We must remember, however, that every black child with a high level of self-esteem may not be focused on achievement. The all too common example is the child who becomes overconfident, does not put adequate time into his or her work, and founders. Feeling too good about oneself without discipline and a mature assessment of life's realities may lead to a dangerous narcissism and ultimately to failure. As Dr. Ladner outlines, these pitfalls can be avoided if black youngsters in late childhood are taught that they must continue to work hard and strive for excellence. Times are rapidly changing, and the demands on black children will change. Although they will grow up without having to fight for the right to vote and without having to participate in a sit-in at a lunch counter for the right to eat in public places, they will face subtle manifestations of discrimination and benign neglect. Therefore, a good self-concept alone, without political awareness, is not a sufficient goal for African American youth.

As a group blacks are still far from feeling the strong sense of community that we would hope for. To my mind, one of the major manifestations of this lack of mutual caring is the excessive black-on-black crime throughout our urban centers. When we really start loving ourselves, we will stop killing each other and direct our energies toward community building and political change. African American youth who commit violence usually have displaced rage and fragile egos. Black children, especially our boys—who are at high risk for incarceration—need help in understanding and constructively channeling their aggressive impulses. Teaching survival skills as well as achievement skills to black children is still one of the most important tasks black caregivers must confront.

Launching Our Black Children for Success is right on target in emphasizing that parenting black youth requires supporting them at home to develop a strong sense of self-worth while working on their behalf outside of the home to bring about social change to ensure equal opportunity for every African American child. Absorbing the lessons outlined in this important book will greatly contribute to the strengths of black children and their families.

Alvin F. Poussaint, M.D.
Professor of Psychiatry
Harvard Medical School and
Judge Baker Children's Center
Boston, Massachusetts

To all parents who are launching black children for success

Acknowledgments

This book would not have been possible had Alan Rinzler not had the foresight to see the overwhelming need. His long-standing interest in the barriers that prevent young African Americans from succeeding helped bring this book into being. Moreover, I appreciate his hands-on involvement in reading and offering helpful critiques of the chapters as I wrote them.

Theresa DiGeronimo, my collaborator, also made *Launching Our Black Children for Success* possible. It was a joy to work with Theresa, who kept me on track with her prodigious work ethic, strict adherence to deadlines, fine eye for details, and good research. She also has the insights of a great mother.

I would like to thank Charles Schaefer, Ph.D., who kindly and generously contributed his expertise to the chapter on discipline.

I want to thank my sister Dorie Ladner Churnet for discussing every facet of this book with me. Her insights as a social worker were invaluable. My sisters Willa Tate, Billie Collins, and Hazel Mimbs shared important insights and recollections as well. My late mother, Annie Ruth Perryman, taught me more about parenting than she realized. My son, Thomas Ladner Carrington, and my niece, Yodit Churnet, were my "human subjects" when it came to my queries on many aspects of their own growth and development. I am also fortunate to see my nieces and nephews—Tommy, Kanini,

Ayanna, Pamela, and Tonya—use many of the tried-and-true formulas for parenting we were taught.

Over the years, and on this specific project, many members of my family and some of my many friends have contributed enormously to my understanding some of the complex challenges of raising children to become well-brought-up adults and successful workers. I realize that the shortcomings of my memory will cause me to omit more names than I have included. However, I will take the risk of naming some: Kay and Ronald Springwater; Brenda and Courtenay Miller; Jean Smith; Horace and Dessie Garrett; Adah and Richard Pierce; Carol Randolph Jasmine; Dorothy Smith; Gwen and D. E. Magee; Julia Poussaint; Martha Norman-Noonan; Regina Drake; Sharon Harley; Gladys Hall; Arvel and Mildred Greenwood; Del Richardson; Henry and Eleanor Ramsey; Sandra Gregg; Woodrow and Sondra Ladner; Arlene Ackerman; Gerri and Phillip Brookins; Fred and Edna Perryman; Constance Newman; Rose Singfield; Peter and Marian Wright Edelman; Carole Daly; Judith Light; Barbara Vance; Alice Rivlin; Barbra Wiggins-Matthews and Clarence Matthews; Loretha Davis; Hassan Minor; E. J. Dionne; Dianne Kenny; Isabelle Sawhill; Constancia "Dinky" Romilly; Dan Reznick; James Forman; Della Ladner Wilson; Roscoe Dellums; LeDrester and Otis Bullock; Kamili Hemphill-Magee; Dolores Clemmons; Marjay Anderson; Tonya Bolden; Carrie Dailey; Madelyn and Don Coleman; Walter Stafford; Edward and Patricia Singletary; Alfred and Janice Fisher; Vicki Sant; Flower Briscoe; Walter Carrington; Bernice Reagon; Susan Stewart; Gladys Hall; Clarice Walker; Rose and the late Ralph Wooden; Lynn French; Christine Dixon; Alonza Ladner and my late uncle, Thomas Fontaine Ladner; Ann Ashmore Hudson; Ethel Sawyer Adolph; Colbert and Gwen King; Florence and Charles Tate; Ann Robertson; Mildred Dickerson; Amy Billingsley; and many, many others.

I also want to thank the members of the Potomac Chapter of the Links, Inc. My "sister links" are superb mothers who have given me a wealth of knowledge about the straight paths and the bumpy roads in raising black children for success. Our chapter's High Expectations project for girls at Jefferson Junior High in Washington, D.C., has been a national model for launching black girls into success for almost twenty years. Audrey Hinton, Thomasina Costley, and all the other members of the Potomac Chapter of Links, Inc., deserve hearty thanks for showing me what longevity in black children's lives really means.

I am grateful to my many friends at Trinity Episcopal Church who are my extended family. Father John Harmon and Keiva Harmon are exemplary models of black parenting with their three little children. Through the pressures of deadlines and in other times of need, all of my Trinity friends have been extraordinarily supportive.

I have also been blessed to have the support of a dear friend, Bill Thompson, who did everything possible to help me to meet the deadlines—from shopping for groceries to running errands. Thanks, Billy.

Of course, all points of view are my own. It is my hope that parents can use this book to help them to navigate the oftentimes difficult challenges of raising their children. Although the book is written primarily for African American parents, many of the issues discussed here cut across all boundaries and are relevant to non-black parents as well.

Joyce A. Ladner
Washington, D.C.

Launching Our Black Children for Success

Introduction

In launching our black children into the successful and fulfilling lives we all want them to enjoy, we parents know that they face many problems that white children do not—because race most definitely still matters in America. A black person may have two degrees from Harvard and be a wealthy Wall Street investor, but he or she may still be followed around a department store by security staff. It still happens to me! On many occasions, salespeople have followed me closely, asking, "Can I help you?" over and over again, fearing, I suppose, that I'm going to steal a pair of shoes. And in larger life situations, we are still discriminated against in housing, employment, and education. That's why we have to teach our children from the earliest age that skin color does matter—for both good and bad.

As black parents we are always juggling several balls in the air. On the one hand, we're trying to teach our children that if they study hard and are good citizens and human beings, they can have successful careers in all areas of life like so many accomplished blacks before them. On the other hand, we know that because they are black and often stereotyped as lazy, intellectually inferior, and criminally inclined, the road to success for our children will not always be that simple or easy. Because of the color of their skin, internal and external obstacles will block their paths to success if they do not know how to move the obstacle or go around it.

Institutional racism, combined with many social problems, makes parenting a black child an incredibly difficult task. Negative media images, violence, drugs, intractable poverty, unemployment, single parenting, addiction, and HIV-AIDS thwart the ambitions of far too many young black people. They also destroy too many fragile families long before they have had a chance to succeed. These life situations can be more difficult to bear than pre–civil rights segregation. Fewer black men died at the hands of the Ku Klux Klan than are dying today as a result of crime, drugs, and violence. Moreover, too many black parents are outliving their children who have fallen prey to life in the streets. This is an unprecedented occurrence for a people who fought the devastation of slavery and institutionalized racial discrimination and then acquired the legal protection of the law through U.S. congressional legislation that barred discrimination in all areas of public life. No doubt many parents wonder: How could a people who endured and prevailed against this torrid chapter of our history end up with children who kill each other?

Although there are no easy answers and no one-size-fits-all solution to successful parenting of black children during these difficult times, through the long process of working our way from slavery to mainstream acceptance, we have learned something important as parents: anger alone will not help our children flourish in a society that often attempts to diminish them because of their skin color. Anger alone will not teach them how to cope with and to transcend the obstacles that may be placed in their paths. Our task as parents is to be proactive and affirmative by using every tool at our disposal to assist them to grow into healthy, stable, educated, successful, and secure individuals. Throughout this book I will suggest positive parenting skills that will help you do something about the racism that can have lethal effects on your children and can prevent them from becoming healthy, educated, and successful adults.

Traditionally, black parents have taken a very family-oriented, commonsense approach to parenting. Their parenting values and skills were based on tradition passed on through each generation. There was no Dr. Spock guide for parenting black children. (Benjamin Spock's *Baby and Child Care*, first published in 1945, was the standard guide for many middle-class parents.) When I became a parent in 1974, I relied heavily on my own family experiences as the third oldest of nine children. I also relied on an extraordinary woman, Dorothy Smith, who was our child-care provider. As a professional caregiver, she gave me the best on-the-job training I could have hoped for. I learned how to parent by observing my parents in action and helping them. I also relied heavily on the advice my mother and my sisters so freely gave. In those days child rearing was just a matter of knowing my child and doing what common sense, my heart, and my family said was right. I know that's a fuzzy description of a parenting style, but that's what my experience told me was best. It never occurred to me, or to most of the black parents I knew, to consult a book to learn how to be a good parent. But times have changed, and we all know now how much we can find out through reading about the wisdom and experience of many other parents like us.

The old oral tradition of passing down wisdom that is so common in the black community secured a generational bond and a sense of historic culture in many black families. But for all the good this tradition gives us, it also has its drawbacks. Without giving up on family advice and experience, it also is important in these modern times to reach out for other more specialized resources that so many black child-rearing specialists offer us. With so much information available on topics like education, medicine, psychology, equal rights, and career opportunities, minorities should no longer rely solely on oral tradition. To be empowered to help our children navigate their way through the roadblocks of racism and discrimination, we need to know and use the most up-to-date information available.

Moreover, we need to do it continuously. Launching our children on their way to productive and self-fulfilling life paths is not a onetime, sit-down conversation. It is a lifelong, ongoing process. From the moment of birth, your child needs to feel your unconditional love. Your preschooler needs to view the black people in her family as her source of strength, love, and encouragement. Your school-age child needs a sense of self-worth to rely on and black role models to look up to. Your teenager needs coping skills, family values, and support to remain on track to reach the high goals set earlier in life. It is my hope that the composite family stories in this book, which are based on many years of teaching, research, and personal experience, will show you that you can do something at every age to improve the quality of your child's future. May this book add to your family traditions and give you information that will help you raise proud, confident, and successful children.

1

Know Thyself

Do you know yourself? Really? Before you try to help your child find the right life path, it's a good idea to take a close-up look at yourself first. Your beliefs and attitudes, your background and experiences, and your upbringing all play a role in how you guide your children to a successful future.

A personal inventory like the one in this chapter allows you to come to grips with the question: "Who am I?" Not "Who was I reared to be?" but "What happened to me?" and "Who have I become?" It pushes you to ask yourself difficult questions about how your own experiences have affected you, what you believe in, what you want for your children, and what you're prepared to do to help them reach their full potential. These questions will help you more clearly see if you provide them with opportunities or obstacles in their journey to adulthood. To strengthen the foundation of your family support program, use this self-assessment to evaluate your assets and liabilities. You may be surprised to find that you have strengths you didn't realize, as well as areas of weakness that may be holding your children back.

Ask yourself the questions posed in the following five sections before you go on to other chapters. Think about them carefully and honestly. Then, before you let yourself be satisfied that you truly know yourself, get some feedback from others. Talk to your siblings about their recollections. Talk to your spouse or your child's other parent even if you're not living together. Ask your parents and friends to give their opinion. We tend to see ourselves one way, whereas others who know us may not see us that way at all. You might even ask your kids for their thoughts and opinions if they are old enough to have an idea of who you are and where you're coming from. You do not need to sit down with a clipboard and pen, but in casual conversation talk about your upbringing, the special problems and issues that you might have had, your strengths and weaknesses, and your hopes for the future. Finding out if others see you the same way you see yourself can be interesting.

This chapter gives you an introduction to many of the topics that are explored in more detail throughout the book. Find out first where you stand and where you need to go.

Five Sections of Self-Assessment

A look at the past
A personality assessment
A reality check
The bottom line
Looking ahead

A LOOK AT THE PAST

Each one of us is a product of our past, for good or bad. That's why we can't really know who we are today unless we take time to consider where we came from. It is a gift to our children when we make the effort to reach back and celebrate how far we've come. The following questions will help you begin to think about the relationship between your own upbringing and your child's future.

A Look at the Past

- What issues and problems related to race did my parents face when they were growing up?
- In the community where I grew up, what kind of expectations and messages did young blacks receive regarding the potential for education, training, work, and careers?
- Did my family encourage me to work hard and reach high?
- What kind of career coaching did I have when I was growing up?
- What obstacles have I had to overcome in order to achieve my dreams?
- How have things changed from my parents' generation, to my generation, to my children's generation?

What issues and problems related to race did my parents and grandparents face when they were growing up? Because of the civil rights movement, most young black parents today and certainly their children have no idea what living in a segregated society was like. Not many people today remember knowing someone who was actually born a slave. Only some of us may recall a grandfather or great-grandmother who actually lived through that terrible legacy. But that doesn't mean you should shut the book on that page in your family history. That heritage runs through you to your children. If your family members have been closemouthed about their trials and tribulations, ask them to talk to you. Tell them you want to know about the sacrifices they made, the struggles they survived, and the racism they faced. Knowing these things gives you a legacy to pass on to your children that they can honor and respect by conducting their own lives with pride and a sense of responsibility.

This can be an extremely motivating factor in raising black children and inspiring them to reach high in life. Use this information to help your children understand that because their ancestors succeeded with so much less than what is available today, they have an obligation to their legacy to do the best they can. After all, if their grandparents and great-grandparents could prevail against such odds, how can they do any less?

In the community where I grew up, what kind of expectations and messages did young blacks receive regarding the potential for education, training, work, and careers? I was lucky. I grew up in a community where my family and neighbors made me feel that I had a responsibility, a duty, to fulfill the expectations of my rural Mississippi community and my race. I clearly remember one example of how that expectation was communicated.

On report card day, all the mature women in my neighborhood would stop me on my way home to inspect my grades. They gave me a dime for every A I earned, and they always told me that I was going to be somebody when I grew up. It didn't matter that they themselves probably hadn't finished grade school or that I was someone else's daughter. They showed me that they had high hopes for the progress of my generation.

This community interest in the upbringing and ultimate success of its children continues today in many areas. I remember one young man from Milwaukee whom I had the opportunity to know when I was president of Howard University. On the day he was to graduate with a degree in engineering, his mother and father arrived with an entire busload of hometown people. This young man was a community investment made by church members, neighbors, former teachers, and extended family members. They were all there to share in his success.

If, when you think back on the community's influence on your upbringing, you see that there was a history of high expectation and support, you too are one of the lucky ones. You know how important this support was to you, and you're now in a good position to make sure you continue that kind of traditional support system for your child and other children in your neighborhood.

But if you feel that you were not encouraged by your community, you are part of a radical departure from a long-standing black community tradition passed down through the ages. It's time to bridge that gap. Reach back into an earlier time and grab hold of the tradition that was denied you. Even if you did not benefit from the strength of community support, it is not too late to reach out for that legacy. I believe very strongly that an integral part of future success for our black children is in reestablishing a community expectation of achievement.

Did my family encourage me to work hard and reach high? If you grew up knowing that your family expected you to earn good grades in school, graduate, get a good job, and be a self-sufficient contributing member of society, then you know how influential these expectations have been on who you are today. You will very naturally pass on this model of ambition to your own children.

On the other hand, if your family did not place a premium on education and achievement, then you need to think carefully about how this influenced the outcome of your own life. You might wonder if life would be better or different if your parents had sat you down and watched you do your homework each night, if they had punished you for bringing home failing grades, or if they had insisted that you take a college prep program in high school rather than letting you load up on vocational courses.

If your parents were not actively involved in your education and goal setting, you may be letting this fact influence how you raise your own children. Look this situation directly in the face and recognize the need to take a different course with your own children. Tell your children, "Even though I did not have someone to push me or show me the way, I can and will do it for you." If you do not communicate this desire to give your children more than you had, your children may grow up thinking, *My parents didn't go to college, why should I?* or *My mother had her first child when she was sixteen; why shouldn't I?*

Family support for reaching high goals is vital. If you look back and realize that you did not have this advantage, promise yourself that it will not be denied your children.

What kind of career coaching did I have growing up? The answer to this question will help you avoid the negative and repeat the positive of your own upbringing. This question asks you to think back and trace the steps that brought you to where you are today. In some families parents map out a life plan for their offspring without ever asking for the child's input. Did this happen to you? Were you expected to follow in your father's footsteps? Were you expected to uphold a family tradition or meet established expectations whether you wanted to or not?

Other parents leave their children alone to find their own way. Ask yourself: Did you head down a life path without guidance or companionship? Did you have to figure things out for yourself? Did you fall into the first job that came along, without any long-term plans?

Some parents suggest possibilities and then give the children the resources they need to explore each one. Did your parents use your interests and talents to guide your career options? Did they talk to you about your hopes and dreams? Did they encourage you to reach high?

How, if at all, did your family guide you? Examine this part of your upbringing; then pull out the good and leave the bad behind.

What obstacles have I had to overcome in order to achieve my dreams? We all live through various ups and downs that get in the way of our life plans, but try to identify the things that were most difficult for you. Was it lack of money, bad peer influence, weak family support, bad advice, or your own poor attitude or stubbornness? The possibilities are endless. Which ones stand out in your life?

In some instances your greatest obstacle may have been the color of your skin. Before you begin to help your child navigate around the obstacles of racism, think about your own experiences. Being black in a white society may have caused you to be treated unfairly. Maybe you were sometimes the victim of public humiliation or even physical violence. Did the attitude and actions of white people in your life deny you opportunities? Did you ever feel unwelcome or scorned in your own school or community? Have you experienced the degradation of discrimination in housing or employment? Although you may have overcome the problems, that fact doesn't diminish their importance in the big picture of who you are and how you will parent your own children.

Honestly assess how you handled these obstacles. Did you successfully overcome them, or did you fall short? Take time to think about how a situation, person, or event has affected where you are today. Knowing and facing your own life obstacles is the best preparation for steering your children around the same roadblocks in their own lives. If you've been there and recognize your mistakes as well as your triumphs, you will have empathy for your children's difficulties but little tolerance if they try to use them as excuses for not achieving.

How have things changed from my parents' generation, to my generation, to my children's generation? This question is particularly important in black families. Things have changed so dramatically over the last few generations that it's essential to be aware of how these changes affect who you and your children are today. Although black children are now more assimilated into America's mainstream, they still carry the burden of history—the legacy of slavery and the continuing burdens of racism and discrimination. They also owe a debt to the Emancipation Proclamation of 1863 and to the Civil Rights Act of 1964. They should know this.

Take a stroll down memory lane and think about how different your life and your children's lives are from those of previous generations, thanks to the hard work of those who came before you. Pull out stories about your parents and your grandparents and share them with your children. Let them know where they come from and how far they've come. Draw on the strengths of your ancestors that have been passed down to you. What survival skills did they have? How did they take a salary of thirty dollars a week and raise eight children (as my father did)? And be honest about the failings in your family line that you expect your children to avoid or overcome. We now live in a society that does not practice legal discrimination but still harbors vestiges of racism. What in your family history will help you teach your children how to live in this kind of world and still reach their full potential?

A PERSONALITY ASSESSMENT

Your innate personality can influence your parenting skills. Your personality creates a comfort zone around you, dictating what you're likely to do as well as what you may be unwilling to do. The following three questions focus on traits that affect your ability to advocate for your children and make sure they have all the resources and opportunities they need to reach adulthood successfully.

A Personality Assessment

- Do I reach out or keep to myself?
- Do I stand up or sit down when I see a problem?
- Am I self-confident or fearful and anxious about my children and myself?

Do I reach out or keep to myself? To borrow a phrase from Hillary Clinton's book, it does take a village to raise a child. Not even the most educated and accomplished people I know try to raise their children without help. We all need to be proactive in finding the people, the programs, the organizations, and the institutions that can help our children. We need to network with other parents about parenting strategies, school information, the college application process. We need to be active in groups like parent-teacher organizations, church lay ministries, and community boards. Raising your child effectively comes down to who you know, how you can work the system, and how well you hone your networking skills. You can try to go it alone, but a community network out there can give you the advantage—*if* you reach out to it.

This is especially true for black parents. Until thirty or forty years ago, black neighborhoods were very stable, and families shared such information informally. This segregated community formed strong bonds that made sure each child knew what was expected of him or her, and each family knew it could rely on the help of neighbors, church members, and an extended family to guide its children through to adulthood. But as these neighborhoods became integrated and close friends and extended families moved apart, many black families were left proud and independent—but alone. They had to find support beyond the black community.

Black parents now need to get out of the house and use the resources that are available to all Americans. They have a responsibility to their children to hunt down all resources that can help their children. If you have not been making this effort, you need to reexamine your reasons for holding back. Doing this will challenge your comfort level if you have had no experience with outside organizations and programs, but you have an obligation to your children to go beyond what is comfortable and reach out for assistance.

Do I stand up or sit down when I see a problem? Traditionally, black parents have tended to defer to those in a position of authority. In the past the number of professional careers open to blacks were so restricted due to racial discrimination that those with professional ambitions grew up to be preachers, teachers, undertakers, or small-business owners. These people became revered and highly respected figures in the community, and their word wasn't questioned. In some homes today this tradition of passive respect has been passed down, and some black parents still hand over their parental authority and control to those in positions of authority. This is especially so for less-educated parents who still see these people as having more knowledge and wisdom.

Be honest with yourself. Do you simply accept what those in a position of authority say? What would you do or say if a teacher said your child should be left back a year (or even jumped ahead a year)? What would you do if your child were put in a class for learning disabled children? When these and thousands of other questionable events happen in your child's life, what will you do? Will you stand up and get involved to find out all the details and to make sure that the person in authority is considering your child's best interests? Or will you sit back, assuming that those in charge know what they're doing? The choice you make will affect your child for life.

If you expect to be a positive influence on your child's future, you have to stand up and be heard. You have to feel empowered to act on your child's behalf. You have to be able to determine if the person in authority is acting in a positive way on behalf of your children or in a way that exploits them. You can do this only if you give yourself permission to examine and when necessary challenge the views of authority figures. Are you ready to do this?

Am I self-confident or fearful and anxious about my children and myself? Child development experts tell us that if we want our children to be emotionally strong and self-confident, we must model that behavior ourselves. That sounds reasonable and doable—unless you're a black parent. The black community has a long history and sound reasons to be fearful of white authority figures, and it is very difficult and maybe even unwise not to pass this cautious feeling along to our children. The days when a black male in the South would not look a white woman in the eye for fear of losing his life are not far in the past. Many were lynched for the slightest smile, eye movement, or perceived act of boldness. This fear is not easily forgotten.

I am a self-confident woman, but I cannot help feeling fearful as a parent. The 1955 death of Emmett Till in my home state of Mississippi was a defining moment in my life, and I don't think I will ever be able to separate that experience from the way I parent my son. I was twelve years old when fourteen-year-old Emmett from Chicago came to visit his uncle in Money, Mississippi. One day he and his cousins went to a local grocery store owned by Roy and Carolyn Bryant. Carolyn was working in the store while her husband was away on a trip. It was alleged that Emmett made a pass at Carolyn Bryant by asking her for a date. He had boasted to his cousins that in Chicago he dated white girls. They challenged him to make a pass at Carolyn Bryant, and he did. When her husband returned a few days later, he learned about the incident because the news had circulated widely in the community. Bryant and his step-brother J. W. Milam went to Emmett Till's granduncle's home and over his protests they took Emmett away with a warning to the uncle that his life could be endangered as well. They took young Emmett to a barn and beat him to death. They also shot him once in the head, then tied a cotton-gin fan around his neck to weigh him down and threw his body in the Tallahatchie River. His uncle and other black people began to look for him. His body surfaced three days later on the banks of the river. I was scared to death that the same thing might happen to one of my brothers. That is an indelible experience, and I will never be free of the fear I felt.

This fear has passed through me to my son, and experiences in his own life have added to this sense of anxiety. He once told me that his defining moment came when he watched the video of Rodney King being beaten by the police. Even in this integrated and supposedly enlightened era, we have reason to fear for our children's safety as long as some people harbor the stereotypes and myths about black inferiority.

Yes, we can be both self-confident and fearful at the same time. The key is to take time to examine how we feel and to try to make our sense of confidence balance our sense of fear.

A REALITY CHECK

Day in and day out we go about our lives in an often blind routine. We don't realize that the things we do and say each day without really thinking can have a profound effect on our children. It's good to do a reality check once in a while to see if basic life occurrences like work, marriage, and daily experiences are all working together to benefit rather than hinder our children's growth. The following questions will help you sort out how your own daily actions trickle down to affect your children.

A Reality Check

- Does my marital status affect my child's chances of success?
- If my child's other parent and I both work, how does that affect my relationship with my child?
- Am I letting my own disappointments influence my expectations for my children?
- What kind of role model am I for my children?

Does my marital status affect my child's chances of success? Your marital status does affect your children, not necessarily only for good or only for bad. Children are influenced in many ways by whether you are single, separated, divorced, married, or remarried. Whatever the situation, it's important for you to stop and assess whether both parents are meeting your child's needs; if you are not, assess how you can improve the situation.

Many black families are now headed by women only. If you are one of these women who is head of the household, ask yourself how this may be affecting your child's future. It is my belief that even the best mother cannot take the place of two parents. You have a parental obligation to do everything you can to give your children the benefit of having both parents or their surrogates.

Being married, on the other hand, can benefit your child—but only if you make the effort to make sure both parents are actively involved in the child's life. Whether married or not, take inventory. Ask yourself: Are both parents involved in this child's life to the greatest extent possible? Are we both consistent in our expectations of our child? Can I do anything to help the other parent become more informed about what's going on in our child's life? Can I do anything to improve the state of my marital situation to help our child?

If, for whatever reason, your offspring's other parent cannot be involved in the child's upbringing, then you need to assess how you can fill the gap left by the absent parent. If you want your child to have all the advantages in the world, you need to start looking outward to community resources that can help you give your child the positive advantage of both male and female influence.

If my child's other parent and I both work, how does that affect my relationship with my child? It is likely that both parents work in many black households, just as in any household these days. If this is so in your family, you'll have to be careful that this factor not be a negative influence on your child's upbringing. When both parents work, they will have less time and energy for cooking a sit-down evening meal, for volunteer activities, for parent-teacher meetings, for interacting with others in the community. These are the facts; what's important is what you do about them.

If you are not putting in adequate family time, reevaluate how you can. Ask yourself if you can pencil in appointments with your kids every single day. Can you give up some of the overtime you work? Can you travel less? Can you muster the energy when you come home to call your children to your side and talk about their day? In order to influence the future of your children, you have to spend face-to-face time with them. There is no way around this.

Am I letting my own disappointments influence my expectations for my children? You may have faced many obstacles in your life that have prevented you from achieving your goals. It's possible that those disappointments are affecting the way you guide your children into the future. If, for example, you were denied certain opportunities because you were black (even though you worked twice as hard as white people), this can make you bitter. You may pass this bitterness on to your children without knowing it and affect their life expectations. If you say, "Look at what happened to me. I could never get a break in this world. Nobody will let a black person be successful," what will this lesson mean to your children when you later say, "I expect you to do well in school"? Why should they do well if they have understood your implied message that the world is going to hold them back anyway? Passing on a "chip on the shoulder" does no child any good.

When I think back on my life, there are many instances of discrimination that I have faced that all these years later could still negatively influence my expectations for my son. I have faced prejudice in my education, my work, and my social life. But, most particularly, I remember how I felt when discrimination against black voters continued long after the law gave us the legal right to vote. By law, I was "allowed" to vote, but in my home state of Mississippi I first had to pass a very difficult literacy test that white voters did not have to take and that most black people failed—including myself when I was a senior in college. Of course, this made me very angry. This kind of disappointment could have turned me away from the system and given me a very harsh attitude about being an American. I could have become very cynical and decided that I would never jump through hoops again for these people who were no better or more educated than I was. But if I had, could I possibly expect my child to go out and fight a good fight against today's forms of discrimination and racism? My disappointment would have kept him from moving forward, and that would have served no purpose for either of us. In fact, it's those who fought against the injustices that led the federal courts to pass the Voting Rights Act of 1965.

This is not to say that we should shield our children from our experiences with racism and discrimination. We need not deny the past or tell our children that life is completely fair and equal. They need to know what we went through and how we managed. They need to know, in the appropriate context, about our disappointments and the things that hurt us badly. But they also need to know how they can emulate the positive things we did to counter these disappointments and avoid our negative or nonproductive reactions. Our children should gain a sense from our conversations that life disappointments are painful, but if we let them, those disappointments can make us stronger and more determined. Remember: if your past disappointments dictate the way you live your life now, you're not likely to rear your child with a sense of optimism about the relationship between good outcomes and hard work.

What kind of role model am I for my children? Later in this book I will talk about the importance of giving your children positive, realistic, and tangible role models. But we cannot overlook the fact that you are your children's first role model. What does your life say to your children about your values and your own ambitions? If you have earned a college degree and have worked your way into a good life position, you are modeling the kind of life you most likely wish for your children. Talk to them about your experiences, your difficult times as well as your victories. Talk about your decision to go to college or the reasons you did not go to college. Show them through your actions and deeds the kind of life you want them to also enjoy.

If you feel like you haven't achieved anything worthwhile for your child to copy, you will have a hard time convincing your child of the value of hard work and accomplishment. You must look at your strengths, in whatever life position you hold, and use those strengths to encourage your children. My own mother finished only the fourth grade in school. She dropped out because her family needed her to work on the farm. But she was a wonderful role model. She never allowed her low educational achievement to limit her ambitions for her children. Eight of her nine children finished high school; seven of us went to college and are successful in life. My mother always told us that if she had had the opportunity to finish school, she would have become a nurse. (If she were alive today, she would be telling us she would be a doctor.)

Falling short of your life's ambition does not make you a failure. Having ambition is what is most important. Let your children know what your dreams are and why you may not achieve them. Let them know that you will not let these same obstacles stop them from reaching their goals. Determination and optimism may be the most important life model you can pass on.

THE BOTTOM LINE

When talking about life goals and future dreams, it's impossible to ignore the fact that being black in America adds a degree of challenge to the journey. Take some time to consider how you have been influenced by your heritage by asking yourself the questions in this section.

The Bottom Line

- What did my parents teach me about being black in the United States?
- What kind of discrimination or racism have I faced in my own life?
- Am I happy with my life?
- What is my attitude about being black in America?

What did my parents teach me about being black in the United States? Think carefully about the answer to this question. Undoubtedly, you were raised with certain attitudes and beliefs about your race and how it would influence your chances of success. Through direct instruction, implied messages, or their actions and behavior, your parents gave you certain messages about what it means to be black in America. What were they? Do you still carry those messages with you? For good or bad, are you passing them on to your children?

When I think back, I remember that my parents were very direct in their teachings about what it meant to be black. They made sure that my brothers and sisters and I knew that being black did not mean being dumb, dejected, or less able than anyone else. They also warned us when we grew older that we might be treated unfairly in the workplace because of our color. But we went out into the world knowing that black people were not responsible for the racism perpetrated against them and that our parents would never accept racism as an excuse for lack of achievement. My mother taught us that we were to play the hand we were dealt: we were to recognize it and fight against it but never allow it to cripple us. I have carefully passed these same messages on to my son and hope that he will do the same if he has children of his own.

If you were taught these kinds of lessons about your race, make sure you pass them on. Don't expect that because your children live in a more integrated world, they don't need to understand that being black can affect their life in a negative way—if they let that happen. They need to hear you say that you will never accept the prevalence of racism as an excuse for failure. Let them see through your own convictions that being black in America may be a challenge but never an excuse.

When you ask yourself this question, you might find that you were one of the children of the post–civil rights movement who was raised to see yourself as a victim of a racist society, without the power to change your life. Some black people bought into this mindset and allowed others' view of them to determine their own outcome. If you grew up with this victimized view of black people's role in society, you may or may not have fallen in line with this self-defeating outlook. But either way, by recognizing the power of attitude in your own life, you'll be in a far stronger position to pass on to your children a more empowering attitude that will allow them to take control of their lives and never be victims.

What kind of discrimination or racism have I faced in my own life? If your child comes home crying because he was jumped by a group of white kids or because he was not accepted into an advanced-student program even though his academic record made him eligible, you face a tremendous parenting challenge. Your response to these kinds of situations will have a lot to do with your own experiences with racism and discrimination. Seeing the hurt that prejudice causes your own child can bring back strong feelings that you may have thought you left behind a long time ago. You may get angry or feel an overwhelming sense of sadness or resentment. What will you do with those feelings when your child looks to you through his or her tears?

You'll be in a better place to react with empathy and wisdom if you have already thought carefully about your own experiences with racism, taken the time to understand how these experiences shaped who you are today for both good and bad, and determined how you will use those experiences to teach your children how to deal with what is still inevitable at some point in a black person's socialization, schooling, and employment. When you have given serious thought to your past experiences, you can offer empathy when you say, "That happened to me too when I was your age." And then you can talk about how it made you feel and how you reacted—being careful not to pass on your own anger or prejudice.

You must be careful, however, not to allow your experiences with discrimination to cloud your judgment. White and black kids get into fights for reasons other than race. Your child may have been kept out of a school program for legitimate reasons. Your child may be playing the racism card where no racism exists. But it's hard to consider these things when your own experiences cause you to jump to race-issue conclusions. Pain and emotional assaults that you have buried deep down within you may surface unexpectedly when your child says, "My teacher doesn't like me." You may immediately assume it's because of your child's color, but don't let your own past vulnerabilities and natural sense of suspicion dictate how you respond. Go with the facts; focus on what happens to your child in each instance.

When you do this, you'll be able to decide how best to use your own experiences as a positive teaching tool. If you did not get your dream job because of racial discrimination, if you have been unfairly accused of shoplifting, or if you were randomly stopped by police while driving, think about how you will explain these experiences to your child. Will you use them to discourage her from dreaming about reaching the top and becoming successful in order to avoid the frustration of racial roadblocks? You would probably not do this intentionally, but that's the message she may receive if you haven't yet learned to deal with your own disappointment. It's very easy to inadvertently pass on the message that there's no point trying because racial discrimination will beat you in the end anyway. Think carefully about your own experiences. Deal with them emotionally now and prepare yourself to encourage and support your child despite these obstacles.

Am I happy with my life? The way you feel about your life—your situation, your job, your progress—has a tremendous impact on how you raise your children, because children model what they see. If you go off to work every morning saying, "I hate this job, I wish I didn't have to go to work," your children will adopt their own negative feelings about work. If you are upbeat or at least optimistic about your future, your children will learn to hope for the best for themselves too. Pay attention to what you say and how you act; you're being watched very closely.

The reality is that you may not like your position in life. Being honest with your kids and letting them know that you don't feel fulfilled can be good. But whining and complaining don't move your children to feel for you and comfort you; these actions move them to create their own negative and hopeless view of the world. Instead, use the facts of your discontent as a base on which to encourage your children to reach higher, do better, and have more than you. You can talk about the circumstances that have put you where you are and use that information to guide your children down another path.

How you feel about your life will determine to a great extent how your children view your role in life and life in general. So think hard about the attitude about life you're passing on.

What is my attitude about being black in America? Some black parents are very comfortable with their blackness; others are still struggling to fit into their own skin. Obviously, where you stand on this point affects how your children feel about being black, and this directly affects their future. So it's important to take time to honestly assess, from your point of view, the assets and liabilities of being black.

If you find that you are happy and comfortable being a black person, your children have a great advantage in their efforts to achieve their goals. They will know from watching you and listening to you that being black is not an obstacle or an excuse. They will be raised knowing that their black skin is a source of family pride and a reason to feel empowered to reach high.

However, if you harbor strong resentment because you feel you are a black person in a racist white world, you will pass on a legacy of hate. You will rear children who themselves practice prejudice and believe in stereotypes. You will give them an excuse for failing. You will teach them to expect nothing. To raise happy, accomplished, and successful children, you need to deal with your own anger and resentment. Face it, name it, and then try to replace it with more positive and optimistic expectations for your children. Sure, let your children know that their parents and grandparents were the victims of discrimination, but encourage them not to repeat the wrongs that so deeply hurt their own kin. Point out that they now have opportunities to rise above the racism of some, *if* their judgment is not flawed and hardened by resentment and hate.

LOOKING AHEAD

The personal insights you gain from self-assessment give you a good foundation for looking ahead. They can help you see more clearly where you want your children to land and how you can help them get there. Ask yourself the following question before you begin the hands-on job of career coaching: Do I have clear expectations for my children?

Of course, as parents we all say we want our children to be successful and happy. If you have reached a level of personal and professional success, you expect the same for your children. But do they know about these expectations? You must tell your children what you expect. Think about and try to remember if you have directly told your children things like this: "I expect you to get good grades." "I expect you to behave in school." "I expect you to meet all the academic requirements to get into a good college." "I expect you to be a self-supporting adult." Have you assumed that your children know these things? If you have, then it's time to speak up: tell them what you expect and then tell them over and over again.

If you do not feel personally or professionally successful, ask yourself if you have let that influence what you expect of your children. You may feel that you want them to accomplish more than you have, but that doesn't mean you really expect them to reach that goal (although you may never have admitted this out loud or even to yourself). Without meaning to, you may be conveying messages such as this: "This world just won't let a black person get ahead. What's the sense of trying?" Or "I tried so hard but just kept getting knocked down, so why should I expect my children to do any better?"

You can't let that happen, no matter how disappointed you may be with your own life or with society in general. My earliest memory is the day my mother took me to school when I was three years old. She asked the principal, Mr. Travillian, if I could go to school with my sister Dorie, who was a year older than me. It seems that I wanted to go to school, and my mother saw no reason why I shouldn't. "If you have this little girl bring me a cigar tomorrow," said Mr. Travillian, "I'll see what I can do." So the next day, my mother dressed me and my sister Dorie up in ruffly dresses and patent leather shoes. And then she bought a cigar, and we walked to the school. I looked up at this tall and imposing man and gave him the cigar. He then called for the teacher, who took me by the hand to the classroom, and I was in!

My mother, who had to drop out of school in fourth grade to help on the family farm, let us know from our earliest age that school was the most important thing in the world. I would feel guilty if I even thought about the possibility of not becoming successful. She also told us directly what she expected. She told us straight out that she did not want us to end up like so many of the girls in our area of Mississippi who dropped out of school, married early, and had kids at a young age. Her high expectations were clear: "You're going to make it out of high school." And eight of us did.

In past generations black parents expected their children to do better than they had done. But I don't see that tradition continuing in some black families today. Instead, I see parents burying their children early due to violence in our streets. I see parents who have given up on themselves and therefore on their kids. I see parents who are afraid to tell their children "no." I see parents who blame society for their children's failures. These are the things that now keep black children back more than racism, more than the repeal of affirmative action laws, more than standardized tests that are biased against poor black children. The push to success must begin in the black child's home, and that is why I have written this book.

TAKING THE NEXT STEP

Each of the points highlighted in this self-assessment test will be discussed in greater detail throughout the book. But first, the following chapter will help you take a good look at your children to better know who they are, what they need, and where they're headed.

2

How Well Do You Know Your Child?

Family guidance does not mean picking out a career and setting a child down on that one road to success, full steam ahead with no detours or dead ends. Instead, it means a slow, ever changing process of discovery that relies on a clear understanding of who that child is. It means using what we know about our children's strengths and weaknesses to supply them with what they will need to overcome personal, social, and racial barriers to their future success and happiness. Long before you attempt to steer your children in one life direction or another, take time to get to know them.

To really know your children, you will have to be an acute observer. You will have to step back and look at who your child really is, not who you want him or her to be. You will need to be brutally honest, give up some assumptions, and even put aside your own dreams and consider instead the dreams of your child.

This can be especially hard for black parents who themselves were raised in a culture that has traditionally been authoritarian. In many traditional households, parents pushed children to the sidelines and did not take their views seriously. Parents took charge of all decisions without eliciting any response from the children.

This method of child rearing probably accounts for the many freshmen I have seen enter college with unrealistic or inappropriate goals set by their parents. Even from our children's earliest age, we have to have a certain amount of respect for their talents, feelings, and desires before we can offer support.

MAKE IT AN INDIVIDUAL AND ONGOING PROCESS

If you have more than one child, beware the one-size-fits-all method of child rearing. It's not enough to know that your children are well mannered, are good students, or are going to go to college. All that may be true, but knowing these things does not mean you really know each child. Love and protect each one equally, but adjust your expectations to match each child's unique self. You can best do this if you first take time to evaluate each child individually—to think about his or her personality, temperament, likes and dislikes, talents, skills, and goals.

This individualized evaluation should be a continuous process from the day the child arrives in your arms through to adulthood. Your children are constantly changing. What you know for sure about them today may not be the same tomorrow because there are peaks and valleys in their developmental process; children do not progress in a straight line, and it's a mistake to try to make that happen. The challenge for parents is to understand and decode the messages we receive from our children, both verbally and nonverbally, from one day to the next.

Be alert, pay attention, look for hidden messages in body language and in silences throughout their lives. And talk: talk to your children about your deepest feelings or talk about the weather, but keep the flow of free communication open each and every day of their lives. Then listen: listen with your ears, your heart, and your soul to what your children are saying.

TRY AN HONEST EVALUATION

You can get to know your children better in a hundred ways. At home, at school, and during recreational activities, you can watch, listen, and learn. The following questions will give you some ideas about the kind of issues you can examine when getting to know your child. Read through them and decide which areas of exploration need further work and study in your family.

Getting to Know Your Child

- What is my child's temperament?
- What are my child's talents and interests?
- Does my child value honesty and integrity?
- Does my child have strong or weak social skills?
- Do I know my child's friends?
- How is my child doing in school?
- Where does my child get information about the world?
- What are my child's work habits?
- Does my child have a can-do spirit?
- Does my child feel safe?
- What problems is my child currently facing?
- What does being black mean to my child?
- How does my child envision his or her future?

What is my child's temperament? Some children are very compliant and easygoing, no trouble at all. Others are stubborn and difficult. Some are shy and withdrawn. Some are assertive and outgoing. Some are fearless and others cautious. And on and on. No two children are exactly alike, and no one temperament is better than the others in determining later success in life. But it's important to know your children's temperament so that you can better understand them and work with who they are—rather than with who you'd like them to be.

As a toddler and preschooler, my son was a jumper, a climber, a hopper, a runner, and a bundle of constant movement. He drove me crazy. But that was who he was at the time. Understanding this, I looked for opportunities to let him run, jump, and climb in safe environments. I enrolled him in tumbling classes. I took him to the park, where he could safely run around. And I childproofed the house, leaving him many wide-open spaces. The abundant energy, extraordinary balance, and sense of daring were gifts in my child that I could have disciplined out of him if I wanted to make him change who he was to fit my view of who he should be.

I could have insisted that he stop climbing. I could have punished him for his daredevil antics. I could have broken his active spirit. I could have insisted that he become a calm, well-behaved, docile child. Today I thank God that my instinct was to let him follow his nature. As he grew he became an excellent athlete. He played football, field hockey, soccer, and basketball. And as a child with a learning disability, the victories he achieved in sports fueled his self-esteem; they made him feel whole because his physical abilities were an important part of who he was at that time.

This one example shows why it's so important to work with, rather than against, our children's nature. Throughout the child-rearing years, it is so often tempting to guide (or push) our children in the direction that is best for us, without stopping to consider what is really best for their particular temperament. To know what is really best for them, we all need to step back and get to know our children—know where they are right now, not yesterday and not tomorrow but now. We need to also consider their place in the family: stereotypically, firstborns often are supposed to be resourceful, self-reliant, and tough; middle children are cooperative and social; and children born last are indulged, dependent, relaxed, and fun. Have you noticed whether your child's birth order has affected his or her temperament?

Many factors can influence your child's temperament; you'll recognize most of them if you keep your eyes and ears open. Remember: the more you know, the better you can encourage areas of strength and support and fortify areas of weakness.

What are my child's talents and interests? Let's say an imaginary dad named John knows his son is athletic and that the boy loves to play baseball. John has bought his son the best equipment. He has signed him up for off-season traveling teams. He even pays for year-round private instruction. John knows his son's talents and interests, and he supports and encourages them. Unfortunately, John's focus on this one talent may be the very reason his son will never truly know his full range of potential.

Too often parents jump wholeheartedly on the first sign of talent and steer their children down that path in the hope of giving them everything they will need to succeed in this area. This frequently happens in areas such as athletics, the performing arts, or academics. We too soon label our children and use our own tunnel vision to deny them the right to explore other areas of life. We fill their days so full of lessons and practice sessions that they have no time to wander into other areas.

We also make the mistake of assuming that their strengths as grade-schoolers will continue to be their strengths as high-schoolers. But how many standout child scholars, dancers, musicians, actors, athletes, and artists fall from the spotlight in their teens? Far more, I'm afraid, than continue to progress on to careers in those areas. When that happens, what does the child have left? Often only a sense of failure and disappointment.

This common scenario is unnecessary if we allow our children the time and space to choose personal interests and if we support those choices without getting stuck on them. If your child loves dance class for three years and then wants to drop them cold for guitar lessons, let her. The dance lessons weren't a waste of time and money; they were good for her during that period of growth and development. To guide your child to a positive and satisfying life path, you must first let him or her go down many roads. Your eight-year-old may be good in math, but that doesn't mean he will be a rocket scientist. It's not necessarily a signal to sign him up for math camp and put him on track to be an engineer. He has a lot of growing and exploring to do. He may find when he turns ten that he loves art and then at age eleven that he wants to be a veterinarian. He may love baseball with a passion and then drop it completely for a skateboard. We have to make an effort to keep up with our children's ever changing interests, strengths, and skills, rather than hang our career guidance efforts on one and refuse to allow our children the opportunity to move on to new interests. No one's career future is cast in stone—especially not a child's.

As you watch your child's interests and talents develop, try to be flexible and go with the flow. Let your child explore, try different things, put some things aside, and try others. Unlike our ancestors, our children enjoy the benefit of having many life and career options. Don't take that away from them by putting them on any career track too early.

To allow your children this freedom, you will have to be careful that you don't mix up your own needs with theirs. Although every generation wants the next generation to be better, that doesn't mean your child is obligated to make up for what you couldn't do. In the past, career options for black people were limited, so you might now feel great hope that your child will take advantage of the opportunities to make a high income as a doctor, lawyer, or Wall Street broker. If you're honest with yourself, you might find that deep down you harbor hopes based on your own shortcomings: "I didn't have the opportunity to be a doctor, but my child will." Or "I wasn't good enough to be a professional athlete, but my child will be." Despite your own dreams, you must give your child the freedom to choose his or her own life direction based on his or her unique talents and interests.

I know from experience that this is not always easy to do. I was sure my son would be a trial lawyer. He was smart, quick, and could argue with a signpost and win! This was the life I dreamed for him. Today as a young man, he has taken his quick mind and strong verbal skills and moved to California to become an actor. This is not what I had planned, but this is his life, not mine. Fortunately, I know him well enough to be sure that he has the confidence, the determination, and the will to find a secure and self-satisfying place in this world. In the end that's what matters.

Does my child value honesty and integrity? Integrity is the firm adherence to a system of values. People of integrity stand by their moral code, and they are incorruptible. African American history is full of stories about the people who made the decision that being able to live with themselves is the most important thing of all—far more important than wealth and status. Material gain was never the motivation for our outstanding black activists such as Muhammad Ali, Nat Turner, Harriet Tubman, Fannie Lou Hamer, Ella Baker, Ida B. Wells, and countless others like them.

However, although our children still have such admirable black individuals to emulate, it is more important that we ourselves become models of honesty and integrity. Your child needs to know that you tell the truth and hold high your family values. Only then can you expect your child to do the same. Have you developed this kind of mutual respect for honesty with your child, or is this an area you both need to improve on? Integrity, after all, is the bottom line in evaluating the quality of one's life. We must grow to feel proud of ourselves, knowing we have done our very best.

Does my child have strong or weak social skills? Social skills play a strong role in career choice and ultimate life success. That's why it's important to know how your child relates to his or her peers. Is she a leader or a follower? Can he make friends easily? Is she loquacious or quiet? Does he like to get involved in social, recreational, and athletic events? Is she withdrawn or too aggressive?

Before you jump to label your child's social skills, take time to watch him or her on the playground or at sport activities or other recreational situations. Pay attention to how he or she interacts with others. It's not unusual for a parent to begin this little exercise absolutely sure that his or her little Tommy is very outgoing (because he is at home and with his close friends) but then end with the surprising discovery that in unfamiliar surroundings, Tommy is very withdrawn and uncomfortable. Or a parent may swear her child is shy (because she used to be and is now stuck with that label) and then be shocked to see her interacting with assertive confidence. Don't assume you know your child's temperament; take time to watch and learn.

Whatever you learn about your child's social skills is not necessarily good or bad; the leader today may be the follower tomorrow and vice versa. The point of identifying your child's social personality is so that you can help him or her play to the strengths and compensate for weaknesses.

Do I know my child's friends? To truly know our children, we must know their friends. Do you know who your child's friends are? What about them is attractive to your children? Gathering this information gets harder as they grow, but if you stay involved in their school and recreational lives, you'll learn plenty about who they hang around with. Go to ball games to see who else is on the team. Go to school activities to get to know other parents. Introduce yourself and strike up a conversation about the kids. Create an environment in your home that makes your children feel comfortable about bringing their friends home. If they don't bring their friends home to meet you, find out why.

Then, if you see your young children are in with the wrong crowd, you'll have an opportunity to do something about it. The road to a productive and fulfilling life travels through experiences populated by high-achieving children whose parents have expectations similar to your own. Because it is so important, helping your child choose friends wisely is an issue that will be explored fully in later chapters.

How is my child doing in school? Approximately four times a year, you see a report card that grades your children's schoolwork. Although these reports give you important information, do not rely on them alone to understand your child as a student. You should know much more about academic accomplishment, opportunities, and potential. Run down this list to help you better know your child and to judge where there's work still to be done:

> Meet one-on-one with all your child's teachers. Make sure each one knows that you're interested in your child's success and

that you want to be informed of any exceptional problems, accomplishments, or changes in performance.

To expand your view of your child as a student, ask for the teacher's point of view: "What kind of student is my child? What are his weaknesses? What are her strengths?"

Know the teacher's expectations, educational philosophy, and requirements.

Understand the state and local laws that govern advancement from grade to grade and eventually graduation. (It is not unusual for a child to be denied a diploma for lacking proper credits; make sure you know where your child stands at all times.)

Understand the standardized tests your children take. Know the dates they are given. Know the concepts and subjects they cover. Make sure you see the results and fully understand how to interpret the scores. Ask what the results are used for.

Where does my child get information about the world? The way we view the world is colored largely by the source of our information about that world. I've often heard parents say, "Where did he get those ideas?" or "He hardly knows what racial discrimination is. Why does he act so victimized?" The roots of personal beliefs and attitudes are often found in sources outside of the family. Do you know what those sources are?

As you begin to examine outside influences, explore these questions:

- Does my child take in an exceptional degree of information from the TV?

- Is my child's day filled with rap music or music videos?

- Does he or she spend a lot of time with children from families who do not hold values similar to my own?

- What books, magazines, and other literature is my child interested in?

- What is he or she learning in social studies and literature classes?

If you hope to influence your child's beliefs and attitudes, you'll need to know what other sources of influence you're competing against.

What are my child's work habits? Our children develop work habits that sometimes grow from their personalities. They may be eager and industrious, or they may be sloppy and procrastinating—or anywhere in between. Knowing how your child approaches work is important because good work habits are the foundation of responsibility; they ensure that we will fulfill obligations, meet deadlines, and do the best job possible. Go over the following list of questions to begin your evaluation. The more often you answer "no," the more help your child needs to prepare for a positive work experience:

- Does my child get his or her homework done without being nagged?

- Does my child rarely need help with homework assignments?

- Does my child do expected chores without being told?

- Does my child get work assignments done early rather than late?

- Does my child get work done in a reasonable amount of time?

- Does my child always do her absolute best rather than just enough to get by?

- Does my child stay with a task until it is finished rather than drop it when he gets bored or challenged?

If you find that your child's work habits are less than admirable, you'll know that this is an area for future work. These habits are not unchangeable. They may be part of the child's personality, but you can still nudge them into a more productive direction.

Poor work habits may also be messages from your child that you need to listen to. If your child does most of his homework quickly and easily but drags out his math assignments, complains about them, and often even skips them entirely, he is telling you something. If your child repeatedly does not do chores you ask her to, more than just a work ethic is involved here. These are the kind of issues that I'll discuss in later chapters, so knowing where your child stands will help you better benefit from that information. Although we can't dictate the career road our children will eventually travel, we can give them the tools, like strong work habits, that will serve them well in any area of life.

Does my child have a can-do spirit? Black people have a long history of resiliency. We certainly got knocked down a lot, but most of the time we got back up. There's no doubt that without a can-do spirit we would never have survived slavery and its aftermath. Have your children developed the kind of attitude that allows them to recognize life's obstacles but trust in their ability to triumph anyway?

Do they get up when knocked down, or do they sulk and quit? How will they react when they become a victim of racism? Do they have the survival skills they need to soothe the bruised egos caused by painful racial epithets? Will they have the optimistic and positive attitude they'll need to overcome these inevitable injustices?

The answers to these questions depend to a great extent on your own attitude in these circumstances. If you realize that your child underestimates his or her ability to get past barriers, take a good look at your own reaction to adversity. If you mope and moan and act defeated in tough situations, this is the lesson you may be teaching your children.

Very difficult issues affect many families, including unemployment, impoverished single parenting, and lack of education and training; to keep a can-do spirit in these circumstances is a great challenge. But life does go on, so if you want your children to rise above the negative influences in their environment, you must show them how to feel positive about life's possibilities.

Does my child feel safe? All children, regardless of color or race, have a basic need to feel safe. However, providing this sense of security has been a challenge for black parents because historically they have not had this protection themselves. The collective racial memory holds the fear of losing children to slavery, of not being able to keep them close by and protect them. This fear embedded in the consciousness of today's black parent arises again in the modern-day equivalent of not being able to guarantee protection for our children from experiences such as street violence, the drug culture, and racial profiling.

Ask your children: "Do you feel safe at home, in school, at play, on the street?" Delve deeper and ask why. Get to know exactly how your children equate the color of their skin with their sense of personal safety. And then provide reassurance, understanding, and support.

What problems is my child currently facing? Knowing the various difficulties your children face each day can tell you a lot about them. If you know, for example, that your daughter is being bullied by a small group of classmates, you can use that circumstance to learn about how she deals with difficult and uncomfortable situations. You'll learn whether she can handle it alone or needs your help. You'll see problem-solving and coping skills in action. You'll get a good idea of what she needs to learn and to what degree you need to be involved.

If you carefully watch the way your children face problems, you'll also gain another insight into their personalities. You'll see if they are overly passive or too aggressive. You'll learn if they are able to depersonalize hurtful comments and actions, if they are sensitive souls who take it all to heart, or if they react with a bit of both. You'll find if they are able to manage their anger or if they are quick to lose control. All of these responses to problematic situations tell you something about your children that can help you better understand and raise them.

What does being black mean to my child? Not all children feel the frequent sting of overt racism, but even our youngest children know they are black and others are not. In my own family, I can distinctly recall when I recognized that people were treated differently according to their color. When I was about four years old, I noticed that the school bus took all the white children to a different school and that that school was much nicer than mine. Even then I knew that wasn't right, and sometimes I felt upset because of it.

Fortunately, my son's moment of awareness was a more positive one. When he was six years old, we moved to Senegal, West Africa, because his father was the U.S. ambassador there. One Saturday morning we were driving from our residence to downtown Dakar when Thomas proudly announced, "Senegal is a black man's town, and New York is a white man's town!" We had never pointed out to him that his new homeland was run by black Africans, but he saw it immediately. He didn't attach a sense of better or worse to this, but he knew it was different, and judging by the beaming smile on his face, it filled him with pride. I'm quite sure he brought that pride with him when we returned to the United States.

How do your children feel about being black? The best way to find out is to ask them. Be direct. You might ask, "When we go out in a crowd, like at the amusement park, do you feel proud or ashamed of the color of your skin?" Or "Have you ever felt uncomfortable because you're a black person?" Or "Have you ever felt that being black has influenced the way people treat you?" If this is something your children don't want to talk about openly or something they haven't yet really internalized, watch for signs of racial awareness by keeping your eyes open for the answers to these questions:

- Does my child prefer white dolls over black dolls?

- On the playground does my child prefer to play mostly with black or white children?

- Does my teen admire primarily black or white celebrities?

- Is my child comfortable being with other black children?

- Is my child defensive about being black?

- Does my child say things like "What's the point in try-ing" that indicate he or she believes skin color will be an obstacle to future success?

- Does my child ever make comments about being black in "a white man's world"?

When answering these questions, keep in mind that most children (and adults as well) have a healthy sense of self-esteem as black people when they can relate to everyone in the diverse world in which they live regardless of color and have a sense of pride in who they are in that world. You can suspect a problem if your children isolate themselves with only white or black peers.

How does my child envision his or her future? It's important to know how your children envision the future. To guide their career and life choices, you need to know if your children are ready to reach for the stars or if they have set their sights too low. Do they dream of great achievements? Or are they starting out with a predetermined sense of defeat? Do they imagine a life of achievement or one of struggle? Or are they totally unconcerned and uninterested in thinking ahead? These are things you should know so that you can encourage high hopes and head off despair and negative thinking.

Ongoing conversations about future plans are also important because these are the only way to discover if the two of you share a similar vision. Your child may have very definite plans for his future, but they do not match your plans for him. You may be grooming your child to step into the family business, and she may be planning to pack her bags and head off to college. You may be assuming your child will get an advanced college degree, whereas he is planning to open his own local business.

Talk often with your children about the future. Find out where they want to go before you map out the route. You can't lead your children down a particular life path if they have no interest in heading in that direction.

Another Point of View

When you make the effort to get to know your children throughout their lives, look for other viewpoints as well. Parents need to have a conversation about who their children are. Every once in a while, it's a good idea to share your observations. If you see a change in your child, bounce it off the child's other parent. Does he or she notice the same thing? Has the other parent observed something that you have not? In the midst of talking about day-to-day child-rearing responsibilities (such as who has to be where at what time and what's for dinner), make an effort to talk about who that unique child really is and where he or she is headed.

APPLYING THIS INFORMATION

When you've answered these questions and feel you really know your child, you'll naturally ask, "What am I to do with that information?" On a most basic level, that information will help you better parent your child in all areas of day-to-day life. But now you can also use it through each of the stages of his or her development and through each of the following chapters to know which information and parenting steps are applicable to your child's needs.

3

Building Strong Identity and Positive Self-Esteem

Questions like "Who am I?" and "What is my worth?" are complex and difficult to answer, but it's important to try. The answers to these questions are the foundation on which your children will build their future. A positive self-identity will give them the confidence they will need to shoot high for a rewarding career, financial success, personal service, and fulfillment. That is why parents must make a conscious decision to help children develop a strong sense of self and worth. Even a good education and privileged opportunities will not compensate for a low sense of self-esteem and the lack of personal identity. These are as crucial to your child's future success and happiness as anything else you can give them.

Our children are individual human beings. They are Americans. And they are black. These multiple and sometimes conflicting pieces of identity can make it particularly difficult for many of them to achieve high levels of esteem. As early as 1903, W.E.B. DuBois wrote in his book *The Souls of Black Folk* about a double consciousness in which "one ever feels his twoness—an American and a Negro; two souls, two thoughts, two unreconciled strivings, two warring ideals in one dark body whose dogged strength alone keeps it from being torn asunder."[1] This is true even today; we live in two cultures, and that can tear us apart—especially when some individuals and groups in one of those cultures are still undeniably racist.

Of course, some black children will encounter far less overt racism in their day-to-day encounters than will others because of where they live, their social class, their economic status, and so on. But none will completely escape, if not the obvious, the subtleties of today's racism. We can't hide from our children the fact that some people will view them as inferior and less capable than their white peers. They must learn to live with these stereotypes without losing sight of their goals and dreams. To do this, they must learn at a very young age a strong sense of self and self-worth. It is absolutely vital that we teach our children how to feel positive about their racial, cultural, and individual identities.

A PROUD HERITAGE OF BLACK IDENTITY

We have made major advances in building a strong black identity since my early days in times of legal segregation. At that time some blacks had a negative self-image, low self-esteem, and general feelings of inadequacy and worthlessness—and no wonder: racism, negative stereotypes, segregation, and poverty all diminish one's sense of value and worth.

Still, we can't overlook that in spite of these negative influences, many brave and motivated black individuals and parents fought to instill pride in the race throughout black American history. In the early twentieth century, Marcus Garvey organized the Back to Africa movement, seeking respect for black people and solidarity among the race. Then in the 1960s, Malcolm X, the Black Muslims, and the Black Panthers revived the cry for equality and the ideology of Black Nationalism. And civil rights leaders and activists also challenged the negative stereotypes that had come to define the black community. This growing emphasis on black pride gave many young people a much-needed boost of self-esteem. During the 1960s and 1970s, black Americans throughout the nation called for black pride, black consciousness, and black power, largely as a result of the need to turn the traditional definition of blackness on its head and redefine black as beautiful. They made deliberate efforts to discard negative self-images and labels and to replace them with powerful role models. At this time independence was equated with being separate and apart from whites. Nationalism flourished as an ideology and as a way of life. The overwhelming emphasis was placed on developing a healthy racial and ethnic group identity.

As the pendulum swung back for greater balance, there was a need to make room for both our racial and our individual identities. Your children need to know who they are as members of the black community, as Americans, and as individuals.

THE ROOT OF THE NEGATIVE BLACK SELF

Creating a solid foundation on which to build your child's sense of an integrated self is not easy. Color never escapes the child. Despite your insistence that they are as good and capable as anybody, it is difficult for children to escape the stereotyping and labeling that continues to haunt American blacks and chip away at self-esteem. After all, the children in an ethnic group that holds the legacy of slavery will be the recipients of negative labels and stereotypes through no fault of their own.

Unfortunately, unwarranted labeling has the tendency to produce aggressive, hostile, and mistrusting responses in children. Oftentimes, when children have been stigmatized as dumb (educationally disadvantaged) or bad (antisocial), they turn their anger into behaviors that justify the label. The imaginative, creative, and active five-year-old who is quickly labeled "bad" in school, and therefore ridiculed and punished each time he jumps from his seat, will soon turn into a true disciplinary problem and fulfill his teacher's expectations. This creates a vicious, self-fulfilling cycle, a cycle fueled by the stigma of skin color. This cycle of expectation turning into reality occurs in many educational, social, and even legal situations throughout a black person's life.

Because the larger society has historically viewed and treated people of color with inferiority, these labels of "dumb" and "bad" and the more sophisticated-sounding labels of "culturally deprived," "culturally inferior," or "culturally disadvantaged," and so forth are not merely psychologically harmful badges that are attached to an individual at one time and later removed; for black children they can determine destiny. Being a person of color can easily cause a child to view him- or herself negatively, without ever clearly knowing why.

Consider seven-year-old Kyle. Kyle is rambunctious; he is loud; he is a bundle of nonstop energy. His first-grade teacher has put his desk out in the hallway because he is a "bad boy." She says she wants to stop his disruptive behavior before it gets out of control. Of course, Kyle is embarrassed and hurt, but he knows only one way to retaliate. He gets louder, more active, and less manageable. He becomes the bad boy his teacher says he is. As Kyle goes on through school, he will probably continue to be the class cutup without ever knowing how or why he got that reputation.

It is not far-fetched to assume that if Kyle were white, things would be different for him. His teacher would be more likely to recognize his need for positive reinforcement and for medical attention perhaps. She would have a meeting with his parents, and they might map out a plan to help Kyle adjust to the controlled classroom environment. But as a black boy, Kyle fits very neatly into the stereotype his teacher has learned over the years from the media and the society at large: black boys are trouble.

Such labeling and stereotyping are a direct consequence of racial and social class discrimination, and they are often the root of a black child's negative identity and poor sense of self-esteem. Our job as parents is to counter the effects of these insidious forms of racism so that our children grow up believing in themselves rather than in what others say about them.

THE ROOT OF THE POSITIVE BLACK SELF

Developmental experts well understand that a positive self-image grows from the early, consistent love and support of parents and significant others in a child's life. Every hug, encouraging comment, and kiss tells a child: "You are valued. You are worthwhile. You are loved." All children use these early experiences to decide who they are and how valuable they are. They rely on the family to establish their secure place in the world, to create a positive view of self, and to define their exceptional worth.

For the black child, this early stage in the development of self is particularly important. Derrick is one dad who knows this. Derrick works hard as a printer in his own shop fourteen hours a day. He comes home dirty and tired, but after a quick shower and dinner, he always spends time with his three-year-old son, Marc. He sits down on the floor and plays games; he reads from Marc's favorite books; he asks his son about his day. "There are so many people out there who will try to make my son feel inferior," says Derrick, "that I want him to hear from me every single day that he is special and he is loved. Nothing I do each day is more important than that." It's a simple but priceless plan for giving our children what they will need to shrug off the negative labels society may pin on them. After all, if your child does not receive early support and love in the home, where will he or she find it?

I'm No Nigger

When I look back over my life, I have no doubt that my mother first gave me the love and encouragement I needed to rise above the negative influences in my environment. I remember that from the earliest grades in school, for example, my mother was very interested in my progress. She set her expectations high and then showered me with praise when I brought home good report cards. I would dutifully hand her my report card, and she would hug me saying, "This is so good, Baby. You keep it up and you will go to college!" I knew I was a valued and loved person. I don't remember ever going through a period of self-hatred that the so-called experts at the time said was so common among black people in the pre–civil rights era. My mother and my entire extended family reaffirmed my positive sense of self.

This love that taught me that I was a valued and worthy person is what got me through some very difficult times. I remember one instance when I had no trouble at all holding my head up high—even though it meant losing my job. When I was about fifteen years old, I worked on Saturdays as a maid. I cleaned house and washed clothes for a white family in my town for two dollars a day. The daughter in this family, named Jolee, was my age, and she was a very spoiled and nasty girl. One day she was lying in bed, and she called to me to tell me to make her pancakes. When I brought in her breakfast, she pointed at a pair of bloody underwear that she had thrown on the floor (apparently, she had her period), and she told me to pick them up and clean them. I hesitated because I didn't want to pick them up, and then she called me a nigger. "Don't you ever call me that," I told her directly. "Oh yeah?" she laughed. "You just wait to see what happens to you when my mama comes home."

When Jolee's mother came home later in the day, I told her what had happened. And I told her that I would not let anyone talk to me that way. Her only response was to say, "You can't talk back to my daughter." So I left that day and never went back—not because I was embarrassed or ashamed, but because I wasn't going to let someone who was no match for me put me down. I was a high achiever; I knew I would make something of myself and doubted she would do the same. Because my family and community had convinced me that I was a worthwhile person, Jolee could not weaken the faith I had in myself.

A Daily Dose of Love

There's no doubt that all black children are in great need of daily doses of love and encouragement. But do we actually provide that feedback to our children consistently? Think back over yesterday.

How often did you say something positive to your children? How often did you compliment or encourage them? The days go by quickly, and we often get so caught up in the jobs of parenting, including providing, cleaning, and disciplining, that it's easy to overlook the good things our children are doing and to forget to give them the extra boost of encouragement they may need to feel good about themselves each day. Make a promise to yourself to give your child positive reinforcement at least once every single day. We all can do at least that much.

THE BLACK SELF IN A LARGER WORLD

In the normal process of emotional and intellectual development, our children will gradually begin to pull away from us and look to people and ideas outside the family for their identity and measure of self-esteem. When this happens (usually beginning in adolescence), the parental role in building identity and self-esteem is still very important—in some ways even more important. Although we must give our children the freedom they need to grow into thinking adults, when they begin to spend more time with their peers than with family, it's time to double our efforts to stay involved, aware, and connected.

At this stage, in addition to a family identity, children look outward and strive to identify with a peer group through its physical characteristics, language, clothes, music, attitudes, and behaviors. Unfortunately for today's parents, many factors outside the home have an insidiously negative influence on black children. This is especially true of today's black subculture and media. Through film, videos, video games, and music, the media have created a look, an attitude, and a vocabulary that work against the positive messages from home that affirm our children's strong identities as good people, valuable individuals, and responsible members of their race.

While growing up, my son Thomas was protected to some extent from negative external influences by his strong family support and ongoing family involvement, but I realized that he was also receiving many inconsistent messages from the rest of the culture. I could not always compete with the more interesting and compelling messages he received from society and the media—from the sometimes violent, misogynistic lyrics of rap music to the violence of the black culture itself. (See Chapter Six for a more detailed discussion of the media's influence on black children.) But that doesn't mean I gave up and turned him over to the streets. We all must keep in touch with our growing children and maintain a relationship in which they feel free to talk to us about what's going on in their lives. Of course, they will always withhold some things from you, but you can still develop a strong tie through ongoing personal involvement and conversation.

Admittedly, this isn't always easy to do. Kids tend to clam up during adolescence. Suddenly, everything you have to say is ignored. And they sure don't want you hanging around when they're with their friends. But you'll have a better chance of cracking their wall of silence if you alter the dynamics of your conversations. This is a good time to play a less-aggressive and opinionated role. When they do talk, try to remain nonjudgmental. Do more listening and less talking. By taking a more passive but always involved role in your conversations, you'll be able to monitor their still developing identity and sense of worth; in addition, you'll have opportunities to continue offering praise, support, and encouragement to these kids who no longer look to you alone for information about who they are and how valuable and worthwhile they are.

Acting Black in a White World

When your children begin to process their identity through the filter of the larger world and their peer culture, make sure they know that being black does not mean acting black.

Acting black is a relatively new social attitude that tries to separate a unique black identity from the white world through antiwhite dress, language, and behavior. This identity requires our children to dumb down in order to be accepted. They adopt the dress, language, and behaviors that have come to be associated with being black. They might, for example, dress in hip-hop style with oversized clothing, baseball caps turned backward, excessive and large gold jewelry. They might walk with a contrived bounce and sway that conveys an attitude of noncompliance, and they might talk so-called black English to separate themselves from whites and middle-class black peers. Our children need to know from an early age that being black does not mean being separated from the mainstream of American culture.

When the black leaders of the 1960s and 1970s called for black pride and nationalism, they wanted to show that they were just as good, just as smart, and just as capable as white people. They were tired of being treated like second-class citizens; they wanted recognition and full realization of their rights. They did not expect that black youths thirty years later would turn their call for a black identity around to cause further isolationism and to create even higher roadblocks to success. To honor the efforts of blacks who sacrificed to give us all the opportunities we have today, we cannot turn our backs when our children begin to equate being black with acting black.

Standard English or Black English?

In the current world, we are first judged by our color; then we are judged by the way we speak. Our kids already have a strike against them in the job market due to their color. Don't let poor language skills compound the bias. Speaking Ebonics or black English is not part of the black identity. Our children must learn that speaking proper English is not a put-down on our race but a way to improve our standing and reach our goals.

If you want your children to have secure futures in any type of professional job, insist that they speak proper English. If they go to a school where classmates do not speak standard English, they will undoubtedly want to be accepted by speaking the jargon and style of their friends. You can't win that battle. But you can be ever vigilant about insisting that proper English be spoken in your home. (You yourself may occasionally use some form of black vernacular among your friends, but try to model proper English in front of your children.) And make sure that your children learn when using standard English is expected and appropriate. They must know from the day they begin the acquisition of language how to speak the kind of English that successful people in America speak, regardless of race. Phrases such as "You be going now," and "Hey, bro, you ain't dissin' me no mo'" do not put kids on the fast track to success.

Don't ever doubt that language plays a critical role in your children's future. They may have an A average in school, but if they can't or won't speak correct English, they won't be considered for top jobs or promotions. That's just the way it is for people of all colors and races in this country. Strong language skills are perceived as a sign of intelligence and capability.

The Black Dress Code

Among all races and nationalities throughout time, kids use the ways they dress and wear their hair to distinguish themselves from adults. Your kids will probably do the same. However, as with language, our kids need to know that disheveled, oversized clothing and dirty hair covered in a bandanna does not distinguish them as black people, it simply makes them undesirable as college applicants and employees. On a college or job interview, black kids need to be especially careful to appear neat and presentable. They cannot walk in with their pant waist hanging around their butt, with their underwear showing, and with tattered hems dragging on the floor. They must learn what is appropriate dress in various life circumstances.

In his article "The Difference Between Yes and No," Earl G. Graves, publisher of *Black Enterprise* magazine, makes it clear that casual, trendy, or street-style fashion is not a choice for black businesspeople.

> One look at the professionals on our latest list of the *Black Enterprise* Top 50 Black Executives in Corporate America,

will tell you that playing in the big leagues of American industry still requires a uniform that communicates confidence, competence and professionalism. . . . Many people point to sandal-clad millionaires produced by the information technology industry as proof that if you deliver the goods, it doesn't matter what you wear. But before you decide to grow dreadlocks and ditch your suit and tie for a FUBU jeans and "05" football jersey ensemble, you need to ask some honest questions about the price you're willing to pay for the sake of personal expression in a business environment. . . . We can never forget that for African Americans, excellence is not only a prerequisite to success, it is often necessary for our survival.[2]

This level of excellence may be easier for white kids to attain, but they are not pardoned from expectations in appearance either. Yes, the hip-hop dress and attitude have spread into the white community among even affluent kids. But you can be sure that on college and job interviews, and on the job, these kids dump the baggy jeans, the backward caps, and the street jargon in a flash to present themselves as intelligent young men and women. We must teach our kids the same adaptability.

Acting White in a Black World

When you encourage your kids to give up the dress, language, and behaviors that they identify with being black, they may complain that you are asking them to deny their heritage, to act white. In his article "Black Intellectual Development," writer Jeffrey Brown reveals the ugly truth about this attitude by interviewing high school students. One young lady from a high school in South Carolina told him that *acting white* was easy to define: "Speaking grammatical English or wearing Polo clothes, plaid shorts or button-down cotton shirts is acting white," she said. "So is listening to Bach or the Beatles.

Acting white is playing clarinet in the school band, reading *Seventeen* magazine, taking advanced courses, or making good grades."[3]

Brown goes on to describe the most heartbreaking story he heard from a young black man in Greenville, South Carolina, who was attacked in the parking lot one day after class during his junior year. Two black schoolmates, whom the young man hardly knew, punched and kicked him. "South Carolina Court of Appeals Judge Sam Stilwell, then a Greenville lawyer, who represented one of the attackers, said his client told him the beating occurred because the other young man was 'too white.'"[4]

These horrifying stories and others like them are relatively new in the black community. Historically, blacks have admired high achievement. Those who graduated school were held in high esteem by their peers and the adults in the community. Parents worked hard to make sure their children did better and achieved more than they had. And their children felt a sense of obligation to repay their parents for their sacrifices.

But this cultural value system sometimes seems to have been seized by alienated young people in inner cities, suburbs, and rural areas alike who feel helpless and hopeless. They have turned the old value of achievement on its head because they have not been able to meet those expectations of accomplishment. They have redefined success and the attributes and values that lead to it as white, and they have kept the image of failure for themselves. This is a very sad picture of blacks keeping blacks down that comes out of a strong sense of negativism and low self-esteem.

Fortunately, the acting black–acting white movement is not as widespread as the popular media would have us believe. Many black kids are graduating high school and college and building successful lives for themselves. This would not be happening if the majority of black kids believed that hard work, proper English, and acceptable dress were for white kids only.

But the acting white philosophy takes up entirely too much space in the black community. Consequently, we must be aware, connected, and involved with our children to make sure they do not use the pretense of honoring their race by acting black to sidetrack their goals and dreams.

This skewed view of black identity is as destructive to the future of our children as is white racism. It is a detrimental and insidious part of a subculture that we all need to fight. To avoid its hold, our kids need to build a sense of self-worth that is stronger than the need to be accepted by a group doomed to failure.

THE CHOICE WE ALL MUST MAKE

Blacks cannot escape feelings of inferiority for not being members of the majority or the struggle with questions like "Do I measure up?" We are born into a society that makes a strong distinction between white and black and even between light and dark skin within the race. Therefore, our identity and our self-worth are tightly entwined in our color.

Even the most emotionally stable black person is open to feelings of humiliation and degradation because of color. No one is truly safe. For example, Robert Johnson, who founded Black Entertainment Television and was the first black billionaire in this country, tells his own story of embarrassment. When Johnson went out to the stables of his Virginia horse farm to ride, a staff member who didn't know him stopped him; he had mistaken Johnson for a stable worker.

We all have stories of this kind to tell. Our children will also. The point of focus in your family must be: What can we learn from dealing with the burden placed on us due to our color? Can we use it to build a positive identity and strong sense of self-esteem? Or will the lessons we learn have a negative impact that will cause us to feel victimized by factors out of our control and lead to self-hatred? The choice we make creates the core of identity and self-esteem. Which will your children choose?

SMALL BUT IMPORTANT STEPS

Parents today are more aware than ever of their role in helping children develop a positive self-image as a black person. However, so many live such tiring, hectic, and problem-filled lives that they do not make the time or effort to empower their children through their own actions, example, and hands-on activities. This is one of the reasons so many black children are floundering without a strong and clear sense of who they are. I often wonder why parents who don't work overtime to provide children with positive self-images are surprised when their children have negative ones.

I feel strongly that the burden of our history places on our shoulders the responsibility for raising children with a strong sense of self and pride. Here are a few ideas that will help you give your children these most valuable possessions.

• Differences in skin color are not always obvious to young children. It's not unusual for a child who is in class with many white children to say he is white. If this happens, don't get upset. Just show that child that people come in different colors. When a child is learning her colors, point out the color of her skin. Compare her skin color to yours. Compare her skin color to a white doll's.

• Create a play group for your young children with black children from families who share your values and goals.

• Create an extended family. If you live in an apartment house, look for neighbors who share your values, teach their children the same lessons you do, and reinforce your beliefs.

• Bring into your home the many wonderful books about black heroes. Show your child that the world is full of positive, accomplished, and successful black people. This will affirm a black child's positive sense of self.

• Involve children in black cultural events such as celebrating Kwanzaa, an African American Christmas tradition, or Juneteenth, which commemorates the end of slavery in Texas. Expose them to black literature, dance, and music. Go to museums and festivals that celebrate black history and culture and join a place of worship that has black members, especially black children.

• Expose your children to the diverse culture of the broader society outside your immediate environment. A key ingredient in helping a child feel good about him- or herself in today's society is not only pride in one's own culture but also pride in an ever changing society without stereotypes and prejudice. Take your children to multicultural festivals, museums, art galleries, and events that celebrate other cultures: Asian, Native American, Irish, Italian, Spanish, and on and on.

• Let your children see you interacting with people of different races in a friendly and kind manner. This will show them that we can be friends with people who are different from us—not better or worse, only different.

• Spend quality and quantity time with your child. Provide the day-to-day and ongoing teaching and reinforcement of strong sense of self. Do not substitute material things for your time and attention. To build a strong sense of self in children, nothing can substitute for you.

Many factors and experiences create a child's identity and sense of esteem. The ideas explored in this chapter give you a place to start. In the next chapter, I'll further explore the foundation of future success that lies in family values. And in later chapters, I'll add important things to do involving role models, education, friends, and networking that all boost self-esteem.

4

Family Values

Fourteen-year-old Jake isn't the best student in his class. His family is not the wealthiest in the neighborhood, and he sometimes gets in trouble at home for forgetting his chores, but everyone who knows Jake says he's going to be successful.

"Jake is the kind of boy every teacher wants in her classroom," says his English teacher. "He works hard; he brings his homework in on time. He's very reliable."

"I've watched Jake grow up," says the pastor at his church, "and I know he is a good boy who won't be swayed by the temptations of the street."

"Jake always has a smile for me," says his elderly neighbor. "He's such a nice boy."

Yes, everyone admires Jake.

In Jake's city is another fourteen-year-old boy named Robert. Robert's parents are very wealthy, and they send him to a private school. But everyone who knows Robert says he's headed for trouble.

"Robert is incredibly rude," says his math teacher. "He talks back and uses profanity whenever he feels like it. He does his schoolwork OK, but he's very lazy. And if I try to correct his work, he laughs in my face."

"I wish I could get Robert to come to church," says the minister from the neighborhood church, "before he ends up in trouble with the law like those kids he's hanging out with on street corners."

"That boy seems so angry," says his elderly neighbor. "One time he bumped into me without even saying 'Sorry' or 'Excuse me.' I think he's headed for serious trouble."

Of course, we'd all like our kids to be more like Jake, who is reliable, good, and nice, and less like Robert, who is rude, angry, and no good. But how do we influence what some people say are personality traits? Was Jake born naturally kind and happy, and was Robert destined from birth to end up a troubled kid? No, I don't believe so for one minute. I believe the positive things that people admire in Jake are learned behaviors. They developed slowly over time because Jake's parents cared enough to pass along to him family values that they themselves treasured and practiced.

The problems Robert faces in the way he interacts with people are also learned behaviors. Somewhere along the way, Robert's parents did not give him the lessons he needed in things like responsibility, respect, optimism, and love. He is a clear example of the way family values, or lack of family values, have more influence on a child's future than any item we can buy or special school we can afford.

That's why if we're going to help our kids succeed, fulfill their dreams, do their best, get into the better schools, get the better jobs, and have a good life, we have to provide them with family values that will empower them to face the inevitable obstacles of life and racism.

A FAMILY GIFT OF LOVE

As you think about the strategies you will use to give your children an advantage in this world, stop and think consciously about your family values. These are the attributes you believe make your family honorable and proud. They give you a clear inner sense of the right thing to do and the right way to be. They are built on deeply ingrained rules of conduct. Every black generation learned these values in a uniform, crystal-clear fashion. But with each passing generation, they seem to be less and less important. We can't let family values be forgotten if we want our children to be successful, happy, and contributing members of the next adult generation.

Without any doubt, we are prospering today in ways that our Jim Crow–era ancestors would never have thought possible. We are able to give our children many material comforts and advantages: music lessons, vacations, cell phones, cars, and so forth. Yet despite all that we've given our children, I see now that the gifts our own parents gave us were of far greater worth: practical dos and don'ts, the shoulds and oughts and musts, as well as the ought nots and should nots that they instilled in us as toddlers, children, teens, and even as wholesome adults—traditional values of the black community.

These values molded the character of a people who fought their way out of slavery and the poverty that followed in the rugged years after emancipation. Many of our grandmothers and grandfathers, and mothers and fathers, held them dear, used them daily for their very survival, and taught them determinedly to their children.

Now it is up to us to reach back and call our values by name so that our children and their children can learn them in a conscientious way. After all, children are not born with family values intact. They learn each value slowly over the years through example in the home and through specific lessons and hands-on involvement. Passing those values on does take an effort, especially today when the young, who are strongly influenced by a me-first and money-first society, reject old-time values. But although sometimes difficult, teaching family values is not a burdensome parental obligation; it is a gift of love we give our children that will stay with them for the rest of their lives. It is a foundation on which they can build a secure future filled with a sense of accomplishment and pride.

The values discussed in this chapter give you a place to start thinking about family values and the ones that are most important to you. Although you might like to add many others to the list, these are ones that have brought our ancestors through many hard years and will fortify our children against the years ahead as they leave home and strike out on their own:

- Respect for elders, for the family name, for self

- Responsibility and accountability

- A strong work ethic

- Optimism and resiliency

- Love

The Shield of Integrity

The overall goal of teaching family values is to give children a strong sense of integrity. A person of integrity has a secure value system that is not swayed by evil and corrupting temptations. This person knows right from wrong, stands tall with pride, and brings honor to the family name. Integrity is an attribute that encompasses all the other values—respect, responsibility, accountability, and others that grow from them such as honesty, sincerity, loyalty, trustworthiness, and dependability. I strongly believe that success and integrity are inseparable.

RESPECT

Respect involves a sense of consideration for and deference to other people, for our own family name, and for ourselves. Unfortunately, in today's rushed, me-first society, respect is too often forgotten, but we must be careful to keep it alive in our own families. Kids who have no sense of respect often find it very hard to successfully work their way to a secure and promising future.

This is especially true for black children because respect holds an important place in the lives of all black people. We have been fighting for this elusive respect for hundreds of years. Respect from one human being to another is the bottom-line solution to all forms of racism. But some in the black community find it hard to balance their desire to be treated as equals with the need to be respectful. Some carry a chip on their shoulders and feel anger rather than respect toward white people in authority. It's common today for kids to act shamefully, with no regard for the damage they do to the family name. And in the black community, it is still too easy to lose respect for self in a racist world. All these things add just one more roadblock along the road to accomplishment.

Respect for Elders

Children were once taught to respect all adults. Children knew from the youngest age that they could not talk back to an adult—not to a teacher, a salesclerk, or a parent. Children would open doors and carry packages for adults. They would not use any profanity in front of an older person. They knew that adults were adults and kids were kids. The lines of demarcation were sharply drawn; by definition, adults and children held unequal statuses. Children who got outside the child's role were disciplined. It was also considered shameful to the parents if they acted "fresh"; such a child did not have good "home training."

Today the lines are blurred. Adults, whether aunts or teachers, encourage children to call them by their first names and to interact with them as though they were on the same level. I recall how unsettled I felt when my friend's eighteen-year-old son called me Joyce and proceeded to talk with me as though we were two equal adults. I think we can have age-appropriate conversations and other relationships with young people without violating old customs of deference or embracing a new culture that does not recognize or respect the differences.

In the past the elderly especially were shown respect without question. We valued their experiences. We admired that they had survived very difficult times. We placed value on their experiential wisdom. No one would ridicule or demean the failing memory or abilities of older folks. Engaging in disrespectful behavior toward an elderly person brought dishonor not only on the offending individual but also on his or her entire family.

Today I see a breakdown in these values. In appallingly unprecedented numbers, some black children curse in front of their elders and tell their parents they hate them at the slightest whim. "Good" children refuse to give elderly ladies their seats on public transportation and don't think twice about interrupting adult conversation. Children routinely talk back to their teachers, and they are rude to anyone who steps in their path. They think nothing of giving the finger and using profanity to express their anger to adults.

Some say that that's just the way kids are today, but I don't think we should so easily let go of the value of respect for adults. This lack of common courtesy seems to me to be the root of some of the problematic deviant behaviors that keep many of our children from reaching long-term, positive goals. Teens taunt and harass the old man who hangs out at the corner store because no one ever taught them to respect other people—even strangers and especially the elderly. They frighten passersby because they think it's funny to make threatening comments. They mug old ladies on the street to steal their purses because they're easy targets. Without any foundation in the value of respect, they become discipline problems at home who terrorize their own parents with vile language and even physical abuse. And they do poorly in school because they talk back to their teachers and refuse to accept their authority. Far too many kids who have no respect for adults end up in trouble and get sidetracked from their goals.

To avoid this problem, we need to give our kids opportunities to interact with adults and set a good example of respect. If you say, "My child would never be disrespectful to adults," ask yourself why you're so sure of that. The only way you can be even partly sure is if you have been persistent and relentless in your efforts to teach your children the value of respect.

We establish an accepted manner of treating adults through the way we allow our children to treat us as their parents. Do you let your child say "Shut up!" to you? Do you let your child ignore you or ridicule you? Talk back? Do you insist that your child hold the door for you and let you pass through first? If we allow our children to be disrespectful toward us, we cannot expect them to show respect for others.

There is a twist to this lesson in parental respect. If we insist (as we should) that our children show us respect, we in turn must show them that we follow our own rules by respecting others. The most effective way of teaching this family value is through example. How do *you* treat the elderly and adults in authority? Think about it. How do you talk to your own parents? How do you talk about your boss? Do you ridicule them? Put them down? When your child complains about his teacher, do you join in his gripe session and also put down the teacher, or do you insist that you both treat the teacher with respect even when you disagree with her actions? Do you give up your seat to an elderly person on the train? Do you run errands for elderly members of your family without moaning or complaining? Your own examples of respect or lack of respect teach your child more about this family value than any lecture in the world.

Respect for the Family Name

Traditionally, a good name was the most precious and valuable commodity black people had. If you lost your good name, you lost your reputation for being an honorable person. Years ago if you got into drugs, got drunk in public, or got pregnant out of wedlock, your whole family suffered the shame. This is a recurring theme in the black value system: although money and material comforts were not readily accessible, recognition as a respectable and honorable person was not only available but was considered a worthy reward. In small communities where neighbors knew one another well, upholding one's good name became very important. Therefore, adherence to traditional values meant attempting to avoid dishonor at all costs.

Unfortunately, today the honor of a good family name has lost its power to control the actions of our offspring. Talk-show hosts like Jerry Springer and Maury Povich allow guests to refer to all the women who come on the show as "bitch," "slut," "ho," and other degrading names without blinking an eye. Reality TV programs focus on people who do revolting and disgusting things with no apparent regard to how this reflects on their family and upbringing. A good reputation doesn't seem so important anymore. In fact, the media, and therefore our kids, glorify those who get involved in fights and shootings and who have been incarcerated. They no longer look for heroes whose names represent what is right, moral, or decent. This changing view of what is admirable makes it tough to instill the value of a good family name—but not impossible.

How highly do you value your family name? If you treasure this legacy from your ancestors, pass that feeling on to your children. Remind them repeatedly that they are wearing a proud name and you want them to respect that name and never bring shame to it. Point out instances in your own life when you could be dishonest or deceptive but choose not to "because I don't want to hurt my family name." For example, when you point out to a salesclerk that she forgot to charge you for the belt that was hidden under your other purchases, your kids may ask, "Why did you tell her that? You could have gotten the belt for free!" You can tell them that honesty is important to you, and "I don't want ever to do anything that would shame our family name." Use that phrase often so your kids grow up knowing they wear a name of value that deserves their respect.

Respect for the family name comes with a bonus: when your kids respect the family name, they have a better chance of going to college and finding future success. This may sound like a far-flung connection, but it is a true one. Children who have a deep respect for their family name are far less likely to get involved in activities that will embarrass or shame the family. They have a strong reason to stay away from drugs and alcohol. They are less willing to risk a teen pregnancy. They strive to achieve high grades in school. Their avoidance of dangerous and self-defeating behaviors is based not only on what will happen to them when they fail to meet their family standards but also on how their behavior will affect the entire family. They also know that a good family name will be a great asset in helping them to get into college and into careers. A good family name is a strong motivator that throughout black history has kept many kids from falling victim to the ills of society.

Respect for Self

Many black parents carefully plan for their children's future. They learn how to invest and save for college. They know how to navigate the educational system. They involve their kids in extracurricular activities that teach them valued skills. But how much time, I often wonder, do they put into teaching their children self-respect? This is the one factor above all others that keeps our black children from buying into the victim status that causes them to drop out of the race for getting a college education and a competitive job with a good salary.

This is a hard lesson to teach when our kids live in a world that values money over self-respect. It's not easy to convince a seventeen-year-old that a fancy new car isn't worth the price of your self-respect when his or her friends have already made the trade without a second thought. Our kids see so many people who get rich quickly through illegal activities like drug dealing, prostitution, gun running, and so on. They also see people get rich through their work in the sports and entertainment industries. These are not illegal occupations, but I feel that our culture unrealistically idealizes them too often and with too much gusto. Our children will continue to see themselves as the next Michael Jordan unless their parents give them continuous and consistent reality checks. Sober advice about respectability and personal worth will keep them on the right path to success.

I don't have an easy answer to how we can make self-respect more valuable to our children than the attractions of the streets, but I do know that without our own good example, it will never happen. Remember, a person with a strong sense of self-respect can look in the mirror with no regrets. He or she can look into a child's eyes and say, "Do as I do." We all have to remember this when we're tempted to cheat on our income tax return and when our children ask us to lie to a teacher or coach to get them out of trouble.

Our children learn how we feel about self-respect from day-to-day experiences. They learn we value it even when life would be easier or more profitable without it. I learned to respect myself by watching my parents' many examples of self-respect. I remember coming home at lunchtime one day and finding my stepfather, Daddy Bill, at the kitchen table. Daddy Bill never missed a day of work, so I thought right away that something was wrong. My mother took me aside and told me that some ignorant white person at work had called him a cruel name and that he had walked off the job. Daddy Bill took his responsibility to feed eight kids very seriously, but he also knew that without self-respect, he had nothing beyond material things to offer us. Later that day my dad's supervisor, who was also white, called and apologized for the coworker's behavior. He treated my father with respect and asked him to come back to work. When my father returned to the job the next morning, he left behind an indispensable lesson for all his kids: if you want others to respect you, you have to respect yourself.

Self-respect is a worthy value that all our kids need on their journey through life. Children with self-respect know who they are and where they're going. Peer pressure does not so easily sway them to give up what they have worked so hard to achieve. They stand tall among the crowd, and that is like having a life-success insurance policy.

RESPONSIBILITY AND ACCOUNTABILITY

When children learn to respect others and to have respect for themselves, they are much more likely to understand the meaning of responsibility and accountability. These are core values that also help determine a child's life chances and potential for success in the adult world. But unlike the value of respect, your example alone will not teach your children these values. This is one case in which you must consistently hold them accountable for their actions if you want them to grow into responsible human beings.

At age-appropriate levels all our children need to be taught lessons in responsibility and accountability. They should be rewarded for good behavior and punished for bad behavior. (See Chapter Five for a detailed discussion of discipline strategies.) I know this is hard to do consistently, but that's how children learn accountability.

Let's say you tell your toddler to put away his toys, and he says "no." You sigh heavily and pick them up yourself because you figure that it's easier to pick them up yourself than to take the time to teach your toddler. Or perhaps your preschooler takes a snack without asking permission, even though he knows that's breaking a rule, and you say, "Tsk. What am I going to do with that child?" Then your grade-schooler runs away to hide after breaking the neighbor's window with a baseball, and you shake your head, saying, "Boys will be boys." You rush over to reimburse the neighbor without taking your son with you to formally apologize for the accident. If you miss these kinds of early opportunities to teach your children responsible behavior, you're likely to end up with high-schoolers who do whatever they please, take no responsibility for their actions, and don't really care what you or any other adults think about it.

When this happens, it's not the teen's fault. The blame must be laid on the shoulders of the adults in that child's life who made no effort in the early years to make him or her face the consequences of unacceptable behavior. No one ever said to that child, "You can't do that, and if you do, this will be your punishment" (and then followed through on the punishment). Kids who haven't been taught to value responsible behavior and who don't know that the larger community will hold them accountable for their actions when they leave the shelter of their home have a very difficult time becoming successful in this world.

Do your child a favor today by starting these lessons in responsibility.

- Don't take your child's responsibilities on yourself. If she waits until the last minute to do a long-term school project, don't jump in to get it done yourself. How will your child learn how to meet deadlines if she never feels the consequence of procrastination?

- Don't make life too easy for your children. Give them chores, ask them to help you do things like set the table for dinner or clean their own rooms, and then make sure they do these things—even when they complain.

- Don't make excuses for your children's failures. This takes away any sense of accountability and destroys their ability to function well as adults. If your child forgets to walk the neighbor's dog as he promised, don't blame it on his busy schedule. If your child is cut from the basketball team, don't blame the coach. If your child fails a test, don't blame the teacher. If your child is caught smoking in the school bathroom, don't blame his friends. Don't try to cover up your child's mistakes because you fear they make you look bad. If, through your own example, you teach your children to blame everyone else for their problems, you teach them how to be victims and therefore how to fail. Child victims grow into adult victims.

- Don't be inconsistent with discipline. If you say your child cannot go out socializing on school nights, stick to the rule even when your child begs and cries. If you say he will not be allowed to visit his friend if he does not clean his room first, don't give in and take him to his friend's house even though the room remains a mess. Every time you state a consequence for unacceptable behavior but don't follow through, you are teaching your child how to be irresponsible. At some point, our children need to learn that they have to take responsibility for their actions. When will that time be for your child? Today? Or twenty years from now, when the consequence is loss of a job, the destruction of a marriage, or worse?

While teaching your children how to be responsible for their own actions, you can also teach them the value of collective responsibility for the welfare of others—especially those less fortunate such as the elderly, frail, impoverished, disabled, and abused. Our children need to know that the community can be only as strong as each part of it. And we all have a social responsibility to add to its strength.

Your children may want to know why they have to help others when they're having a hard enough time getting ahead themselves. Be sure they understand that we all stand on the shoulders of others who came before us and made sacrifices that allow us to have all that we have today. This has always been an accepted part of black history. When I was growing up, our teachers, preachers, and parents taught us about the heroes like Frederick Douglass and Harriet Tubman who fought against slavery. They made sure that we knew that the black scientist George Washington Carver invented hundreds of products from the peanut, and that Benjamin Banneker, the inventor and astronomer, helped to design the nation's capital. We can't drop this legacy now that we have what we want. It's up to each one of us to look back to our community and offer our help to others who haven't yet reached our own level of success.

Then move from talk to action. You can write out a check to your favorite charity if you like, but it would be better to teach your children how to give of themselves; regardless of economic wealth, we can all give back something. For example, several times throughout the year, Martha would bring a bag of groceries to her church to help stock the food pantry of the social services ministry. She always did this while her kids were at school because it was much easier to quickly run through the store, buy the items, and unpack them at the church without her three grade-schoolers running circles around her. But then one day Martha decided to bring her children along to do her good deed on a Saturday.

"I realized that it would be good for my kids to be part of this kind of community service. They should know that our family helps the poor, and they should be part of that effort. Now they come with me every time, and they help pick out the food. They're learning that helping others isn't a chore; it's just something we regularly do because we care about other people. I hope they take this lesson with them into their adult lives."

Martha's children will very likely continue to give back to their community throughout their lives because she is raising them to be socially responsible. You have lots of opportunities to do the same. Volunteer your children to help your elderly neighbors do chores like raking leaves or running errands. Take your children to a family shelter and read stories to the children who live there. Gather up your old but gently worn clothing and donate it to the Salvation Army or other such organization. Do something and do it often.

We all need to remember something that I have heard Marian Wright Edelman of the Children's Defense Fund say in her speeches: "Giving back is the rent we pay to live on this earth." My own mother used to say that we have to "earn our space on earth," and we do that by helping others. Show your children through your own enthusiasm that although giving to others is our responsibility, it is not a burden but a joy that has its own reward.

A STRONG WORK ETHIC

The myth of the lazy Negro has dominated popular culture and lore for generations. I cannot emphasize strongly enough how far this myth is from the truth in the history of our people. In times of prosperity and times of scarcity, the labor of blacks has been a persistent feature of American life. Slaves were never compensated for their labor. The slaveholders provided them with a wooden shack to live in and the simplest and most inferior food to eat, but little else. Still, our forebears produced the cotton crops and built the plantations in the South. They helped build the cities in the North. Their entire lives were organized to produce as much as they possibly could for a rapidly developing economy from which they derived no benefit.

Not only did the black workers not benefit from their labor, but they were denigrated and denied the most common courtesy due to all human beings. They were beaten if they learned to read or write. They were not allowed to practice their African religions, and yet they were also denied the right to practice Christianity except under the watchful eyes of a white preacher. They could not legally marry or own property. They themselves were the property of slaveholders in the same way as were the land and the crops. Despite these denigrations, slaves named their children for other family members; they created their own marriage ceremony by jumping the broom (a practice that has been rediscovered by young black couples who marry today); they ran away from the plantations rather than suffer the painful humiliation of being beaten or sold to a distant plantation or breaking the strong bonds between parents and children. Frederick Douglass, the noted abolitionist, describes in *Narrative of the Life of Frederick Douglass, An American Slave* one occasion when his own mother, who had been sold to another plantation, slipped into their home in the night to see him. "I was grander upon my mother's knee than a king upon his throne. . . . I dropped off to sleep, and waked in the morning to find my mother gone. . . . My mother had walked twelve miles to see me, and had the same distance to travel again before the morning sunrise."[1] Throughout history, despite many disadvantages and obstacles, blacks were never lazy.

After the emancipation of slaves, the great migration north brought masses to the cities of St. Louis, Chicago, Detroit, Milwaukee, Los Angeles, and New York, where blacks found work in factories in the newly industrializing America. They also moved westward to Texas, Oklahoma, California, and other points. For the most part, job opportunities were severely restricted, but that did not quench blacks' desire to work and achieve the American dream.

There was no such thing as unacceptable work then because blacks usually didn't have alternatives. They were simply glad to get a job at all. Without the opportunity to get a formal education, most blacks had little to barter for subsistence. Work was the key to being honest, meeting one's family obligations, assuming responsibility for one's upkeep, and making a contribution to one's village of neighbors. The only line my parents drew on the type of job they did was whether or not it was honest.

In years past and before the years of integration some fifty years ago, a ditchdigger could earn almost as much respect for doing his job *well* as a teacher did. There was no such thing as looking down on people who worked in unskilled "dirty" jobs, because people measured success by the success of an individual's efforts. Dr. Martin Luther King Jr. supported this work ethic when he said, "If a man is called to be a street sweeper, he should sweep streets even as Michelangelo painted, or Beethoven composed music, or Shakespeare wrote poetry. He should sweep streets so well that all the hosts of heaven and earth will pause to say, 'Here lived a great street sweeper who did his job well.'"[2] Even as we work to create more opportunities for our children to get jobs that put them on a level playing field with white youngsters, we must teach them that any honest job is a good job.

An Honest Day's Work

It is now our turn to teach our children the value of a strong and honest work ethic. A work ethic is the understanding that we all have a responsibility to work and to be self-supporting. It is the belief that there is honor and value in all honest work. To do an honest day's work means appreciating the way our forebears turned hard work into opportunities for achievement. Success begins with the initiative to get a job and then doing the very best you can.

In some environments teaching kids to work hard is like teaching them to swim upstream: you can do it, but it's difficult. Today, a rapidly transforming economy requires greater technical competence. New immigrants from Asia and South America are eagerly taking the unskilled and semiskilled jobs that blacks once dominated and now often turn down. The attitudes of some of our people toward what is now regarded as menial work (unskilled and semiskilled) is changing. Many of our young people in particular feel they shouldn't have to do the same kind of work that their fathers and grandfathers did. They cannot understand why they must start at entry-level jobs at the low end of the service industry. As a young Washington, D.C., man named Richard asked: "Why do I have to work at McDonald's? Why can't I get into one of those computer-training programs?" Too many kids like Richard laugh at their classmates who work in fast-food restaurants. They think that only a fool would put in that much time for that little amount of money. Hard work and pride in work are not as valued as they used to be; quick, easy money is the goal in our society.

Our challenge as parents is to acknowledge our children's frustration with the dead-end jobs that pay minimum wage and to advocate that more jobs that provide promising careers be opened up to young black men and women—while at the same time teaching our children to view all work as honorable. To do this, our kids need to hear family stories that emphasize the value of hard work. I remember my Grandmother Ida, who worked for many years as a maid to a white family that owned a furniture store. She was never paid more than two dollars a day plus twenty cents bus fare. It therefore came as a shock even to her family when we learned that she had saved enough to pay for tuition, room, and board for my cousin to go to three years of nursing school. Grandmother Ida was the kind of ordinary hero that Martin Luther King Jr. would have respected.

Although we cannot turn the clock back to my grandmother's time, we can teach the same values that made her into one of my heroes: the value of education, the value of saving or preparing for the future, pride in one's work, sacrifice, and a belief that the next generation should be able to get the formal education she was denied on account of her race or skin color.

Building the Foundation of a Family Work Ethic

We know the streets are luring our kids away from family values with promises of fast money. The question we need to ask ourselves is this: What are we doing to counter those promises? We have to be proactive by talking to our kids about the importance of our family work ethic, and we must give them concrete examples in our own lives and family history. Unless we do so, we can't expect them to resist the temptation to do as little work as possible for the most amount of money—a temptation that entices many of today's young regardless of race or color.

Here are some ideas to help you open up family discussions on the subject of the value of hard work.

• Talk about the kind of work your children's grandparents and great-grandparents did, even if it was not professional or so-called skilled work. Talk with pride about their determination and persistence in the face of a racist society that kept black workers down. When you have this conversation, tell your children that each generation is expected to achieve as much education as or more than the last. "Although your grandpa had to shine shoes," you might say, "you don't have to do that kind of work because you have more opportunities than he did." Tell your children that you hope they get a good education and combine that with the strong work ethic that Grandpa had, the kind of strong character trait that pushed a man to get up every day and do his absolute best to support his family and save for their education. Tell them that their grandmother may have worked in menial jobs by today's standards, but she did what she had to do to survive. She also created the opportunities for them to do better. Therefore, they are standing on their grandparents' shoulders. Let them know that with a good education and the family work ethic combined, nothing can keep them down. We all owe our hard-working ancestors the debt of our own hard work. Make sure your children know that.

• Tell your children about your own work. Whether you earn a living working behind a desk or scrubbing floors, take them with you when they have a school holiday and let them see where you work and what you do. Then they'll understand what it means to have a hard day, a busy day, or a good day at work. Talk to them about the benefits of getting up each morning and going to work. They need to see the connection between work, the roof over their heads, and the clothes on their back. Work is a form of providing, and that's an honorable task, no matter what the job is.

• You can also use the unskilled laborers in your neighborhood as examples of hard workers to be emulated. The landscapers, the ditchdiggers, the road workers, and the sanitation workers who pick up the garbage are all examples of people who work hard despite the sometimes limited potential for advancement or great riches. But that does not make them inferior to you or your children. Imagine how far these people could go if they had the educational opportunities your children have. Make sure your children know that there's nothing wrong with working with your hands, or doing unskilled jobs, as long as you do it with pride, as long as you understand the value of a strong work ethic: no cutting corners, no getting lazy, no kicking back and letting others pick up the slack. In any job in any environment, a strong work ethic is key to success.

The family work ethic is another core value that determines children's futures. They must be taught that doing legitimate work to be self-sustaining is honorable and that those who cut corners and try to earn a fast buck without hard work may face serious consequences (such as going to jail for selling drugs). Unlike working for a quick buck, honest work makes you feel good about your ability to accomplish something useful.

OPTIMISM AND RESILIENCY

People who see themselves as helpless and hopeless victims in an unsympathetic world will never reach for the stars, and they rarely reach their goals. This pessimistic attitude makes people feel they simply can't achieve because the powers of the universe are against them. This attitude is an invisible obstacle to future success that is creeping into the black community at a time when the efforts of the civil rights activists of the 1960s should be paying off at a premium.

Where do kids get this idea that there's no point in even trying? I believe that the message is all around them: they are inundated by media that project negative, stereotyped images of young black men and women. Many children are in inferior schools that can point to far too few models of success. And some of our kids feel the discouragement of their overworked and overburdened teachers and counselors.

Despite these obstacles, parents have a special obligation to try to put on their best face for their children. This means finding ways to be optimistic even when it is difficult, preaching success and achievement even when children are bombarded with negativity, and, in effect, finding that silver lining in all the clouds. I once had a girlfriend who was always complaining, moaning, and dwelling on everything that was wrong in her life. I eventually grew weary of her negative personality and stopped associating with her, but before we parted company, I could clearly see how she was passing on her negative attitude to her children: all of them were complainers too!

Models of Optimism

My own mother and father were exactly the opposite; they both had a strong can-do spirit. "It's not important that you fall down," they said to us kids repeatedly, "but that you get back up and dust yourself off and keep going." They had little tolerance for people who complained a lot, especially about minor things they could fix. "Stop whining," my dad would command. "People get tired of hearing someone complain all the time. Do something to fix your problem; then you won't have to complain." Each time a problem confronted my parents, they found a way to bounce right back. Much of their resilience was forged in the throes of stark economic deprivation, which required them to keep functioning in the midst of adversity.

"Don't expect anything to be handed to you on a silver platter," Mother often chided us. "Colored people don't have the luxury of wallowing in our problems or thinking about ourselves all the time. I want you children to learn how to handle just about anything that happens." And we did. I have carried my parents' optimism, reassurance, and can-do spirit with me through a life that has seen both tragedies and triumphs.

This is the spirit that shines throughout black history. One of the best examples of resilience I have encountered is the life of the late civil rights activist Fannie Lou Hamer. Hamer was the youngest of twenty children in her Mississippi sharecropper family. Her life was marked by one tragedy after another. She limped when she walked because she had polio as a child. She had surgery to remove a lump from her abdomen, only to find that the white doctor had given her a hysterectomy as well—without her knowledge. Her adopted daughter died of malnutrition, and Hamer battled breast cancer during the last years of her life. But Fannie Lou Hamer never used any of this as an excuse to give up her fight for equality.

Hamer became a leading figure in the civil rights movement in Mississippi. In 1962 Hamer and seventeen others took a bus to the courthouse in Indianola to register to vote. On their return home, police stopped their bus. They were told that their bus was the wrong color, and they were all arrested and jailed. After she was released from jail, the plantation owner paid the Hamers a visit and told Fannie Lou that if she insisted on voting, she would have to get off his land—even though she had been there for eighteen years. She left the plantation that same day. Ten days later night riders fired sixteen bullets into the home of the family with whom she had gone to stay. This only made Hamer more determined to continue her work with welfare and voter registration programs.

In 1963 Fannie Lou Hamer and other civil rights workers arrived in Winona, Mississippi, by bus. They were ordered off the bus and taken to Montgomery County Jail. Then three white men came into her cell and said they were going to make her wish she were dead. They ordered two Negro prisoners to beat her with a black-jack. She left the cell bleeding and battered but more determined than ever to continue her struggle for the rights of all blacks.

In 1964 Hamer made a memorable speech at the Democratic National Convention in which she pleaded with the delegates to unseat the racist all-white Mississippi delegation and seat the integrated delegation of civil rights activists. Although she suffered one defeat after another, she had the strongest faith I have ever seen. Her battles caused her to get weary, but she always reminded the poor blacks with whom she worked that she was "in no ways tired" and would never abandon her struggle for civil rights for her fellow black Mississippians.

Here was a woman who always looked to the future with unwavering optimism and the assurance that people have the ability to solve most of their problems themselves. Fannie Lou Hamer often chided those who gave up instead of fighting their entrenched problems. The lesson she taught my fellow 1960s civil rights activists and me is a lesson worth teaching today to the new generation, which unfortunately does not seem to know its inner strength.

Readers might well ask if this isn't a special burden carried by blacks and not by other Americans. The answer is "yes." The color of one's skin poses a lot of burdens and hardships that should not exist. But as long as they do exist, parents must find ways to navigate the road to achievement for themselves and for their children with an optimistic spirit.

This is not to say that you must be a constant model of joy and optimism. No one can or should be. Our children need to see that we experience the full range of human emotions. We're sad when there's reason to be sad. We feel grief and anger when appropriate. But we don't let these feelings throw a shadow over our everyday lives. A sunny disposition in general is indispensable for teaching children to be optimists, to believe that the future holds great possibility for them. It tells them that they can have interesting and fulfilling careers. It pushes them to work toward a goal that they believe is attainable.

From Dependence to Resiliency

An optimistic attitude is also valuable because it gives your child a sense of resiliency. When you have faith that tomorrow will be better than today, you will get back up and try again when you fall down. If you do not have that faith, what's the point of getting back up?

A can-do spirit is what has kept the black community on its feet for hundreds of years. "Been Down So Long, Seems Like Up to Me" is the title of an old Negro spiritual that speaks to this virtue. Being knocked down is nothing new to black people, but manifold numbers of our young and elderly alike are finding it more and more difficult to get up off the ground in these modern times. Families that are not resilient have become dependent on social workers, judges, parole officers, educators, and every manner of social service program to extricate them from their difficulties. People who might have functioned on their own in the past—with the help of family and friends—have traded in their independence and coping abilities for entry in social service programs that they hope will solve many of their problems. This culture of dependency must be broken. But the poor cannot break it alone. They need help in getting their children educated and in finding job-training and placement programs for themselves that pay a living wage.

Developing an Attitude

Are your kids resilient? How do they react to failure or disappointment? If your child strikes out at a baseball game, does he say he's no good and wants to quit the team, or does he practice harder so that he can get a hit at the next game? If your child fails a test at school, does she throw up her hands and insist she's just stupid, or does she decide to study harder the next time? Look for these kinds of situations that highlight a person's optimistic or pessimistic tendencies.

If you notice your child is quick to give up, don't write it off as a personality trait. Optimism and resiliency can be taught. First, check out your own attitude. For one entire day listen closely to what you say. How often are your comments negative? How often are they positive? If you find that you are more often negative, take time to consciously stop those thoughts and replace them with something positive. Instead of saying to your child, "You'll need a miracle to get that part in the school play," say, "I know you'll try your best. Good luck!" It's really as simple as that. Turn all negative remarks around so that you more often sound encouraging and hopeful.

Then help your child break the habit of pessimism by working on problem-solving skills. Talk about how truly frustrating failing is, but how important it is to take control of that failure and use it as a lesson to do better in the future. There are plenty of opportunities for this lesson in your child's life. If your young child becomes frustrated because her block tower keeps falling down, help her figure out how to make a more solid base to support the weight. If your grade-schooler is struggling to learn a new skill like ice skating, skateboarding, or tuba playing, before he gives up completely, help him brainstorm actions that might help him get better—maybe taking lessons, reading a how-to book, or asking a friend for help. If your high-schooler begins to feel overwhelmed by the college selection and application process, help her understand that when the total picture looks too large and insurmountable, taking it one small step at a time is best. Ask her, "What is one thing you can successfully do today?" Small victories are far better than one large defeat.

Lessons in problem solving help a child develop an optimistic attitude that looks for solutions rather than giving in to the problem. This attitude alone can mean the difference between success and failure in life.

LOVE

Want your kids to succeed? Teach them how to love. So many of life's obstacles can be overcome with a strong, unshakable belief in the power of this most basic human emotion. Because it is so basic, we tend to think that love is something that just comes naturally, but sociologists and psychologists know that it is learned. Yes, love as a family value needs to be taught to children. Our children cannot grow up and develop loving relationships if love is not modeled in their home. They need to be loved unconditionally, and they need to see adults who love each other, who show respect for each other, and who give that love freely, without any strings. Throughout their lives they will need to be able to access a store of many different kinds of love: love of humankind, love of friends, love of a spouse, love of their own children. All these feelings are learned from those who love them when they are young.

Our kids also need to learn about unhealthy kinds of love. If they don't, they may follow the road taken by eighteen-year-old Sandra. Sandra was a popular girl in high school who had many boyfriends over the years. But now her mother is sick with worry because Sandra has just moved in with a boyfriend who abuses her. "I just don't understand why she puts up with him," says her mom. "He yells at her, ridicules her, and won't even let her go out with her girlfriends or visit her family. Last week, she had bruises all over her arms, and I just know it's because of him. She says she loves him, but how can she love someone who is so cruel and possessive?"

It's hard to understand these kinds of "love" relationships and often impossible to pull our children away from them. Prevention is the better approach. You should make sure your children know that jealousy and possessiveness are not signs of love. They should know that verbal, emotional, or physical abuse cannot coexist with love. They need to understand that love does not demean or injure. Tell them, show them through your own example, and make no exceptions. It is sad to see how many of our promising young women are lost to dysfunctional love relationships.

Love is what binds durable relationships together over long periods of time. Because future happiness and success are intimately tied to one's ability to feel and express love, this is an important value. No matter what their parents' circumstance—married, single, or divorced—the children need to feel loved and through example learn how to give love back. I believe that all other values grow from this basic human emotion. It is the undercurrent that drives our kids to want to succeed and make those who love them feel proud.

Spiritual Backup

When struggling to teach your children positive family values despite the pull of many immoral values in our society, you don't have to go it alone. Look to your place of worship for backup support. Our religious institutions reinforce the values we work so hard to instill in our children at home. Children raised with religion are given moral and spiritual guidelines. Their religious upbringing often fills them with a sense of responsibility to respect themselves and never bring shame upon the faith community. It also encourages high achievement as a way of praising and honoring the Creator. In a spiritual sense, it is our duty to use all the Creator's gifts to their fullest extent, to bring honor and pride to our families, and to follow the moral codes taught by our places of worship.

The belief in a higher power allows us to have faith that after we have done all we can to help ourselves, things will turn out as they should. For many of us, it is the foundation of our optimistic spirit. It is a source of strength that supports us as we reach toward our goals. It is the root of hope. I don't think it's a coincidence that some of the best students I have had in my college classes are religious. When they graduate, sometimes a whole busload arrives at the ceremony with the church members who have supported and encouraged these children all their lives. I have seen over and over again how the church can anchor a child's family values in a safe harbor where the influence of the street can't damage them.

PASS IT ON

Your family may have additional values that you want to pass along to your children. Think about what they are, how they will better help your children reach their future goals, and how you can best model them. And remember that values are not the kind of thing you can give a onetime lecture about and feel secure that you've covered that base. Values are taught through example over and over again throughout the child's lifetime. Through repetition and reinforcement, they define character, moral fiber, and reputation. They become an integral part of who your children are and ultimately who they become as accomplished, productive, and happy future citizens.

Of course, sometimes children will resist your lessons in things like accountability, responsibility, respect, and hard work; they're not always fun and easy lessons to learn. That's where discipline may play a role in helping your children reach their goals. The next chapter will explore the use and abuse of discipline.

The Power of Discipline

Its Use and Abuse

Undisciplined children will be at an extreme disadvantage when they enter the adult world. These children are unlikely to attain higher education. They may not get or keep good jobs. They will struggle to reach their goals and fulfill their dreams. This sounds harsh, but I say this with conviction because I have seen the truth of these statements over and over again in my years as a parent and educator.

The world we live in expects all of its citizens to follow the rules, know right from wrong, take responsibility for their actions, and show respect for others. How can we expect our children to do this in the adult world if we do not teach them when they are young how to be self-disciplined?

I'm sure that the majority of black parents try to discipline their children, but too often the methods of teaching right from wrong fall far short of truly helping children learn how to function in society. The results are dysfunctional teens and young adults who eventually have to learn from the harsh school of hard knocks or who end up in jail or dead. Consider these far too typical examples:

We want to thank Dr. Charles Schaefer, author of *Teach Your Child to Behave* (New York: New American Library, 1990), who kindly and generously contributed his expertise to this chapter.

On a sunny June afternoon, the playground was filled with the squeals and laughter of happy children running from one activity to another. Four-year-old Kevin and five-year-old Natasha were among them. As soon as Kevin arrived, he ran up the steps of the slide, pushing past the other children in line and knocking one little girl to the ground.

"You do this all the time, Kevin," his mother yelled as she looked up from the book she was reading while sitting on a nearby bench. "Cut it out."

Finished with the slide, Kevin scooped up a fistful of dirt and threw it at a little boy sitting nearby. As the boy ran crying to his mother, Kevin's mom warned him, "You'd better stop it or we're going home." Paying no attention to the warning, Kevin ran up to a little boy on the swing and spat at him.

"Boy, wait until I tell your father how you're acting," said his mom, barely glancing up from her book as Kevin ran off to torment another child.

Natasha saw Kevin running wild and thought that looked like fun. She ran up behind him and pushed him hard, knocking him to the ground. Kevin let out a scream, and Natasha's father came running. He grabbed Natasha at the elbow, spun her around, and slapped her full force in the face. "Every time we come here, you misbehave," he yelled. "You can't go around hurting other children."

Yanking at her arm, he marched Natasha over to the parking lot and literally threw her body into the backseat of the car. As he started the engine, he yelled back to his daughter. "You don't know how to play with other children so you can't stay here. I'm gonna give you a good beating when we get home."

Both Kevin and Natasha's parents need to teach them how to play with other children, how to follow the rules, and how to control their impulses. But neither the very lax nor very strict discipline strategies they used that day on the playground are going to teach these important lessons. So when or how will the children learn them? Unfortunately, too many kids never learn the dos and don'ts of good behavior. When parents repeatedly fail to instill the roots of self-control in their children at this young age, what chance do they have of influencing the behavior of their children when they grow into their teens? Very little. That's why we see so many out-of-control young adults in our communities.

Fortunately, there is an effective middle ground of discipline between apathetic leniency and physical or corporal punishment. This chapter will take a look at how you can use this middle-ground discipline to help your children grow into highly functioning adults who are able to work hard, attain their dreams, and become successful in the work world.

A BRIEF HISTORY OF BLACK DISCIPLINE

Across color lines the discipline of children has long stumbled along a rocky road. Throughout most of recorded history, children were considered the property of adults. They were exploited physically, emotionally, economically, and sexually on all socioeconomic levels without any notice or outcry. In fact, it was not until the seventeenth century that the concept of childhood was even recognized as a status separate and distinct from adulthood.

Even recognition as a human entity, however, did not bring relief for children. The prevailing religious beliefs of many Christian denominations of the seventeenth and eighteenth centuries convinced parents that children carried the burden of original sin. Christian parents had the duty to use sternness and whippings to purge their children of this sin. "Spare the rod and spoil the child" was the motto in many homes.

In late eighteenth-century America, the Society for the Prevention of Cruelty to Children was founded to promote the idea that children were more than property to be beaten and whipped into shape. Houses of refuge were established for neglected and abused children.

But it was not until 1962 that the government took up the problem of child abuse and neglect, establishing protective service agencies and mandatory reporting laws in all states. Now children were viewed as human beings with rights who require special protection and treatment.[1] Unfortunately, due to slavery, racism, and poor role models, the black family has historically lagged behind in the move toward a gentler method of child rearing.

The Roots of Black Punishment

Black people have a culture and a history that is laden with corporal punishment. As beasts of burden, slaves were routinely beaten and whipped. Slaveholders used violence to uphold discipline on the plantations, often ordering one black to beat another slave for an alleged misdeed.

This brutal existence was the only model of discipline black people had to emulate. They adopted it in their own families, and for many it was an effective way to keep their kids alive. The consequences for misbehavior among black children on a slave owner's land were harsh. Children needed to learn quickly the dos and don'ts of life; there was no room for trial and error. A small infraction could result in a brutal whipping or even lynching. So parents whipped their own children to keep them from being beaten more severely by white people.

After the end of slavery many black parents continued to discipline their children with physical punishment, often for the same reasons as their ancestors. The consequences of a social infraction for a black child were often much more severe than those for a white child. Black children were much more likely to be dealt with more cruelly by teachers, shopkeepers, the police, and the courts.

To prevent their kids from facing the wrath of individuals or the long arm of the law, parents disciplined their children at home very harshly as a strong incentive to keep kids in line so that they wouldn't end up arrested, beaten, or lynched by white people.

This intense need to protect their kids from outside punishment sustained the black community's use of corporal punishment. And it instilled in the race a strong need to have disciplined children. In her study of 729 families, Shirley A. Hill, an associate professor at the University of Kansas, asked parents to choose which they felt was their most important parenting role: being a teacher and guide, a disciplinarian, or a provider. She found that black parents were about three times more likely than white parents to give disciplinarian a top ranking.[2]

A Turn Toward Nonviolence

There was a time when I believed in corporal punishment. I was raised that way by my own parents, who did the best they could with the education and training they had. But as I grew older, I realized that they could have handled my misbehaviors differently, certainly without violence.

I had an epiphany about the destructive quality of physical punishment as a nonviolent activist during the civil rights movement. I felt strongly that violence was not the way to send a message, to create change, or to make anything better. At the same time I became concerned about the increasing violence committed by younger and younger children in the black community. I saw that home violence was laying the groundwork for how our young people learned to deal with problems. They were learning that if someone upset them, they should react by hitting that person.

Looking back, I can see that corporal punishment may have been effective in my parents' day, but that was in a time when violence was not so pervasive in our world. Today kids live with violence in their music, video games, and movies. Violence has lost its sting. Slapping a child or shoving a teen against the wall teaches that violence really is nothing more than an expected part of everyday life. This just reinforces the idea that life is violent.

In recent years other black parents have also been reexamining this tradition of violence in the home. However understandable it may have been to use physical punishment at one time, many are now using new methods and finding them far more effective. We can now see that stopping the violence in our communities will be difficult if we practice it in our homes.

In this chapter I recommend a nonviolent method of discipline that, according to Charles Schaefer, Ph.D., a child psychologist from Fairleigh Dickinson University in New Jersey and the author of *Teach Your Child to Behave*, has proven to be more effective than physical punishment in teaching children the dos and don'ts of the society we live in.

PUNISHMENT VERSUS DISCIPLINE

Child psychologists tell us that physical violence (spanking, hitting, slapping, whipping, beating, and so on) is a commonly used method of punishment and yet is rarely as effective as other less aggressive approaches to discipline. Dr. Schaefer believes that there are many reasons to look beyond physical punishment for better means of disciplining our children. He tells us that physical punishment

- Does not encourage children to develop self-control

- Does not nurture a close parent-child relationship

- Does not guide children to choose right over wrong instinctively

- Does not teach children the logical and natural results of misbehaving

- Does not change negative behavior to acceptable behavior in the long run

Furthermore, says Schaefer, physical punishment may

- Make children angry, hostile, and fearful

- Teach that violence is a way to handle problems

- Lead to physical and emotional abuse

- Show children that you don't believe in the Golden Rule ("Do unto others as you would have them do unto you.")

- Break down positive family interaction and replace it with hostility and fear

- Teach that it's OK to vent anger by hurting others

Discipline and punishment are an inevitable part of day-to-day child rearing. What kind of discipline problems have you faced in just the last few days? Temper tantrums? Sibling fights? Bedtime battles? Lying? Talking back? Cursing?

The possibilities are endless. The question is, How did you handle these problems? Most parents will use some kind of punishment—scolding, spanking, or loss of privilege—and yet the problem reoccurs a day or two later. This happens because most parents believe that discipline and punishment are one and the same thing. They are not.

Although some types of punishment can be effective in making children behave, punishment alone is actually only one part of effective behavior control. Discipline, on the other hand, is a broader concept, which includes punishment and also a collection of other, often more effective methods that can be used to teach children appropriate behavior. So rather than thinking of yourself as a drill sergeant barking out commands and cracking a whip, think of yourself as a teacher who wants to guide, encourage, and motivate by using a variety of methods and techniques.

Think back to your child's first year of life. How did you teach him to clap hands, to talk, to walk? Parental intuition told you that you wouldn't help your child learn these skills by yelling, spanking, insulting, or threatening. You probably used positive teaching techniques, like showing him through example, offering encouragement, and giving lots of opportunities to practice. You quite naturally prompted your child to master the skills by rewarding even awkward efforts with smiles, hugs, and praise. These natural tendencies toward positive teaching methods prove that you have what it takes to be a good teacher. You can now extend these natural skills to your methods of discipline. You will be amazed by the results.

THE HOW-TO OF DISCIPLINE

Good discipline based on teaching rather than punishing has many advantages. It can give children a most valuable trait: self-discipline. It can strengthen the bonds of the parent-child relationship. It can also give children a sense of right and wrong that will guide their actions and foster a sense of self-control throughout a lifetime.

Before you go through one more angry outburst when your child breaks a family rule, step back and think about your system of discipline. If it's not working for you, consider this three-step plan.

1. Teach through example.
2. Set limits.
3. Enforce rules with penalties and rewards.

Step One: Teach Through Example

Children are the world's greatest mimics. Four-year-old Marcie sees her mom throw things in frustration, so she too throws her toys when she is angry. Seven-year-old Karen has never heard her parents use profanity, so she doesn't use it either. Ten-year-old David hears his mom lie to his dad about how much her new shoes cost, so he lies to his mom and dad without feeling guilty at all. Twelve-year-old Casey sees her parents always use good manners and speak politely to each other and to their children, so Casey too is kind and well mannered. Seventeen-year-old Daniel sees his dad hit his mom, so he is quick to hit his girlfriend when she bothers him. For good or bad, kids have learned most of what they know about socially acceptable behavior through imitating and absorbing the behavior of their parents. Because this is the case, the example you set for your child will be as powerful a teaching tool as any deliberate discipline technique you may use.

The philosophy of "Do as I say, not as I do" does not work well with children. Children are very aware of any discrepancy between what their parents tell them is morally right and the actual behavior exhibited in the home. Do you preach the importance of honesty to your child yet fabricate an excuse to get out of a social function? Do you give lectures about the value of being responsible and then fail to keep your promises to your children? Do you hit your young child to punish him for hitting his playmate? If you want to teach your child how to behave in our society, you must be careful to avoid contradicting your words with your actions.

You can set positive examples for your children in a number of ways. You can face daily problems with good judgment, common sense, and a willingness to accept the consequences of your actions; use good manners and model kind and sharing behaviors; maintain control over your emotions; and endeavor to become more aware of the ideals and values that give meaning and direction to your life.

Take a good look at your own behavior and ask yourself if that is what you want to pass on to your children. This can be especially important and especially difficult in black families. Black parents have good reason to be worried about their children's safety in a racist society that is still able to treat their kids with violence just because they're black, a society that has different standards for black and white children's behavior. And so strict discipline is often necessary. But more often than not, many black parents were brought up with a strict disciplinary style that included physical punishment. This lifelong model makes it more difficult for us to be a good example of nonviolence for our children—but not impossible.

There's no way around it: if you want your children to be non-violent, self-disciplined, and mannerly adults, you have to *show* them how it's done while they are still young. No one ever claimed that parenting is easy, and consistently modeling disciplined behavior may be the hardest job of all.

The Discipline of Athletics

When my son was growing up, I found that his involvement in athletics supported and reinforced our family lessons in discipline. I remember watching my son in a crowd of eight-year-old basketball players who were all running around after the ball hoping for a chance to throw it through the net. They knocked each other down and broke all the rules trying to stand out as the best player in the gym. But after a while most of them learned the discipline of the sport. My son learned to take turns; he learned teamwork and respect for others; he learned that hard work was expected and laziness was not tolerated. He learned how to lose with dignity. All of these lessons supported my efforts to teach my son to be a self-disciplined person.

Step Two: Set Limits

Limits are family rules; without them your children have no way of knowing where the boundaries of life are. It seems simple enough to say, "This is right and that is wrong," but limits that teach children to behave take a bit more planning and discussion. Consider this example from the adult world of rules and regulations. It points out the fact that the way in which rules are presented to us often affects the way we feel about them and how well we can follow them.

For example, Carol has just accepted a new job, and the personnel supervisor has handed her a list of employee guidelines. These inform Carol before she starts working what the company expects from her and what she can expect from the company in return. Carol notes that the company gives her six paid sick days, one week of paid vacation, medical and dental insurance coverage, a holiday bonus if she meets her production quota, and a pay raise based on her yearly review. The company in turn expects from Carol such things as a given level of productivity, professional decorum in dress and manner, an agreement to work overtime two days each month, and an acceptable attendance and punctuality record. Carol now knows what is expected of her and what she will get in return. Because all of this is clearly spelled out in advance, Carol feels secure that she will do well in her new job.

Dan has also started a new job. He was not given any employee guidelines, however. He was simply told to start work on Monday morning. When Dan arrived in the jeans, sweater, and sneakers he had always worn at his previous job, he was severely reprimanded and sent home to put on a suit. The following week Dan's boss gave him permission to take a day off to attend his brother's out-of-state wedding. Dan was later shocked to see that he was docked a day's pay. No one had told him that employees were not paid for days off until they had been with the company for three months. Dan was furious; he felt that he had been treated unfairly and was being punished for breaking rules he didn't even know existed. Then on the following Wednesday night, Dan put on his coat to leave work (he was meeting his wife for their anniversary dinner) when his boss told him, "Relax. You're not going anywhere. It's your night to work overtime." Dan finished buttoning his coat, walked out, and never returned. He didn't want to work for people who hadn't enough respect for their employees to tell them the rules before they broke them.

To do a good job, all people need to know the rules. Children too need to know what's expected of them, what they can expect when they follow the rules, and what will happen when they don't. Here's how to set your limits so your kids are more likely to follow them.

Set Limits in Advance

Your children can't behave if they don't know in advance what you expect of them. That's why you should give your child limits *before* he gets into trouble.

Some limits will become long-standing household rules that your child will know by heart, such as "You can have dessert only if you eat all your dinner," or "Bedtime in this house is eight o'clock." But other limits will be set as the need arises. If you are going on a picnic near a stream, for example, tell your child *before* you get there that she can fish in the stream, but she cannot put her feet in the water because it's too cold to have wet feet. If you're going shopping, tell your child *before* you get into the store that candy and toys are not on your shopping list for today and that you will not be buying any. When you visit relatives for the holidays, tell your children exactly what kind of behavior you expect from them *before* you get there. Think ahead to help your child practice self-discipline.

Be Consistent About Your Limits

You and your parenting partner must agree on the rules. If you do not, you have little chance of teaching your child discipline and will end up punishing the inevitable disruptive behavior.

When parents have different household rules or when they undermine the other's rules, they confuse their child and place him or her in an unpredictable environment. This anxiety can itself produce more active misbehaving, and it can also teach a child how to divide and conquer by playing one parent against the other until she gets her own way. If the parents argue over the rules, some children blame themselves for causing the conflict and get a good dose of guilt and insecurity even though they may ultimately get their own way.

For example, Tracy, a thirty-two-year-old mother, told eight-year-old Jimmy that he could not have a new toy when they went to the store to buy his cousin Katie a birthday gift. When they were in the store, Jimmy asked for a toy several times, but Tracy firmly reminded him of the rule she had set earlier. Jimmy accepted the finality of his mom's decision without much of a fuss.

Seven hours later, when Jimmy's dad arrived home, Jimmy immediately went into his begging routine. "Mommy bought Katie a new toy, but she wouldn't buy me one, and I want one. Please, Daddy, buy me a toy." Tracy told her husband, Bill, about the rule she had set before they went shopping: no toy, end of discussion. She kissed her husband and son good-bye and went out to run some errands. When Tracy returned two hours later, Jimmy ran to her, waving his new toy excitedly. "Look what Daddy bought me!"

Bill didn't intentionally defy his wife. He simply had had a long day, didn't want to hear Jimmy's whining anymore, and figured it would do no harm to get the boy a toy. But he was wrong; he did do harm. He sabotaged his wife's ability to set limits for their son in the future. He interfered with his son's ability to accept and understand limits. And he hampered his own ability to give Jimmy a sense of security. Because there will be many more nights when Bill doesn't want to hear Jimmy's complaining, Jimmy will have many more opportunities to get his own way. As Jimmy gets older, the problems will get bigger. The issues of drugs, alcohol, cigarettes, cars, and sex will give him even more leverage to divide his parents and get what he wants. Jimmy's parents need to join forces now to teach their child to accept limits.

Make Your Rules Positive

One goal of disciplinary techniques is to help your child learn what he *should* be doing. Yet rules most often are set with words that tell the child only what not to do. Instead of setting limits in negative terms like "Don't curse," say, "Talk like a well-mannered and educated person." Instead of yelling, "Don't talk back at me!" say, "Speak to me with respect." Instead of saying, "Don't throw your book bag on the kitchen table," say, "Put your book bag in your room."

The difference between a negative limit and a positive one may seem insignificant at first, but the effect is substantial. Continual use of "no," "don't," and "stop that" not only sets a negative tone but fails to give your child a clear idea of what she is supposed to do.

Step Three: Enforce Rules with Penalties and Rewards

It would be nice if children obeyed the limits we set just because they are supposed to, but it doesn't work that way. Children, like most adults, need to know that their actions will be followed by consequences that will either motivate them to do right or make them avoid doing wrong. This consequence can be either a penalty or reward.

Like limits, penalties and rewards must be spelled out in advance. Children are better able to control their behavior and follow the rules when you tell them, "If you do that, then this is what will happen." Applying a penalty or reward after the fact may teach a lesson, but it doesn't help the child prevent misbehaving to begin with. And the goal of discipline, remember, is to promote self-control. So when you lay out your family rules, attach a reward or penalty as well.

Enforcing with Penalties

Penalties are negative consequences. They are the unpleasant things that will happen to your child if she breaks a rule. Parents can use a variety of penalties that do not include any form of physical punishment to teach their children right from wrong. You might try a time-out, loss of a privilege, or the righting of a wrong.

In sports a *time-out* is a brief interruption of the action. In discipline it is an interruption of your child's disruptive behavior. You can use this technique if your child is between ages two and eight to remove him from the area of trouble and place him in an isolated area. Take him away from the play group, for example, and put him in a chair in another room. Have him stay there one minute for each year of age (a four-year-old would stay four minutes). This is effective because it immediately stops the misdeed. It is unpleasant for a child because it takes away his freedom to play and interact with his family and friends. And it is safe because it serves as a cooling-off period for both the child and for you. You give the child time to think about the misbehavior, and you give yourself time to regain control of your emotions so you don't punish in the heat of anger.

The loss-of-privilege penalty says to your child, "If you do something bad, you will lose something that you like." The time-honored discipline tactic of grounding is an example of this penalty. If a child breaks a rule, she loses her right to go out and play. This penalty may be effectively used with children ages two and a half right up into the teens. Some parents also use this kind of penalty when they withhold part of their child's allowance if he doesn't do his assigned chores. Loss of TV or video game time is another privilege that parents often withhold as a consequence for breaking the rules. With older kids other losses can be imposed, like withdrawal of a new clothing budget, use of a car, cancellation of a special trip or attendance at another event, depending on the severity of the situation.

Righting a wrong is a method of discipline that makes a child aware that what she has done is wrong and that she must make an effort to right that wrong. (Most parents exercise the technique every time they tell a child to apologize when she hits another child.) Restorative justice is a penalty that can be used with children three years old and older. It helps them restore a sense of self-worth and also the goodwill of others. Making amends can also teach children to consider how their actions affect others. And it helps a child learn that when he hurts someone or infringes on someone's rights, he should do something to correct it. Righting a wrong, therefore, is an altruistic rather than a punitive type of penalty.

Righting a wrong was the method of discipline that Glenn used when his fourteen-year-old son, Ray, broke his neighbor's window while playing baseball in the backyard. Glenn knew his son didn't mean to damage the window and knew that yelling at him or punishing him wouldn't teach him the lesson needed in this circumstance. Instead, Glenn and Ray went to visit the neighbor and apologize for the broken window. They negotiated a way that Ray could pay for the repair. Because Ray did not have a job, he offered to cut his neighbor's grass and walk his dog. By not rushing in and offering to pay for the damage, Glenn gave his son an opportunity to learn how to take responsibility for his actions. This is how children learn that they are accountable for their actions.

Enforcing with Rewards

Rewards are the positive consequences that help motivate your child to do what's right. Although penalties are appropriate and effective in some disciplinary cases, children who are disciplined with only negative consequences do what they're told with a grudge against their parents and with no internal sense of accomplishment. Children who are disciplined with positive reinforcement and the promise of rewards are much more likely to want to be good and often grow up with a greater sense of self-discipline.

As logical as all this sounds, most parents don't use positive consequences nearly as often as they use negative ones. If a child is told he must put his bike in the garage each night and he does it for five days in a row but forgets on the sixth night, which day do you think he'll get his parents' attention? On the sixth, of course, because most parents are used to a disciplinary approach that stresses the negative. Give rewards a try before you settle back into the habit of dishing out punishment, and see if you don't find discipline a whole lot easier to handle.

These rewards can be either concrete or social. Concrete rewards are tangible things or privileges, such as food, money, toys, or special activities. They can be used to discipline children when they are dependent on good behavior. This works using what is sometimes called Grandma's rule: work before pleasure. The everyday rewards or pleasant events are contingent upon the performance of work or unpleasant activities.

Examples might include the following: "Study for this test for thirty minutes, and then you can have an ice-cream cone." "Take out the trash, and then your friend can come over to visit." "Clean your room, and then I'll let you buy that shirt you've wanted." Kids are far more likely to learn how to be self-disciplined when they want to complete a task than when they are threatened with some penalty if they don't.

Social rewards are positive consequences that motivate children to behave through the use of praise, recognition, approval, and attention. This kind of positive reinforcement is a quick, simple way to promote good feelings and help your child take pleasure and pride in his daily accomplishments.

For example, Joan used a social reward when she looked out the window and saw twelve-year-old Diane giving the dog a fresh bowl of water even though that wasn't her job. Although Joan was busy cleaning the kitchen, she took the time to go out and tell Diane that she was very happy to see her taking such good care of the dog. Diane was delighted by her mother's attention and said she would do that task every day. Praise alone turned a chore into a privilege.

Simple praise gives children a needed sense of worth, competence, and confidence. It increases their ability to absorb failure and take risks. Yet despite all the good that praise can do for children, in most homes words of praise and approval are few and far between. Rather than praising, parents tend to blame and punish, even though this approach to discipline has been proven to have a minimal effect on long-term behavior.

Social rewards have the advantage over concrete ones. The use of material rewards or special privileges needs to be carefully monitored and eventually phased out so that children don't learn to expect a gift every time they do what's right. But social rewards can be given whenever appropriate; they never need to be phased out; they can be carried around with you at all times. They don't cost any money, and most children will work very hard to get you to use them. Start practicing this discipline technique today. Use it by itself; use it along with concrete rewards; use it the next time you see your child. Give him a smile and a compliment today.

A Checklist for Positive Discipline

Use this checklist to support your efforts to raise well-mannered, self-disciplined children.

Step One: Teach Through Example

✓ Remember that the philosophy of "Do as I say, not as I do" does not work.
✓ Show children through your own example how to be self-disciplined.

Step Two: Set Limits

✓ Set limits in advance.
✓ Be consistent about your limits.
✓ Make your rules positive.

Step Three: Enforce Limits with Penalties and Rewards

✓ With younger children, try time-outs.
✓ With older children, try loss of a privilege and the righting of a wrong.
✓ With all children, give positive reinforcement with concrete and social rewards.

Kids are like open vessels. When they are young, they are open for us to fill with our family beliefs and values. They accept our view of right and wrong and take as their own the behaviors we model. Through the use of effective discipline strategies in childhood, we have great influence on their behavior, their attitudes, and the way they interact with other people. This gives them a firm foundation on which to build their lives.

Discipline is a building block that our children can't skip over. No matter what career direction your children choose, they will face limits, penalties, and rewards. To succeed in life, they must learn the rules of personal behavior and understand the consequences of nonconformity. For black professionals this is especially true. Our children will need to work harder than others to claim their piece of success, and we can't allow their hard work to be sabotaged by a lack of discipline that others will interpret as stereotypically lazy, aggressive, or stupid. To climb the career ladder, our children will need a strong sense of self-discipline; we have an obligation to give it to them.

The sources of the stereotypes that our kids must fight off in order to find their place in the world are the subject of the next chapter. There I will explore the influence of the media and friends on black children and further discuss the need for close parental involvement.

6

Countering Negative
Media and Peer Groups

While our kids are young, we have a strong influence over their development. We build up their sense of self and teach them right from wrong. We control who their friends are and monitor their choices of music, TV, books, magazines, and movies. We place them on what we hope is the road to success, set goals that encourage them to reach for the stars, and try to give them the opportunities that support the achievement of those dreams.

But more rapidly than we could ever have predicted, our children move out of the protective home and into the larger world. Here we lose some control, as friends and various forms of media vie for our kids' hearts and souls. In any community these outside influences can sabotage our efforts to keep our kids on the path to success, but it seems especially difficult in some black communities where negative and self-destructive influences can claim far too many promising teens.

Although it's natural for teens to separate from their parents and seek their own identity, when this happens it's not time to toss in the towel or give up on your plans to guide your children to a secure and accomplished future. During these adolescent years it's more important than ever to know where they're going, what they're doing, and who they're doing it with. It's precisely at the time when our kids start to pull away that they need us to stand by in case they falter and to offer consistency, guidance, and love.

The outside influences that are most pervasive and most likely to pull our kids away from their career goals come from the media and from peers. This chapter will help you better understand their impact and consider what you can do to counter their potentially harmful effects.

MEDIA IMPACT

The media speak for our society. They broadcast our lifestyles and our customs; they give us insight into other cultures and belief systems. And they have the strength to dictate style and trends, as well as social, economic, political, and spiritual viewpoints. The media are an integral and necessary part of our lives, but they are also a thorn in the side of all parents trying to help their kids keep their eye on the target of future success.

The media both present and deeply influence the perception of American life, and within that frame, the black community. They influence the content of our racial belief system and frame our view of social reality. Because this view is often slanted to the negative, our kids need guidance to know that being black does not mean being demonized or ghettoized. They need our help to identify the boundaries of what is proper and improper, what is acceptable, what is real, and what is nothing more than commercial hype.

You can begin reclaiming your child's view of life from media control by taking a close look at the influence of hip-hop, rap, and today's TV programming.

The Influence of Hip-Hop and Rap

Rap music grew out of the hip-hop movement of the Bronx black community in the 1970s. Since then it has left its mark internationally on mainstream clothing, language, TV, music, and movies. It has become part of black culture, from housing projects to prep school alike. It is not something that can be avoided or ignored.

As a parent, I have sometimes found myself at odds with the values expressed in some rap music. But I also know that some parents in past generations called jazz and rock and roll "the devil's music," and so I don't want to overreact. Although rap tends to be stereotyped as violent and outrageous, like the generations of music before it, it contains good and bad that mirror the culture of youth.

If you look beyond the most offensive of lyrics, you'll find that a great deal of rap music strongly identifies with the realities of black culture and is a showcase for the traditional black art of verbal dexterity and storytelling. Even the notorious verbal battle between rappers Jay-Z and Nas is nothing new to the verbal one-upmanship that is part of the black tradition. Writing for the *New York Times*, Douglas Century reminds us of the long history of black verbal battles from the taunting game known as playing the dozens, to the trash talk of street basketball, to the verbal jabs of boxer Muhammad Ali.[1] You'll also see that not all rappers fit the "gangsta" mold. Many, such as Will Smith and LL Cool J, fit the opposite type: well spoken, respectful, clean-cut, and mainstream.

Many of the themes voiced through rap are also nothing new. Theresa Martinez from the University of Utah analyzed the lyrics of political and gangsta rappers of the late 1980s and 1990s and found that the key themes were distrust, anger, resistance, and critique of a perceived racist and discriminatory society. She found the music to have a message of resistance, empowerment, and social critique.[2] These same themes are found historically in other forms of black music. Negro spirituals grew out of the pain of slavery. The blues originated in the Mississippi Delta among poor sharecroppers who captured themes such as disappointment in love ("My baby done left me") or about money woes ("The man [white man] is doing me wrong"). Jazz also addressed oppression, as in Billie Holiday's rendition of the song "Strange Fruit," about a black man being lynched. In rhythm and blues Marvin Gaye's classic "What's Going On?" is an anthem for the resistance to racial oppression.

In many ways rap is a continuation of the black oral tradition that discusses contemporary black life. The rappers are depicting the underbelly of poverty, violence, and other problems in inner-city neighborhoods. Many of us don't want to hear about this sordid life, nor do we want the white world to hear it and then stereotype blacks for living that way. But it is the life that many black people live, and the music tells their story.

Many rap songs also convey a powerful black story about injustice, inequality, and pain as well as pride and triumph. Minister Benjamin Muhammad, president of the Hip-Hop Summit Action Network, says, "Hip-hop is making a significant turn in the direction of more conscious lyrics, as well as progressive commentary about the culture itself. It has evolved to the front-lines of political consciousness."[3] If you listen closely (and can interpret the rap slang), you'll hear that today's lyrics often identify the artists' concerns with African American history and traditions, while also emphasizing the importance of their immediate experiences.

For example, in 2002 music mogul Russell Simmons (who owns one of the most successful music recording businesses), rappers P. Diddy and Jay-Z, and several other nationally prominent rap artists led a demonstration of thousands of black public school students in New York City to protest the mayor's proposed school budget cuts. Simmons has said that he hopes to energize people under age thirty to become politically active and socially conscious. Working with the Hip-Hop Summit Action Network, he plans to start a "rap the vote" media campaign with the National Association for the Advancement of Colored People (NAACP) and a literacy drive with the Urban League. The organizations will use hip-hop artists on radio, on TV stations like BET and MTV, and in classrooms.[4] Rap is the voice of this age.

For these reasons, we can't assume that rap is automatically a negative influence on our children's lives, their goals, or our own goals for them. Many very accomplished black young adults grew up listening to rap. A young woman I know in Washington, D.C., for example, is dating a man who received his M.B.A. from Harvard, while she is about to finish her Ph.D. and begin her first teaching job at a major Midwestern university, and she listens to rap. Her taste in music will not interfere with her future success.

Another example of the broad influence rap has had can be found in a recent incident at Harvard. Renowned Afro-American Studies Professor Cornel West angered Harvard President Lawrence Summers by recording a hip-hop CD that addresses his concerns about the contemporary black experience. Summers demanded that West pursue more scholarly activity and further accused him of inflating grades and of missing classes to engage in partisan politics (West worked on Bill Bradley's campaign for the presidency and was an advisor to the black New York City politician Al Sharpton). Soon after, West left Harvard for Princeton because he felt that Summers had insulted him.

Living with Rap

This incident at Harvard is a lesson to us all. If we don't like rap and demand that our kids abandon this form of expression, they'll just push further away from us—where we have even less influence over their future. Instead, you might try the following suggestions to help your child keep the balance between the pull of rap music and the push toward a highly regarded career.

• Be aware. Listen to the most recent, popular rap. Read newspaper and magazine articles about the artists and their songs. Know which rappers spew misogynistic lyrics and glorify drugs, violence, and criminality. Find out if your kids listen to these, and if they do, talk to them about your concerns. Parental discretion labels are helpful, but they do not tell the whole story. Listen for yourself.

• Talk about the use of epithets like *nigga*, *bitch*, and *whore* (or *ho*) that are found in the lyrics of the gangsta rap artists. No matter how casually rappers toss around these names, in your home and the world where your kids will make their future, these words are not acceptable; they are derogatory and hurtful. You can't stop your kids from hearing them, but you can firmly insist that you do not want them used in your home. Teach your kids that they are not to refer to women that way.

• Don't buy your kids CDs with offensive lyrics. Your kids may buy them for themselves, but you can make a point that you will not support rap artists financially who demean the black community and all their ancestors who worked so hard to eliminate the stereotypes that associated all of us with thugs and criminals.

• Don't attack or forbid. The more you complain that you don't like the music, the more your kids will love it. Saying, "This is junk. I forbid you to listen to it" makes the music all the more interesting. Your kids will hear these songs anyway at their friends' houses, at parties, and every time you leave the house.

• Steer your kids to rap lyrics that are self-affirming and constructive. For younger kids, for example, there's LL Cool J's *And the Winner Is*. This book and CD set features LL rapping to the book's words. It teaches kids how not to be arrogant when they win and how not to be insecure when they lose, and it encourages kids to stay persistent and never give up. Many rappers are sending out positive messages. Bring their songs into your home.

• Don't belittle your children's desire to be rap artists. Lots of kids dream of making their fortune in the rap world. Even though the likelihood is slim (as it is for those who dream of making it big in pro basketball), you don't need to squash the goal with a dose of cold reality, like: "There's no way you're going to be a millionaire rap artist, so give it up." Instead, you might encourage (or ignore) your children's musical interests, wish them good luck, and at the same time make sure that they stay in school and get good grades. It is quite likely a phase that will pass.

• Offer your kids a balance. Talk to your kids about the history of black music. Introduce them to rock and roll, classical, gospel, jazz, blues, or your favorite music. Talk to them about the artists who were famous during your adolescence and whose music is still available. Healthy banter between the generations is good. Let them know that rap shares a long tradition of storytelling through music. In your home play other forms of black music such as spirituals, blues, ragtime, jazz, gospel, and rhythm and blues. Also, invite them to concerts featuring rock and roll artists or the music you love.

Rating TV

Ever since Beaver Cleaver moved over to make room for Archie Bunker, parents have debated the good and bad of TV. Experts have long known that this relatively new form of media has the power to shape viewers' attitudes as well as set and break boundaries of acceptability. Because of this influence, many parents have complained and protested the abundant use of violence in children's programming, and many fear it has desensitized kids to the horror of murder, abuse, and addictions. Parents of all races fight this battle.

For black parents, the concern about the negative influence of TV is especially pressing. Not only do our kids watch all this violence, but they quickly realize that most of the criminals and bad guys on TV shows are young black men, giving our kids the impression that black is bad, or, equally appalling, that black gangstas are cool. Knowing that TV has the power to shape one's view of race, we have to be alert to the ways these shows can influence our children's expectations for future accomplishment and success.

Blacks on TV

It's obvious that little TV programming includes black people in positive lead roles, but the situation is slowly improving. In the first few decades of American TV, blacks were virtually invisible. Then in the 1970s and 1980s Norman Lear produced shows like *Sanford and Son*, *The Jeffersons*, and *Good Times*, putting the spotlight on black characters struggling to make it in the white world. Unfortunately, many episodes of these shows peddled blatant stereotypes of the uneducated black buffoon. Although many blacks laughed at

Fred Sanford's antics, they worried that this show would reinforce stereotypes of the uneducated bumbling Negro. *The Jeffersons* and *Good Times* brought black families into prime time, but these characters were also stereotypes.

In the 1980s *The Cosby Show* offered a welcome relief from this negative view. For the first time, a TV show presented a black two-parent family as middle class and successful. The father was a doctor; the mother was a lawyer; and the children faced the same growing-up issues that children of all colors and races struggle with. Here was a show that gave black children positive role models. It showed us that black people do become lawyers and doctors, do have good marriages, do raise their children with care and love.

The Cosby Show was very successful, but similar network shows weren't able to attain the same popularity and longevity. What came to be called black TV (shows featuring black actors in major roles) moved to cable television in the 1980s; cable revolutionized programming and offered more opportunities for shows featuring black actors. In the early 1990s the networks learned a lesson from these cable shows and realized they could draw an audience with programming geared toward black audiences. One of the early shows, *In Living Color*, mimicked the popular *Saturday Night Live* format with a heavily black cast. The success of this show lured other networks to produce more programming for the black audience, and the trend has continued.

However, more needs to be done to give our children TV characters they can admire and emulate, characters who model the kind of successful life they too can attain. To prepare for the future, our children need TV programming that uses black actors as successful professionals in shows that focus on the character's role—and not solely on the color of his or her skin. This kind of generic casting mixes people of all races in real-life situations and gives our kids a glimpse of how they too can find their place among people of other races. Black pride must become part of the world our children live in—not segregated from it.

Living with TV

The NAACP has noticed the problems in black TV programming and has increased pressure for better minority representation in the industry. After a recent diversity hearing in Hollywood, the four major networks—CBS, NBC, ABC, and FOX—pledged to establish minority recruitment programs and hire more black producers, actors, writers, directors, and so on. This is encouraging, but it is no guarantee that we will soon see quality TV shows that integrate people of all races.

The best antidote to counter the effects of bad TV is parental monitoring. It's true that there is no evidence that any one type of TV show will change a young person's aptitude for future success and career happiness. But there's no doubt that the shows that depict stereotypically negative images of black people work against our efforts to convince our children that they are as good as anyone else and have the potential to be successful, regardless of color or race. In your home choose TV shows carefully. Seek out shows that depict blacks in positive career roles. Look for black doctors, lawyers, construction workers, clerks, and architects in shows where the role is more important than the color of the actor.

You might also try some of the following strategies to help your kids learn to balance the depiction of black people on TV with your own family values, high standards, and hopes for your children's future careers.

• Do not use TV as a babysitter. Know what your kids are watching. When they're young, turn the set on only if you want them to see a specific quality show. Otherwise, turn the set off and interact with your kids one-on-one; you have much more to offer them than anything TV executives dream up.

• Assess your family's viewing habits. Do you let TV into your home too often? Some homes now have TVs in the family room, the kitchen, the bedroom, and even the car! Maybe it's time to find other ways to entertain the kids.

• Watch TV with your children. If you don't like what you see, find an alternative show or activity.

• Talk about TV shows that you watch with your children. This will help them think critically about what they see. Discuss the way black characters are depicted. Ask questions such as these: Do you think that happens in real life? Do you notice that the criminals in these shows are often black? Why do you think that is? Do you agree? Help your children recognize that what they see on TV does not always represent the reality of the world they live in.

• Older kids may not want you to sit down and watch TV with them, but you can still strike up conversations about shows you have seen.

• Limit TV watching time. Surveys show that blacks watch TV far more frequently than do whites. It's time for a change.

TV is part of our culture and a daily form of entertainment in almost every household in the nation. It will continue to change and grow, and black people can have a strong role in changing the way this form of media portrays the black community. Until then, help your children view stereotypical black TV with a critical eye and separate it from the real world where they will make their mark in the future.

PEER INFLUENCE

Twelve-year-old Tisha has changed. She no longer brings her long-time girlfriends around the house. She is getting phone calls from young women her parents don't know and may not especially like. They are rude, use street slang, and dress like hookers (what some girls call the Britney Spears look). They seem to be very secretive, and last week Tisha's parents caught her in a lie about where she had spent her Saturday afternoon. Tisha also just received her first failing grade in school. Is this a stage Tisha is going through, or should her parents be worried?

Lots of kids like Tisha try out new friends and new styles when they enter middle school and high school. This doesn't mean these kids are on their way down a destructive path, but the signs point to possible trouble that her parents need to be aware of. For good and bad, friends are the most powerful outside influence on a teen's life. If your kids hook up with peers who have different family values and different life goals, they will have a very tough time eventually breaking away, going off to college, and finding financial success. Instead, they may give up on those goals and adopt dead-end lifestyles. That's why it is so important for you to continually stay involved in your children's activities and friendships long after the kids tell you they'd rather be left alone.

Attachment to peers helps teens let go of old ways of relating to their families and gives them a new identity they can hold on to. "I am a member of this group. I dress like them. I act like them. I look at them and I know who I am." This feeling of belonging is very important to the child's growing self-image, an image that is separate from you.

All of this is very natural. But when kids identify with the wrong friends, they can get involved in activities that interfere with their ability to have a productive and successful future. It's friends who offer the first cigarette, the first joint, the first drink, and the first push to be sexually active. Certainly, alcohol abuse, drug addiction, and teen pregnancy have kept many young people from reaching their full potential. My mother always said, "If you lie down with dogs, you get up with fleas." It's our job as parents to know who our kids are hanging out with and determine if they're headed for trouble.

If you are worried that your child's friends may be a bad influence, take some time to assess your relationship with your child. Is anything lacking that has pushed him or her to look elsewhere to meet a need? Very often, when kids are asked why they like their friends, they will say things like this: "They care about me." "They pay attention to me." "They make me feel important." "They make me feel like I belong." These reasons are especially strong in households where the teens do not get this sense of caring and belonging from their parents.

Kids who do not feel connected to their parents and do not have firm limits on their activities are more likely than others to end up in street gangs that can pull them away from their positive goals. Although families that maintain open communication are more likely to observe early warning signs of gang involvement and do some investigating (see section on street gangs later in this chapter for the tell-tale signs). Some gangs are no more than groups of friends who give each other a sense of belonging. But others are involved in violence, law breaking, and drug selling. You need to find out the following:

What kind of a gang is it?

What does it provide for your child that he or she is not getting at home?

What can school or law enforcement officials do to help you better understand the gang and determine if you should intervene and prevent such membership?

What alternative activities and peers can you offer?

Where can you get appropriate counseling for your child?

Kids who have to look outside the family for love often find it in the wrong places, so be available to your kids. A parent who is distant or too busy is less likely to counteract the bad influence of friends. And make sure your kids know (because you tell them) that they are loved, that they are important, and that you care about them.

This is especially true as kids enter puberty. This is the age when black kids and white kids often separate. Frequently, black kids no longer get invited to their white classmates' after-school get-togethers or birthday parties. The divide develops perhaps from an old notion that white women and black men should not have contact. So what does a black kid do when he is suddenly spurned by his friends? He may turn to whatever group will take him in; this of course can mean trouble.

For this reason, middle-class black parents established a social organization called Jack & Jill of America, Inc. This organization was founded during the era of racial segregation to provide children with cultural and recreational outlets they could not have because of their race. Black parents networked with each other and made sure that their children knew each other. Friendships formed early in life remained an important part of their lives into adulthood. Interestingly, the organization continues to thrive in this integrated world because it fills this gap when black children are still excluded from social activities of white friends. But most important, it is a way for black parents to ensure that their children get the values they want them to have and that they form friendships with other black kids. It gives black kids positive identities and wholesome activities. It also gives them a sense of belonging—so very important to all our kids. (You can find more information about Jack & Jill of America, Inc., in Helpful Resources at the back of this book.)

Even when your child is secure in your love, you can't be sure that he or she isn't hanging out with kids who will have a bad influence, but you can do more than cross your fingers and hope. If you stay involved in your children's lives, they are less likely to choose friends who will lead them astray. Here are some tips you might try to keep tabs on your child's choice of friends.

• Get to know your kids' friends. Make them welcome in your home (this is particularly important if you don't especially like them). Invite them to stay for dinner. Talk to them.

• Get to know the friends' families. When you know the parents of your children's friends, you can determine if their values agree with your family values. Join school organizations; attend school and sport functions. When your child joins a new team or group, invite the members and their parents over for a get-together.

• If your children are hanging out with the wrong kids, do more to keep them busy and give them alternative exposure. Sign them up for after-school sports or classes in martial arts, music, or art. Encourage their involvement in school clubs and activities. Look into the programs at the local Boys & Girls Clubs, the YWCA, or the YMCA. Don't sit back when you see your kids wandering into tough territory.

Street Gangs

Gang membership is not confined to certain types of people in certain locations. Anyone—male or female—from any city, town, suburb, or farm can join a gang and get involved in violent, unlawful, antisocial, or criminal activities. Keep your eyes open. The National Crime Prevention Council advises that if you notice the following signs of gang involvement, you should suspect that your child has joined a gang:

- Changes in type of friends
- Changes in dress habits, such as wearing the same color combination all the time
- Gang symbols on books or clothing
- Tattoos
- Secretiveness about activities
- Extra cash from unknown sources
- Possession of a weapon
- Declining interest in school and family
- Arrest or detainment by the police

SURVIVING REBELLION

Even if you have seemingly lost your child to the street, you can't give up. It's not uncommon for teens to turn away from the values their parents spent years instilling. And there will be times when you simply cannot protect your children from negative outside influences. There is no guarantee for any of us that our children will follow the path we set them on. All we can do is try to balance the outside world with our own consistent positive input. Never forget that many kids go through a period of rebellion when they slam the door on their parents' love but then come around and reclaim their family values as they mature. Despite scary detours, kids who have a loving family behind them usually end up in a good place.

A Checklist for Countering Negative Media and Peer Groups

As your children spend more time choosing their own entertainment and friends, stay involved and aware. Use this checklist to help you balance the negative effects of the media and guide your children to the choices that will further their future hopes and dreams.

✓ Help your children identify the boundaries of what is proper and improper, what is acceptable, what is real, and what is nothing more than commercial hype.

✓ Pay attention when your kids show an interest in rap, which you cannot avoid or ignore.

✓ Don't attack or forbid rap. The more you complain that you don't like the music, the more your kids will love it. Remember that rap contains good and bad that mirror the culture of youth.

✓ Offer your kids a musical balance. Talk to them about the history of black music. Introduce them to rock and roll, jazz, the blues, or your favorite music.

✓ Strike up conversations about TV shows that give the impression that black is bad or that black gangstas are cool. This will help your kids think critically about what they see.

✓ Look for TV shows that feature black characters your children can admire and emulate, characters who model the kind of successful life they too can attain.

✓ Stay involved in your children's activities and friendships long after the kids tell you they'd rather be left alone. When you do, they will be less likely to choose friends who will lead them astray.

After the love of family, the next important factor needed to counter outside influence is the support of a strong education. The next chapter will take a look at what you can do to improve the quality of your child's schooling.

7

Education

They Can't Take It Away from You

Education is the single most important measure of the ability to succeed. It is also the most powerful tool for challenging stereotypes and overcoming racial barriers. A lack of education, more than any other factor, pushes blacks (more so than their white peers) into low-paying, dead-end jobs.

For these reasons the black community has long held the education of its children in the highest regard. Despite a mainstream cultural bias that frequently depicts black parents as uninvolved or uncaring, data from the U.S. Department of Education support the truth: black parents are more involved in school-related activities than are white parents (often in an effort to supplement or compensate for the inadequate education of their children). This survey found that African American parents of eighth graders were more likely than their white counterparts to say that they talked regularly with their child about school experiences and their plans for after high school, that they limited the number of hours of television their children watched on school days, and that they had rules about maintaining a certain grade point average.[1] Still, our true legacy for the education of our children is supported by scientific data and a deep-seated cultural quest for advancement.

Millionaire Scholars

The emphasis on education as a family expectation is ingrained in our people. That's why some notable black athletes who drop out of college to pursue professional sports for millions of dollars still often promise their families that they will eventually go back for their degree. The parents of basketball stars Michael Jordan and Shaquille O'Neal, for example, insisted that the young men finish their college degrees. So they both went back as young adults during their summers off from playing in the National Basketball Association to the University of North Carolina at Chapel Hill and Louisiana State University to complete their educations. Notwithstanding all the money they were earning, the young men knew that a college degree brought pride to the family. Their families knew that a college degree meant security even after their sons could no longer play ball.

Like the black parents in the U.S. Department of Education survey, you have a strong role to play in the education of your children. This does not necessarily mean that you must sit down and teach them their actual school lessons. As this chapter explains, it means you must do these six things:

- Pass on the legacy: make sure your children know how important education has been to the black community throughout American history.

- Support the academic environment your children learn in.

- Strip away stereotypes that keep black children down.

- Raise educational expectations.

- Fight the stigma of so-called acting white.

- Support good teachers.

By doing these six things, you will become an advocate for your children in the school system that is responsible for training them for future success.

PASS ON THE LEGACY

An appreciation for the value of education is deeply embedded in our culture. Knowledge has always been viewed as a passport to a better life, more valuable than money or other material things. After all, money comes and money goes, but an education stays with you forever.

Early Efforts

Most early efforts to educate blacks were initiated by various churches in the hopes of enabling slaves to read the Bible and be Christianized. As far back as the late 1600s, the Church of England established the Society for the Propagation of the Gospel in Foreign Parts to Christianize slaves in British colonies. But there was strong opposition in the Southern states to teaching slaves to read and write. In fact, it was illegal. Southern plantation owners knew that education amounted to empowerment. They feared that if slaves could read and write, they would have tools to influence others and perhaps lead a movement that would take blacks from slave status to free people and even overpower landowners. Although some slaves became literate through their own determined efforts, they did so at risk of extreme punishment or even death.

Immediately following the Emancipation Proclamation in 1863, various church denominations and groups like the Baptists, Methodists, and the American Missionary Association (AMA) founded schools for the children of ex-slaves throughout the South.

In fact, the AMA founded more than five hundred schools for freed slaves in the decades following the Civil War. These schools were open to all students and often operated as integrated institutions during the Reconstruction period. But despite these efforts, the traditions of racism, white hostility toward blacks, and the inability of the black minority to protect itself after Northern troops went home disadvantaged the former slaves from the start.

As the South recovered from the effects of the war and developed public school systems, the AMA concentrated on improving and expanding colleges for blacks in the South. Many of the private institutions now known as historically black colleges and universities began as AMA schools. They include what were traditionally regarded as elite liberal arts schools, including Atlanta University, Dillard University, Fisk University, Hampton Institute (now Hampton University), Howard University, Huston-Tillotson College, Le Moyne College, Talladega College, and Tougaloo College (my alma mater).[2]

Northern religious organizations also promoted the education of blacks after the Civil War. In 1704 a member of the Society for the Propagation of the Gospel in Foreign Parts established the first school for blacks in New York City. As early as 1735, the Quakers were teaching black children to read and write. By the later 1700s, the Quakers opened schools specifically for "colored" children, and later they were instrumental in opening schools in New Jersey and Pennsylvania that allowed black and white children to attend together.[3]

The Struggle for Desegregation

Then in 1896 a landmark U.S. Supreme Court decision, *Plessy v Ferguson*, declared that public institutions should be separate but equal. Justice Billings Brown asserted that distinctions based on race did not run afoul of either the Thirteenth or Fourteenth Amendments, passed to abolish slavery and secure the legal rights of former slaves. Although the phrase *separate but equal* appears nowhere in the opinion, the Court's rulings approved legally enforced segregation as long as the law did not make facilities for blacks inferior to those of whites.[4]

But those facilities were inferior. In most areas black schools were plagued with overcrowding, inadequate materials and supplies, and dilapidated facilities. Typically, black schools received the used textbooks and other supplies from white schools even though they were public and supported with tax dollars. I am a product of such a school and studied from the hand-me-down books from the white schools in my hometown.

Still, despite the educational obstacles born of racism, segregation, and oppression, African Americans expected each generation to be better educated than the last. From the 1910s through the early 1930s, the black community raised millions of dollars from a very poor population to build and staff schools for its children. The desire and respect for education continued to grow throughout the twentieth century.[5]

As the twentieth century unfolded, the debate, the laws, and the consequences of segregation and desegregation became the crucible for the civil rights struggle and defined the experience of blacks in the American educational system. In 1954 another landmark case, *Brown v Topeka Board of Education*, mandated the end of segregation in schools. But this was not the end of the inequities in American education. Instead of desegregating the schools when the Brown decision was handed down, many white legislators decided to build new schools for black people in order to postpone or simply not comply with desegregation orders. So once again blacks had to file suit against the refusal of the Southern states to comply with the Brown decision, and the courts usually ruled in their favor.

Still, the inequities continued. In Mississippi, for example, white children were taken out of their public schools and put into private, segregated schools called SEG (segregation) academies. Only poor white children and blacks were left behind in many public schools. Since the passage of antisegregation laws, I've seen the all-white high school in Hattiesburg, Mississippi (my hometown), transformed into a virtually all-black school. Today the school doesn't have the distinctiveness, the academic and administrative budget, and other critical support that it once had as a white school. Now it is a typical school for blacks: academically inferior to many of the white schools around it, suffering from the same inequities black schools face in poor neighborhoods in the urban North.

The battle for integrated and equal education continues into the twenty-first century. Acquiring a good education today is as critical as it has ever been for black children. The technology-driven global society our children live in requires high-level training, and many concerned and involved individuals are doing something about that. Bob Moses, for example, founded the Algebra Project to teach black children advanced mathematics because he believes that mathematics and science courses are gateway subjects that prepare children to compete in the technology-driven workforce. He asserts that access to these gateway subjects is the hallmark of citizenship just as voting was a gateway legal right for disfranchised blacks whom he helped register to vote in Mississippi in the 1960s. His results have been extremely successful and opened doors to thousands of children who had been deemed unlikely to succeed.[6] As Moses and other educators have found, society is demanding far more from our children than ever before; we must help them be prepared to face and conquer the challenge.

SUPPORT THE ACADEMIC ENVIRONMENT

LaQuesha, Will, and Kwame all attend the same selective East Coast university, yet their educational backgrounds are quite different. LaQuesha went to a large, inner-city, predominantly black high school. She had a few select friends, but some of her high school classmates put her down for having good grades and for thinking she was better than they were when she applied to top-level universities. Will went to a predominantly white, private high school. He kept up with his peers in the classroom and on the athletic field but was rarely included in social activities. Will considered himself a high-achieving misfit when he also applied to elite universities in the East and Midwest. Kwame went to an integrated suburban high school that had an equal mix of blacks and whites. They all got along, and the color of Kwame's skin was not an apparent issue with his friends or in the classroom, so he thought it was no big deal when he applied to the same top colleges as his white classmates.

LaQuesha, Will, and Kwame are all on the road to career success, despite their varied geographical, educational, financial, and experiential backgrounds. Like these three students, the educational experiences of our children today vary widely. They are educated throughout the country in both public and private schools; in urban, suburban, and rural areas; in wealthy, middle-class, and poor districts. Regardless of background, the major universal factor in the successful education of black children these days is the ever-present parental support behind capable students—despite the continuing presence of racism. No matter where our children go to school, they may still have to overcome the obstacles caused by racism, while at the same time struggling to keep a sense of cultural pride. You can help them find this balance by supporting their academic efforts and nurturing their cultural roots in whatever type of school they attend.

Black Children in Integrated Schools

Many excellent integrated schools exist around the country. Aside from having good facilities, equipment, active parents' groups, and competent teachers, these schools are also the laboratories for learning how to survive in an integrated society. They provide a microcosm of the "real" world where our children will make their future. Many of these schools successfully blend children of white, black, Asian, Hispanic, and other ethnic backgrounds in one educational system where they all learn the new ways of adapting to a rapidly changing society. If your children attend well-balanced integrated schools, help them take advantage of this racial and ethnic diversity.

Make sure your children have equal access to all the classes (including advanced placement courses), extracurricular activities, and opportunities the school has to offer. Much of the learning goes on outside the classroom, so be sure that they go on the field trips and exchange programs. Teach them to be good citizens by taking leadership roles in school clubs. Support group assignments that put children of all races together to work toward a common goal, whether it is a community service project to collect food for a homeless shelter or a joint classroom assignment. Encourage your children to participate in integrated and cross-cultural activities. (It is not uncommon for students to segregate themselves according to various preferences including race.) Make sure they respect one another's differences. The black child who finds a comfortable fit in an integrated school is likely to find that same fit in the larger world.

Children in good integrated schools are the beneficiaries of the hard work of the activists in the civil rights movement in the 1950s and 1960s who fought tirelessly for desegregated schools because they knew this was the only way to ensure that black children had the same access to higher-quality education that was available to white children. In fact, separate was never equal. Make sure your children know and appreciate that legacy, while at the same time retaining their own sense of self and a positive racial identity.

Black Children in Black Schools

If your children are in a predominantly black school, you are probably well aware of the effects of racism on your child's education. These schools are most often in poorer communities (whether in the inner city or in rural poverty), and they frequently do not have the facilities and resources they need for students to keep up with the children in more affluent districts. They often lack modern school buildings and advanced-level curricula with the latest technology and science labs; they struggle to keep good teachers, who often go to higher paying and less-demanding environments.

Some children attend these schools because their parents believe in public education and try to support the system. Others are there because they have no choice. In either case these children especially need reinforcement at home to get the most out of their education. Here you need to make it clear to all teachers, counselors, and administrators that you have high expectations for your children. Here you need to demand high achievement from your children and academic excellence from the teachers. And here you need to keep close track of your child's studies and progress. Fill in the gaps if you feel your child is not learning in school. Reinforce all school lessons; buy your own workbooks; and assign your own homework. Do not let the poor quality of your child's school ever be an excuse for academic failure.

Black Children in White Schools

If your children attend a predominantly white school in a middle-class community, where the few blacks are very much a minority in the student body, they may receive a higher quality education with more academic resources than their peers in an all-black school in a poor neighborhood. These schools will have a more varied and advanced curriculum. They often have higher-paid teachers and state-of-the-art facilities. Certainly, these factors give your children academic advantages that will help them realize their future goals.

Even in this environment, however, your children still need your help. Here they are likely to be very much in the situation of minority students. They may lack positive black role models. Also, being the minority student can sometimes put a lot of extra pressure on kids. They sometimes feel that they cannot fall short. They must be on their best behavior at all times to counter others' preconceived negative stereotypes. Many don't want to stand out so dramatically and get tired of playing this role of the token or special kid. They also have ample reason to question whether their peers and teachers really accept them or if there is subtle racism. Some cope quite

well in these circumstances, but some withdraw and voluntarily isolate themselves. Others may act out.

Although your children benefit from the academic advantages
offered in these middle-class, mostly white schools, continue to support their need for a strong and positive identity at home. As discussed in Chapter Three, even a good education and privileged
opportunities will not compensate for a child's lack of a strong personal identity and low self-esteem. Your children also need to understand that being in a predominantly white school does not mean that
they will automatically get a first-rate education or that going to a
predominantly black school is inherently inferior. Always remember
to convey to your children that race and class are closely intertwined
and that no matter what the racial composition of their school is,
their responsibility is to put forth their best efforts to excel.

STRIP AWAY STEREOTYPES

The stereotype of black children as uneducable or hard to teach is
still alive in America. The most blatant example of this kind of
thinking was expressed by, of all people, Francis Lawrence, the president of Rutgers University in 1994, a person in a position of prominent educational leadership. Addressing the viability of using the
Scholastic Assessment Test (SAT) as a primary factor in deciding
college admissions, Lawrence said: "The average SAT for African
Americans is 750. Do we set standards in the future so that we don't
admit anybody with the national test? Or do we deal with a disadvantaged population that doesn't have the genetic hereditary background to have a higher advantage?"[7]

"Disadvantaged . . . genetic hereditary background"? This kind
of thinking is reminiscent of the most egregious type of racist pseu-
doscientific double-talk. The effects of any stereotype that says that
our children are genetically disadvantaged begin in preschool or
kindergarten and follow them throughout their education. The
destruction of the myth must be an ongoing process throughout the

school years on every level. It must also continue when your young adult offspring launches into a professional career.

My mother used to say that we always had to work twice as hard and remember that we had no margin for error because the standards to which racist whites would hold us would be very high. Her words still ring true today.

This negative labeling is especially evident with boys. This is because people often interpret normal and predictably excessive energy in a black boy as acting out. Our boys are often unfairly labeled as being intellectually slow or physically hyper or as having attention deficit disorder (ADD). Sometimes their slow or hyper behaviors are fueled by their teachers' expectations that they are going to cause trouble. In turn, if the black boy sees that he is punished for an act that a white boy is not punished for, he is likely to feel that he is being singled out because of his color. Children respond to racism in the only ways they know how: they withdraw, act out, or become depressed. Too infrequently do they tell their parents that their teachers are mistreating them.

Young children are ill equipped to ignore the insults leveled against them. Even if you have told your children to pay no attention to the racist teacher or the kids who taunt them with racial slurs, they will feel inevitably the stinging blow of being labeled and stigmatized. All children crave acceptance by their peers and the important adults in their lives. When black boys are labeled as difficult or as slow learners in need of special education or of the medication Ritalin (to calm down their so-called hyperactivity), they cannot help but feel excluded and isolated. In many children, once a label is assigned, the negative behaviors fulfill the negative expectations; kids accept the negative labels of behavior problem or slow learner, and they begin to act out the role.

The long-term damage is incalculable. Researchers have found that although black males constitute only 8.5 percent of all public school students, they represent 36 percent of special education students and 37 percent of all school suspensions. They are more likely than other students to be placed in remedial programs and lower-track classes, and their high school dropout rate is as high as 60 percent in some cities. Some say that black male students are especially likely to experience the "Invisible Child Syndrome," where they are ignored and discouraged from learning.[8]

What a waste of potential! We must become our children's advocates on every front. We must fight mistreatment based on stereotypes in the classroom, at parent-teacher association meetings, in the principal's office, in teacher conferences, and in public hearings on the school budget.

We must continue the fight in our own homes by supporting and encouraging high academic performance so that society's low expectations never become self-fulfilling prophecies. Black boys need extra encouragement. We need to show them lots of tender loving care even as they are growing into an adolescent macho phase. Behind a lot of the bravado and machismo is a vulnerable child who desperately needs to know that his parents love, support, and care for him unconditionally. (At the same time, black boys cannot use racism as a reason for not succeeding in life. They must persevere against racial discrimination and work twice as hard to jump each hurdle!)

Black like Me

Pride in one's race comes from lessons in the home at a very early age. Gwen Magee, a longtime friend of mine, told me this story that highlights the way a child with a positive self-image perceives the world: "A few years ago when my two daughters were home from college, they were looking at some of the drawings they did in elementary school. We had a really good laugh because there was one picture that Kamili had drawn of George Washington chopping down the cherry tree. She had used brown crayon to color his skin just like her own!"

RAISE EDUCATIONAL EXPECTATIONS

Today black civic and professional organizations work harder than ever to counter society's biased expectation of black children as so-called slow learners. And we must do the same in our homes to keep educational expectations high. Research studies have found a strong relationship between parental expectations and school success; my parents knew this without any scientific data behind them. Mother reminded us often that she would have studied nursing, but she didn't have the opportunity. "You children have the opportunity that I wish I'd had," she said. "You have no excuse not to get an education."

We have to remember to pass this message on to our own children, starting as early as possible. If you communicate to your children that your family values high grades and academic achievement and that you expect these of all your children, they are more likely to meet those expectations than will children whose families don't.

Next you must make sure that your child's teachers and school administrators hold the same expectations. Unfortunately, scholars have reported that the number of black children who perform below their grade level has been on the rise, and educators typically try to solve this problem by placing the children in special categories and low-track classes.[9]

Don't let this happen to your children. Talk to their teachers. Ask questions. Make it clear that you support the school system. Tell them you intend to be involved in your child's education, and you expect results and accountability from the teachers. Educating your child is a partnership between you, your child, and the teachers. Each person must do his or her part in order for the child to succeed.

What Can You Expect from a Standardized Test?

One common factor in this incessant labeling of black children as dumb is the use of standardized tests, especially and most notably the so-called intelligence quotient (IQ) or the SAT and American College Test (ACT) scores that allegedly evaluate aptitude, achievement, or ability. In many cases across the country, blacks do not achieve scores comparable to their white peers. This has supported the centuries-old belief that blacks are innately inferior on an intellectual level.

Some have challenged this notion by pointing out that the standardized tests used to label, place, and evaluate the intellect of children are culturally biased. Cultural bias refers to the idea that the poor performance of minority and economically disadvantaged children stems from their unfamiliarity with the content and format of the tests rather than their lack of the thinking processes needed for high-level problem solving.[10]

Researcher Jane Mercer has championed the view that all so-called intelligence tests are in fact tests of achievement, because intelligence can develop only in a cultural context. The tests, she argues, tend to be heavily loaded with questions requiring progressively more advanced verbal skills in the English language and knowledge of the history, values, customs, and institutions of the Anglo core culture. The tests assume that most non-Anglo cultural groups have had the opportunity and the desire to assimilate and have indeed absorbed the essentials of American culture.[11]

For some black children, these norms might be a fair yardstick of learning potential because those children are raised in social circumstances characteristic of the core culture. They might, for example, have two parents who have attained at least a high school education, speak standard English, and participate frequently in community activities. These children have been exposed to the kinds of things on which the standardized tests are based.

Some purport that this exposure to the white middle-class culture is a key to high scores on standardized tests. A study of forty-six African American children who had been adopted as infants by middle-class black and middle-class white families is a good example. When tested later, the adoptees in the white families had higher IQ scores than those adopted by black families. This study indicated that black children socialized in the white middle-class system's core culture performed on a par with their white classmates on standardized intelligence tests.[12] However, one can surmise that if the intelligence tests included more material based on the core of African American culture, the children raised in white families might have scored lower.

When black children who are raised in families outside the core culture do not perform well on the tests, authorities falsely assume that they *cannot* do well; that is, they do not have the ability to do well, even though they have lacked exposure in their daily lives to the wider society's expectations of which skills are needed to do well in the dominant white society. This occurrence supports the erroneous belief that IQ test results represent a fixed intellectual potential, that nothing can be done to help today's low scorers become ready for higher levels of education tomorrow. The IQ test often leaves children with the stigma of being labeled innately inferior, unable to develop their intelligence, and permanently doomed. Therefore, authority figures think it best to track them into lower-level, dead-end occupations. This is the dangerous pattern from which we must protect our children.

Regardless of your children's standardized test scores, keep your expectations high. Assess the areas of weakness and get extra help to improve the scores. My friends sent their daughter to a very expensive boarding school for one year after high school in order to help her master mathematics on the level she needed to be competitive. It worked splendidly because of the investment of time, energy, and resources they used to get her on track in this specific area.

Not all parents have the resources to send their child to a specialized school, but you can still find out why your child's verbal score is low while the math score is high, or vice versa, and what to do about it. Be proactive by seeking out the help that exists in the school and community. See what free services may be available or advertise for a tutor at the school, community recreation center, and at your church; hire a college student to help; or consider carefully some of the test preparation classes that are offered everywhere these days.

But be careful. Consult with your fellow parents; shop and compare; make sure you get the best value for your money. And if you cannot afford to pay, look into tutoring programs run by students in the local college, high schools, churches, and volunteer organizations. Remember that although the intelligence and college application tests do not represent the core culture of many Americans, including blacks, it is still important for your child to do well on tests. Moreover, math, science, and reading comprehension are not culture-bound, so your children must develop those skills to be competitive in the white world. If they need extra time because of a learning disability, request that they be given an untimed test (as required by law).

Expect the Best at an Early Age

With the necessary academic skills in hand, your children then need a positive can-do attitude that the negativism of others cannot crush. We can best encourage this attitude when we start early. The value of education should be instilled in children from birth onward. Keep educationally oriented materials in the home. Read books and nursery rhymes to children to help them increase their vocabulary. Involve your young children in family conversations and even in discussions of current events. Encourage them to think critically by asking them their views on subjects of discussion. Show a genuine interest in their feelings and points of view. This is how they acquire analytical skills and a strong sense of self-worth. We all have an obligation to start the process of intellectual growth before our children arrive at school. This prepares them to take advantage of their schoolwork right from the start and avoid the label of disadvantaged that comes with being black.

FIGHT THE STIGMA OF ACTING WHITE

Because I know how long and how hard my ancestors fought for educational opportunities, I find it especially difficult to understand the dumbing down or acting white phenomena affecting the potential of some black students.

Acting white is a charge that some black students levy against other black students who earn high grades and take advanced courses. Some alienated young people feel so helpless and hopeless that they ridicule the value of academic success. They have redefined success as being available only to whites, and they have kept the image of failure for themselves. This is a tragic example of blacks keeping blacks down.

Fortunately, the acting black–acting white phenomenon is not as widespread as the popular media would have us believe. Many black kids are graduating high school and college and building successful lives without ever encountering the stigma of acting white. Or, if confronted with the stigma, they have enough self-confidence to stay on their path to excellence by not succumbing to the desire to be accepted by their racial group. But the problem of acting white is out there, and if the attitude is prevalent in your child's peer environment, it can be very destructive. In their article "Black Students' School Successes: Coping with the Burden of 'Acting White,'" authors Fordham and Ogbu relate the experience of the great college and professional basketball player Kareem Abdul-Jabbar, who transferred from a predominantly white to an all-black high school: "It was my first time away from home, my first experience in an all-black situation, and I found myself being punished for doing everything I'd ever been taught was right. I got all A's and was hated for it; I spoke correctly and was called a punk. I had to learn a new language simply to be able to deal with the threats. I had good manners and was a good little boy and paid for it with my hide."[13]

We must be aware of and connected and involved with our children to make sure they do not use dumbing down in a pretense of honoring their race, thus sidetracking their goals and dreams. At home continue to reinforce a sense of positive identity. Praise your child for his or her efforts to do well in school. Reward good grades and praise high-achieving blacks in your community. Find people and activities that offer approval for achievement. Try to involve the child with other families with high-achieving children. Find after-school clubs, organizations, and activities. You must be proactive because merely saying, "Keep your head held high, and do what you know is right" is too simplistic a response to this complicated situation.

Being Black in a White School

Author Rochell Humphrey wrote this account of her school experiences:[14]

> I was called an Oreo by my friends from the city because I did "white" things like play the violin, sing in the chorus, and I spoke proper English most of the time. My mother did not consider speaking proper English speaking "white." She considered it "speaking like you have sense," and she felt very strongly against her children fitting any of the negative stereotypes that seem to plague the black people of this country. She didn't want us to be white; she just wanted us to recognize that we didn't have to limit ourselves. . . . I remember I resented the fact that no matter how hard I worked I would still be seen as "black," and therefore less than they [white students] were. Without the support of my mother, who was convinced that her children were going to make something of themselves and worked actively at convincing us, too, I would have started to believe that notion of inferiority.

Negative peer influence is especially strong for our gifted children. Researchers have found that academically gifted black students often experience more psychological and emotional problems than do black students not identified as gifted. Gifted black children frequently find themselves having to choose between academic success and social acceptance. When caught in this tug-of-war, some black students attempt to sabotage their achievement by failing to do assignments, exerting little effort, reprioritizing values, and giving more energy to securing social acceptance. They underachieve.

As parents we need to be aware of this social and academic problem. In the general population of gifted children, about 20 percent underachieve. However, more than 40 percent of black gifted students, especially male students, do not work up to their potential.[15] If your children's grades start dropping or if they are not achieving at a level that you know they are capable of, you must find the underlying cause of the problem. You may not get the answers you need out of the child alone. Talk to the teachers. They may notice a change in the child's socialization habits. They will know if the child is being teased in the classroom when he gives correct answers. They may know if your child is being forced to choose between doing his schoolwork and being ridiculed and ostracized by his peers. This is not an easy choice.

To avoid the hold of negative peer pressure, our kids need to build a sense of self-worth that is stronger than the need to be accepted by a group that appears to be headed toward failure. Peer and support group counseling with high-achieving students can be very helpful. See if your school can set up opportunities for black children to meet, discuss coping strategies, and support each other. They might discuss how they feel about being smart, how they cope with peer pressure and low teacher expectations, and whom they turn to for emotional and academic support. In addition to offering information and coping skills, these discussions may lead to friendships and decreased feelings of isolation and alienation.

You can also counter the isolating effect of your child's being a good student by encouraging him or her to participate in extracurricular activities that promote social interaction and leadership. Children need to find activities outside of the classroom that let them interact with their peers on different levels. If, for example, a good student is also an athlete or a member of a musical or drama group, she may find it easier to gain social approval in these activities, thus reducing the isolation at school.

History Lessons

For white children history lessons affirm their positive role in government and society. They learn about the white visionaries who founded the country, the courageous white men who led armies to victory, and the adventurous white explorers who opened horizons. They feel pride in the roots of their culture and lineage.

For the black child, history classes about black achievement are often limited to the history of race-based slavery, discrimination, and intergenerational poverty, and a brief mention during Black History Month (February) of some accomplished blacks. If this is the extent of your child's lessons in cultural heritage, work with school officials to supplement their material with more multicultural resources. Push for the adoption of new textbooks that teach race and diversity. Then take time to bring resources into your home that give your children this information. Talk about accomplished black people. Make sure your children know about the courage of Harriet Tubman, the slave who escaped and went back into the deep South countless times to bring other slaves to freedom; Frederick Douglass, the abolitionist who defied slavery; countless modern-day achievers like Charles Drew, the black physician who created blood plasma; and Thurgood Marshall, the first black to serve on the United States Supreme Court. Our children need to hear a lot more about black Americans' contributions to science, government, literature, architecture, medicine, and so on. This can have a big effect on their own motivation to excel and be different.

SUPPORT GOOD TEACHERS

I went to a segregated school in Mississippi. This school had hand-me-down textbooks and two or three Bunsen burners for what passed as a science lab. Our library consisted of a bookshelf in a classroom. (The school had a book budget of one hundred dollars, an amount set by an all-white board of education that granted the white schools a considerably larger book budget.) The ceiling leaked in my classroom. We did not have a real playground, and we had a dirt court for our competitive basketball games. No one in power seemed to care because this was an all-black, segregated community.

Therefore, I have had to ask myself, How did I excel academically and go on to earn my Ph.D. degree? I can easily answer that the foundation of my success lies in my family's unwavering dedication to education as a passport to a better life, the community support behind my efforts, as well as the dedication of the excellent teachers in my school. My teachers were part of our all-black, self-reliant but interdependent community. Our teachers' values were the same as those of our parents, extended family, neighbors, and church members. This uniformity in values gave rise to high expectations for our educational success.

Although our schools were materially unequal to those of our white peers, it was much easier for us to excel back then because our teachers were genuinely concerned with our learning and believed our scholastic achievement was tied to the continued progress of the race. Our teachers assumed that we could and would learn, and if they failed in their efforts to teach us, they considered it a sign of their own inadequacy.

Things have changed, however. Very frequently, teachers today don't live in the same community as the children they teach and don't know them outside of school. They do not know the parents and their values. They do not attend the same church. They no longer assume their students can learn.

In addition, teachers today no longer have the respect of children or their families. This respect began to decline in the black community in the late 1960s and early 1970s when social problems began to increase in urban schools and when occupations other than teaching began to open up for black people. The latter provided choices to black men and women who had historically been confined, for the most part, to teaching. I have visited countless public schools around the country, and sadly I see that teachers are no longer the undisputed authority figures in their classrooms. Violent and disruptive students, disrespectful parents, and a hostile public challenge teachers to the point where students now attack teachers verbally and physically. How can these teachers care deeply about the success of our children?

The insult is further aggravated by the low compensation teachers earn for this most important job. They make less than accountants, lawyers, and doctors, and often less than waitresses, sanitation workers, and store managers. Given the paltry investment we make in our children's education, it is not surprising that the quality of teacher candidates is often low (especially in the inner city) and that their students enter the workforce without the skills necessary to function in a highly competitive technological society.

Teachers are the pivotal link between our children, ourselves, and the future that we want them to have. This link must be kept strong. You can do your part by going out of your way to know your child's teachers. Don't just walk in one day and demand accountability. Right from the start, be involved in the class and the school. If at all possible, make time to volunteer in the school so that you can work together for your child's best interests. Get involved in school organizations. Groups like the parent-teacher organization (PTO) or parent-teacher association (PTA) give you an opportunity to meet the people directly involved in your child's education, and meeting them will directly influence the way the teachers perceive your child.

Make sure your child's teachers know that your family values education and achievement. Support and praise teachers who nurture and push your children to reach their full potential. Vote for school budgets that reward them financially. Identify teachers who are burned out, prejudiced, insensitive to or unaware of the needs of black children in the classroom and request to have your children kept out of their classes. If that isn't possible, stay closely involved, counter any offensive remarks or experiences your children may have with your own brand of encouragement.

When your child has a good teacher, support his or her efforts. Teachers are facilitators of knowledge, but the responsibility to make sure your child is prepared to take advantage of that knowledge rests with you. The teachers rely on you to reinforce what's being done in the classroom by making sure your children are there every day, are rested and well fed (your children may qualify for free meals if your family's income is below the poverty line), and come to school with a positive attitude about learning. If we all give our teachers the family backing they need to do their job well, our children will reap the benefits a thousandfold.

An Educational To-Do List

Check off each of the main points in this chapter as you incorporate them in the education of your children:

❑ Make sure your children know how important education has been to the black community throughout the history of America.

❑ Support your children's academic efforts and nurture their cultural roots in whatever type of school they attend.

❑ Fight the myth that our children are genetically disadvantaged in the academic arena.

❑ Communicate to your children that high grades and academic achievement are important in your household and expected of all your children.

❑ Find out, if your children are not achieving at a level that you know they are capable of, if they are being forced to choose between doing schoolwork and being accepted by peers.

❑ Look into the reasons why your children may be getting low grades on classroom exams or IQ tests. They may have deficiencies that can be identified and corrected. Do not wait. Do so immediately.

❑ Keep the links to your children's teachers strong. Teachers are the pivotal link between our children, ourselves, and the future that we want our children to have.

MAKE IT HAPPEN

Some children don't succeed because they don't have a pragmatic understanding of the connection between getting an education and succeeding in life. That is why we should view education as a tangible commodity, not an abstraction. Show your children how an education is directly linked to professional and skilled jobs. Talk about the education your child's doctor has had. Talk about the training needed by firefighters and so on. Then set high educational goals and explain how your family can use loans, jobs, savings, and scholarships to finance a higher education. Our kids need to know that further education and good jobs are not out of reach for any one.

They also need to know that the educational opportunities today are far, far greater than they were for our grandparents, great-grandparents, and great-great-grandparents. After completing their guaranteed elementary and high school education, students of their generation can choose to go on to the best colleges and universities in the country. They can and do go on for postgraduate degrees that allow them to be doctors, lawyers, business managers, executives, Ph.D. scientists, and educators. Nothing can stop them as long as they can avoid the lure of drugs and violence that, as the next chapter explains, keep far too many of our children from reaching their full potential.

8

Drugs and Violence

No Place to Hide

At age fifteen Robert was an honor student with a promising future; at age eighteen he was a drug addict shot dead on the street. His family, his friends, his teachers and classmates all stood in shock at his funeral. *How,* they all wondered, *could such a smart and motivated boy end up like this?*

At first the signs were subtle: Robert withdrew from the family and spent all his time at home locked in his room. His old friends stopped coming around, and new friends called on the phone but never visited. Robert quit playing football and basketball at school so that he could work more hours at the grocery store; he said he wanted to save money for college, yet he was always borrowing from his parents against his next paycheck.

Robert's parents barely noticed these small changes. Both were professionals who worked long hours. They also led very active social lives, which frequently kept them out at night with their friends. Robert had always been a good kid, and his parents didn't worry about leaving him alone so much. His father would say, "It's good for a kid to learn to be independent." They also thought that the things they gave him (his own car, computer, video games, and so on) were enough to keep him busy and on the right path. But because they were so preoccupied, Robert's parents didn't pay close attention to the little changes that occurred over time.

But later the signs became more obvious. Robert started skipping school and was fired from his part-time job. When his parents expressed genuine concern, he said his teachers gave him low grades because they didn't like him. He also said he "wasn't learning anything anyway, so what's the big deal about skipping classes?" In addition, he cast blame on his supervisor at the part-time job, saying the man was a racist who didn't like him. Robert was easily agitated and quick to start fights. His moods swept from sullen to hostile.

His parents then realized that their son was in trouble. "You'd better straighten yourself out," his father would say, "or I'll put you out." On the other hand, his mother tried to reason with him without the threat of violence. She knew her son was in some deep trouble, but she was clueless as to what it was. She begged him tearfully to confide in her, but Robert didn't trust her enough to do so. At this point he was too far gone for them to pull him back so easily.

In a moment of desperation after Robert's behavior did not change, his parents decided to search his room for any clues to his behavior. They looked through his dresser drawers and found the source of the problem: marijuana and trace amounts of white powder that they suspected was cocaine. While his mother fell to her knees and cried, his father's initial reaction was anger. Why in the world would their son do this after all they sacrificed to give him a better life than they had?

To think that drugs could destroy the future of their once high-achieving son who had been given so many opportunities was more than they could take. Although they realized that they had never talked to their son about drug abuse, his father felt, *I shouldn't have to tell him that drugs are bad—he should know!* After the initial shock wore off, both parents were crushed. Their reactions were a mixture of anger and confusion: they were angry with themselves for not acting on their suspicions that something was wrong months earlier; they finally realized that Robert had changed before their very eyes and that they had done nothing to stop it. They were angry at Robert for lying to them about why he was so lethargic, stayed locked away in his room, and disappeared for long periods of time. They also turned their anger outward at the dangers of the streets for sidetracking his goals and at a society that expected black males to self-destruct.

When Robert returned home late that night, he discovered his parents' "intrusion" (as he called it) and flew into an uncontrollable rage. He threw furniture across his room as his father tried to physically restrain him. Then he ran out of the house while shouting that he didn't need help from anyone. His parents were distraught. His father drove around the old areas where he hung out to look for him, while his mother phoned all of Robert's friends known to her. What they didn't realize was that Robert no longer frequented his old hangouts, nor did he still see his old friends. He had told his parents so many lies about where he was going and who he was going with that they did not know that he had another life and new friends who were drug users and pushers. Robert had gone to the drug-infested part of the town he now frequented. Two days later the police rang the doorbell at his parents' home to tell them that their son had died when a drug deal went wrong.

Robert's death by drugs and violence is the nightmare that parents of all races and socioeconomic backgrounds dread. But statistics tell us that the problems of drug abuse and violence have a more devastating effect on black teens than on any other group of young people. A *New York Times* article says that in some areas of the country, it is now more likely for a black male between ages fifteen and twenty-five to die from homicide than it was for a United States soldier to be killed on a tour of duty in Vietnam.[1] This is a situation that we, as parents of black children, must not ignore, deny, or hide. We all must step forward and be proactive to protect our children from drugs and violence.

Fortunately, even though drugs and violence are very serious problems, the majority of children do not give in to these pressures. They do not because in most cases, the support systems of their families, schools, communities, and churches have given them values that encourage optimism and hope rather than despair and anger. Colin Powell mentioned the vital role of values in saving our children at the Republican convention in 1996 when he said:

> Our vision first and foremost rests on values—values, because values are the conscience of a society. Values that must be lived, not just preached. Children learn values by watching their parents in their homes, values that are then reinforced in their churches and places of worship, in their schools and in the communities in which they live. Values fuel families, families that are bound together by love and commitment, families that have the strength to withstand the assaults of contemporary life, to resist the images of violence and vulgarity that flood into our lives every day. Families that come together to defeat the scourge of drugs and crime and incivility that threatens us.[2]

This is our charge: to give our kids the family values they need to stay away from drugs and violence. Of all the outside influences that can steer our children off the positive road to career success, drug abuse and violence are the most grave. Addiction, incarceration, and homicide destroy far too many black teens and young adults. Because these consequences are so damaging, we must make a very conscious effort to help our kids remain free of drugs and violence.

DRUG ABUSE

Drug abuse is not something that happens only to other people's kids or only to the urban poor. We all know stories about white suburban kids from privileged families whose lives were ruined by drugs. And it does not occur randomly; there are reasons why some kids fall victim and others do not. Often a key reason lies in the family. Research studies repeatedly show that a child's family has a strong influence over the likelihood of his or her abusing drugs. Parental love, guidance, and support help children develop self-esteem, self-confidence, personal values, and goals—all of which contribute to the making of drug-free kids.

Keep Your Eyes Open

Because the lure of drugs is in most neighborhoods and schools in America, you should be ever vigilant in watching your child for signs of drug abuse. If you notice subtle changes that worry you, do not disregard them as signs of a typical teenager. You know your child very well, and you know when something's not right. Trust your instincts.

The time to talk to your child about the perils of drug use is long before they do so. Do not wait until they have started using drugs. Talk to your child about your concerns (without being accusatory) and keep an open dialogue going. Engage them in conversations about drugs so that you can understand how they feel. Even if what they say offends or upsets you, it is still better to know. Only then can you intervene before the act rather than waiting until they get into trouble. Also, let your children know that their rooms are not off-limits to you. As long as you are paying the bills on the house, no part of it is none of your business. Make it hard for your kids to use drugs.

Keep reminding yourself that preventing drug abuse is far easier than stopping it. Keep your eyes open for early warning signs such as unusual behavior, new friends, a need for more and more money, items missing from your home, and in some cases, poor emotional health.

Unusual Behavior

Kids who are drunk or high look, sound, and act different. We all know that, but it is easy to turn a blind eye when the subject is our own children, who we believe would never do that. Do not deny the possibility: look for glassy eyes, excessive giggling, runny nose, slurred words. Watch for the personality changes and mood swings that accompany some drug use. Your children may become uncharacteristically quiet or loud, active or fatigued, or they may swing from forlorn and sullen to brazen and angry. They might also become secretive and deceptive.

These changes are not always indicators of drug abuse; sometimes they occur as children struggle through adolescence to gain independence. But if they persist, they are a reason to be vigilant and to intervene if necessary.

New Friends

Kids very often get drugs from their friends. So it is critical that you know your children's friends. When they call on the phone, take a moment to talk to them and invite them over. Make your home welcoming and kid friendly. Notice if your children suddenly have new friends. Be observant and honest about what you see: Do they look to you like losers? This might be a sign that your child too feels like a loser or doesn't feel that she can measure up to a higher level of success.

Keep your kids active and involved with highly motivated children. Children who do not have friends or are not involved in extracurricular activities or feel bored or isolated often fill the void with drugs. Make sure you recognize the voids and find positive replacements.

Need for Money and Missing Items

Drugs cost money—lots of it. Be aware if your child is asking for more and money. Is she "borrowing" money without asking? Is he getting an advance on his allowance repeatedly from both parents? Is he working steadily but still asking for money? And do not shrug it off as weird if you notice that things are missing from around the house. Take note if your child begins to lose things like her good leather coat or her CD player. She may be selling possessions to support a drug habit.

Poor Emotional Health

Although as parents we are generally quick to notice and attend to physical disease or disorders, we frequently ignore our children's emotional problems. Left unattended, these problems can lead to substance abuse. Depression, for example, is common but usually undiagnosed in teens. Yet we know that children who are depressed because they are experiencing stress or loss or feeling the burden of learning, conduct, or anxiety disorders are at a higher risk for substance abuse.

There is a connection between depression and drug abuse because, like adults, some teens self-medicate to relieve the pain. Unfortunately, the physical, social, and psychological problems associated with substance abuse give them more reason to be depressed, thus bringing them further down into the hole of hopelessness, isolation, and sadness. They then feel the need to use more alcohol or drugs to pull themselves back up. It is a vicious cycle.

We need to be alert for signs of troubled mental health. Signs of depression can include the following:[3]

- Feelings of sadness or emptiness

- Loss of interest or pleasure in ordinary activities

- Eating disturbances: loss of appetite and weight, weight gain

- Sleep disturbances: sleeping much more or much less than usual

- Change in activity level: slowing down or speeding up of activity

- Fatigue or loss of energy

- Feelings of guilt or worthlessness

- Difficulty concentrating, remembering, and making decisions

When you see your child struggling with what may be depression, you might think it is best to respect his privacy and wait quietly for the blues to pass. But if the symptoms of depression are obvious to you, your teen is probably waiting for you to say something to show you've noticed and care about his pain.

Do not be afraid to be direct. You might say, "I've noticed that you seem withdrawn [angry, sad, or whatever] lately. Let's talk about it." If your child opens up to you, do not jump in with a quick solution; just let him know you understand that sometimes life hurts. Even if your child's problems seem trivial to you, take them seriously and spend time helping him sort them out; offer a story from your own life that shows you understand the problem and that the pain passes and life goes on. Then encourage him to brainstorm ways to change the situation and feel better so that he can gain some control over the situation. Do not be judgmental about his coping plans; just listen and let him think things through.

If you listen intently and show your support, the depression may resolve itself. In most cases childhood depression passes in a few days or weeks and is a valuable learning experience. But if the mood doesn't pass, then your child may be experiencing a deep, despairing clinical depression that needs professional help.

Unfortunately, the black community has traditionally frowned upon psychiatric care because for many years black people were forced to learn to cope by themselves with physical or emotional problems. Few mental health professionals were available. Also, mental illness was often considered shameful and a sign of weakness or an inability to cope. Today we know better; mental health care is widely available, and we must not let this stigma keep us from getting professional help for our children if the signs of depression last for more than two weeks or impair ordinary functioning. To reach out for help, you can begin with your school guidance office, your family doctor, or a mental health professional. If your child refuses help, go for help yourself and ask for advice on how to handle the situation.

To find more information about depression and counseling, contact the National Foundation for Depressive Illness (see Helpful Resources at the back of this book).

Start Early

Do not wait until your child is a teen hanging out with the wrong crowd before you bring up the subject of drugs. More often than not, it will be too late. The U.S. Department of Education's booklet *Growing Up Drug Free: A Parent's Guide to Prevention* says that children in grades four to six should know the following:[4]

- Ways to identify specific drugs, including alcohol, tobacco, marijuana, inhalants, and cocaine in their various forms

- The long- and short-term effects and consequences of use

- The effects of drugs on different parts of the body and the reasons drugs are especially dangerous for growing bodies

- The consequences of alcohol and other illegal drug use to the family, society, and the user

This list gives you a lot to talk about. But before you bring up these topics with your kids, do a little homework. Your kids will laugh you off if you give them outdated or exaggerated information on the dangers of drugs. You can find out the facts through many fine on-line sites that have been established to help parents keep their kids off drugs. You might start with these and check Helpful Resources at the back of the book for more information:

TheAntiDrug.com TheAntiDrug.com was created by the National Youth Anti-Drug Media Campaign to equip parents and other adult caregivers with the tools they need to raise drug-free kids.

Parents' Resource Institute for Drug Education (PRIDE) PRIDE is the largest organization in the nation devoted to drug- and violence-free youth. It offers programs devoted to reach parents and youth at home, school, and work.

Prevention Online The National Clearinghouse for Alcohol and Drug Information stocks many materials that everyone can use to better understand the facts about drug abuse.

The National Council on Alcoholism and Drug Dependence This site offers objective information, including statistics, interviews with medical or scientific experts, and recommendations about drinking and drug abuse from leading health authorities.

Talk to Your Kids About Drugs

Unfortunately, minority youths are overrepresented in the statistics on addiction and drug-related problems. And according to one study sponsored by the Partnership for a Drug-Free America, black parents realize this and are doing something about it. This study found that black parents were more likely than Hispanic or white parents to say they discussed the risks of drugs regularly with their children. Fifty-seven percent of black parents in the study said they did so, compared with 45 percent of Hispanic parents and 44 percent of white parents. And 31 percent of the black children in the study recalled having such conversations, compared with 29 percent of Hispanic children but only 19 percent of white children.[5]

All this talking makes a difference. Another study by the Partnership for a Drug-Free America reported that of the teenagers in the study who said they had heard nothing at home about the risks of drugs, 45 percent said they had smoked marijuana within the last year. One-third of those who said they had learned a little at home used marijuana in the same period. But among teenagers who said they had learned a lot, only 26 percent said they smoked marijuana. Comparable reductions were reported in the use of inhalants, hallucinogens like LSD, and crack cocaine.[6] So even if it appears that your words are going in one ear and out the other, keep talking. Your kids really are listening.

Here are some tips from the book *How to Talk to Teens About Really Important Things* that can help you have meaningful conversations with your kids about the risks of drug abuse:[7]

Let your actions speak for you. Let your kids hear you say, "No, thanks, I'm driving" when offered that extra drink at a family party.

Be open about expressing your beliefs, values, and feelings. Let your children know that your family does not accept any form of drug abuse. Be firm, but do not become hysterical and exaggerate the dangers of drugs; you will seem ridiculous and out of touch.

Be calm. Remember that you are sharing ideas and information about drug abuse. Do not put your teenager on the witness stand or demand a confession. Also, do not try to talk when you are too angry or hurt to be coherent and reasonable.

Keep the discussion focused. Your goal is to talk only about the problem of drug abuse—nothing else. If you stray to a critique of friends, music, or attitudes, your point will be lost.

Remember that a single discussion will not do the job. Reinforce your child's learning with reminders and ongoing discussions.

Praise the good. When your child has acted responsibly in a difficult situation, show your approval. This is especially important when your child follows his conscience rather than his friends.

Encourage your child to stay away from drugs because it is the healthiest choice for her body, mind, and future.

Listen

When you have conversations with your kids about drug abuse, you do not have to do all the talking. This too easily leads to lectures and accusations, and that is how you lose your children's attention completely. Let your children know that you want to hear what *they* have to say about drug use and abuse. Then listen, even when you may not agree.

To get your kids talking, ask age-appropriate questions and listen to the answers. You might try some of these:

- "Some people think the drinking age should be lowered to eighteen. What do you think?"

- "Do you think it is true that nearly 40 percent of teenagers try marijuana before they graduate high school?"

- "If kids know that sniffing glue or nail polish remover can cause irreversible brain damage, why do you think they do it anyway?"

- "I heard that some children are starting to use crack in elementary school. Why do you think they do that?"

Then ask your kids probing questions like these: "What do you mean by that?" and "Can you give me an example?" The more you show you are really interested in their point of view and will listen without judgment or interruption, the more your children will talk.

Use the Media to Open the Door

Sometimes items in the news or on TV create opportunities for discussion; be sure to use them. Scan the daily papers and circle articles related to drug use. Some will show the devastating effects of substance abuse in alcohol-related car accidents, drug-war murders, and lung cancer deaths. Ask your child what she thinks about that. Ask if she knows anyone in the same situation. Use the news item to open the door to further discussion.

You might also use educational TV shows to support your efforts to educate your children about the dangers of substance abuse. This tactic worked quite well for a friend of mine. Mary's daughter, Lisa, was fifteen years old when she first heard the music of Styles P and the song "Good Times." She played it loudly and constantly. She read everything she could find on the group, hung posters in her room, and seemed to admire the lifestyle of hard drugs. Naturally, Mary was not happy with this new idol, but she knew it would be useless to forbid her daughter to listen to that music. But how could she possibly counter the glorification of drugs she knew her daughter was being exposed to?

The opportunity to offer some balance came unexpectedly one Sunday night. Flipping through the TV channels, Mary came upon a PBS documentary on heroin addiction. She made a bowl of popcorn, poured some soda, and called Lisa into the room.

"Come here," she said. "Let's watch this show together. There's so much I do not know about today's street drugs; we could learn something together."

Lisa did a quick U-turn, saying, "Forget it, Mom. I'm not watching that show."

Because Mary knew this could be important, she responded, "Either sit down and watch this with me, or your can forget about going out on Friday night."

With great annoyance, Lisa sat down.

Not long into the show, Mary saw that the images of young people with collapsed veins shooting drugs into their genitals was having the effect she'd hoped for on her daughter. Revolting and yet sad, the show made a great impact.

Years later, during a conversation about a friend who was struggling with drug addiction, Lisa told her mom about a TV show she had seen as a teen that convinced her to stay away from street drugs. "I do not know how I happened to see that show," said Lisa, "but it really affected me for the rest of my high school years."

Lisa didn't remember that her mother had forced her to watch the show; she remembered only its impact. The message is what's most important. So even if your kids give you a hard time when you steer them to informative sources like documentaries, articles, or news clips, persevere in your insistence that they get the information. It does make a difference.

Support School Prevention Programs

In many communities, schools have programs about substance abuse that support the parents' efforts to raise drug-free kids. Find out if your school has such a program. If so, ask your child's teacher when it will be presented to the class so that you can use it to support your own lessons at home. You might say to your child, "I hear a former drug addict came to your school today to talk about drug use. What did he tell you? How did you feel about his message? Do you think his story will keep some kids away from drugs?" When the school is providing the lessons, you do not need to lecture. Just use the experience as a platform to begin a discussion.

If your school does not have a drug prevention program, you can be instrumental in getting one started. To begin, you might contact Drug Abuse Resistance Education (DARE; see Helpful Resources at the back of the book). DARE is the single most widely used substance abuse prevention and safety promotion curriculum in the world for children in grades from kindergarten through high school. DARE promotes healthy self-assertion, positive choices about risk-taking and health-related behaviors, and positive social skills. DARE's curriculum also teaches resistance to substance abuse, gang membership, violence, and destructive peer pressure.

The National PTA also has a program called Common Sense: Strategies for Raising Alcohol- and Drug-Free Children. Designed primarily for parents with children in grades 3 to 6, it also offers resources for parents of younger and older children. You can find more information on the group's Web site (see Helpful Resources).

Be a Good Example

Children's complaints about hypocritical or inconsistent parents most likely stem from parents' own use of alcohol and drugs. Before you set firm limits on your child, take some time to think about your own use of tobacco, alcohol, and drugs. Many adults use them to ease physical and emotional pains. We take drugs when we have a cold, when we have a headache, when we're tired, when we need to relax. Prescription drugs are so much a part of our culture that we don't even think of them as having an adverse effect on our children's perceptions of us. But it's this casual use of legal drugs that gives our kids the impression that drug use is no big deal. They are bombarded with media messages that drugs are good, therapeutic, and necessary. Drugs provide fast solutions to problems, whether it's a headache, a cold, or a backache. It's in this environment that your kids will be listening to your antidrug messages. You can give these messages more impact if you first monitor your own tobacco, drug, and alcohol use.

Explain that some drugs are legal and that using them sensibly is not necessarily bad. At the same time, use prescription and over-the-counter drugs with caution and explanation. When you take medications in front of your kids, you might say, "I'm taking this cold medicine because a drug like this can be helpful if I don't take too much or use it too often." Let your kids know that drugs are only for positive medicinal purposes. Avoid comments like these: "Boy, do I need a cigarette." "What a day! Where are the aspirins?" "When I get home, I'm going to have a stiff drink." Remarks like these convey the idea that it's acceptable to use substances to quickly change one's mood.

Be Honest About Your Past

When you start talking about drugs, don't be surprised if your kids want to know if you ever smoked pot, used other illegal drugs, or engaged in underage drinking. Considering that the media have broadcast even former President Clinton's experimental marijuana use and President George W. Bush's history of alcohol abuse, the use and abuse of drugs is bound to come back to haunt many parents.

If you did use any illegal drugs or abuse alcohol, truthfulness with clarification is the best way to respond to kids' questions. If you lie or are evasive, you'll lose credibility in your kids' eyes when they probe relatives and old friends and find out the real story. Tell them: "Yes, I made a mistake, and if I had to do it over again, I wouldn't." And point out your knowledge of the adverse effects and dangers of your use: "I remember driving while I was high and putting myself and everyone in the car in great danger. Even though all the facts about the dangers and long-term effects of drug use weren't in yet, it was still a stupid and dangerous thing to do." Or "I knew [or heard about] some young people my age who died from drug use. That frightened me, so I decided I would never take drugs again."

Our kids also need to know that the stakes and consequences for drug involvement today are much higher than they were when we were young. Even drug possession can be illegal in some states like New York that send people to prison for interminable sentences because they are caught with crack cocaine. Drugs not only ruin your life, but they can wipe out your future altogether if you spend it behind bars. One misstep today can mean twenty years behind bars without any right to appeal. Take the case of Kembra Smith, a young African American woman pardoned by President Clinton after spending six years in jail. She was a college student who got involved with the wrong crowd. She dated a drug pusher who quickly had her transporting drugs up and down the East Coast. She was eventually arrested and spent several years behind bars facing a twenty-four-year sentence with no chance for parole. Her boyfriend was murdered, and the child born of this union was reared by her parents. Kembra was young, made some bad choices, and paid a heavy price.

Be honest and let your kids know that you and others have made mistakes and that you hope they can learn from these mistakes and avoid the risks of drug use and abuse.

Talk About the Future

Be sure your kids understand *why* you are so firmly against drug abuse. Tell them specifically how drug or alcohol use can destroy their long-term goals and ambitions. You might concede that today's music, movies, and videos make drug and alcohol use look cool. But point out the reality. An arrest record, a driving accident, addiction, low school grades, or teen pregnancy (which are all associated with drug use) make it very difficult for an individual to rise above the rest, to become successful, and to build a secure and happy future.

Time to Act

If you find that your teen is involved with drug use, open, honest communication is your best tactic for addressing the problem. If your teen is arrested for drug possession, if you find drugs in his or her room, or if he or she comes home obviously drunk or stoned, you can't assume this is a onetime mistake that will never happen again, as your teen will promise. You need to address the situation directly and seriously.

Although your first inclination may be to protect your child, don't be too quick to rescue your teen from the penalties associated with drug abuse. A few hours at police headquarters behind bars or being booked on a charge of possession will teach your child a powerful lesson. Moreover, making your son or daughter pay the lawyer's fee in order to get out of the mess your child created should also teach a lesson.

You will also need to be firm about your stand against drug use. Make it clear (again) that your family has a no-drug rule. The National Institute on Drug Abuse advises parents to back up this rule with a clear and consistent set of rules that they are willing to enforce. In countless interviews with drug-troubled teenagers, one hears complaints about parents being hypocritical, inconsistent, permissive, selfish, or aloof, but almost never any complaints about strictness, rules, curfews, chaperoning, or involvement.[8]

When making and enforcing rules to guide your children through this difficult time, do not be afraid to be a strong parent. State firmly: "You cannot use illegal drugs. If you do, you will [insert a punishment that you think is appropriate]." Then make sure your teen knows that if he does not learn this lesson, he will begin therapy for drug counseling and rehabilitation.

To find more information about drug counseling, call the National Clearinghouse for Alcohol and Drug Information (see Helpful Resources for contact information). You can talk to a professional counselor who specializes in your area of concern.

As Robert's parents learned too late, the consequences of drug abuse can be deadly. State your family rules against drug abuse when your children are young; keep the conversation going; and be proactive in saving your child from this destructive fate.

VIOLENCE

Our children live in an inescapable culture of violence that continues to affect black communities more harshly than it does white communities. The facts are shocking: homicide has been the leading cause of death among African Americans age fifteen to thirty-four since 1978. The lifetime risk for violent death for young black males is 1 in 27. By contrast, 1 in 205 young white males and 1 in 496 white females are murdered.[9] These statistics are most alarming when they are coupled with the fact that the fourteen- to seventeen-year-old age group has supplanted eighteen- to twenty-four-year-olds as the most prone to crime.[10]

These statistics no longer come only from the inner cities, where the problem can be blamed in part on the harsh effects of poverty and problem-ridden families. Today moral poverty and a profound sense of alienation leading to teen violence is found in every town and valley. And as these younger teens commit more of the serious violent crimes on our streets and in our schools, they seem to be showing more cruelty without remorse. Consider the school killings in white middle-class communities, killings that cannot be blamed on poverty. The nation must become more concerned about what makes for white middle-class children who commit mass murder and why they kill without impunity when they have no material needs whatsoever. What makes them so angry and remorseless over their actions?

Why the Anger?

We can also ask why many young black people feel so angry and hostile. For many this is the consequence of living in a racist society. When children experience, feel, and internalize racist rejection and contempt from mainstream society, they tend to express contempt for society in turn.[11] Some commit crime to protest their real or perceived unequal social, economic, and political status. Black youths who experience racial profiling when they are followed around retail stores or pulled over on the road, questioned, frisked, and bullied by the police sworn to protect them, for example, do not grow to respect the law or even feel bound by its rules.

The anger fueled by racism creates a cycle of alienation. Black youths, who feel cut off from full participation in the system, find that violent acts on the streets earn them the respect and status that mainstream society denies them. But this glorification of violence further isolates them from their own dreams of success.

It is not surprising that young blacks react to racism with violence; in their world of TV, movies, music, and videos, violence is the answer to all problems. It is so common that they have built up a tolerance that blinds them to the horror and pain of "blowing someone away." American culture has made violence a form of entertainment, and as our children internalize that message, an act of violence becomes more of a challenge—a game—than a serious act with dire consequences.

Parent Power

This is a situation that we cannot ignore as we guide our children to positive career goals because violence can keep them from reaching their potential in several ways. When they are the perpetrators, children risk suspension or expulsion from school, a criminal record, and incarceration, depending on the severity of the act. As potential victims they are at risk for psychological, emotional, and physical damage. However, as they venture out on their own, can we really have any impact on their actions and safety?

Some researchers don't think so. In 1993, for example, the National Research Council stated that the impact of deviant peers is overwhelming during adolescence for African American youth, so much so that parents may be able to do nothing to offset it.[12] However, researchers like Dr. Chanequa Walker-Barnes do not agree that parents are powerless. Walker-Barnes recruited three hundred ninth graders from English classes at a Miami high school. Fifty-four percent of the students were Latino; another 25 percent were black; and the rest were white or of some other race. The students completed a series of questionnaires: a long baseline questionnaire with follow-ups every three weeks for the remainder of the school year. Some of the questions measured gang involvement (defined as hanging out with gang members, wearing gang colors on purpose, and flashing gang signs), as well as gang delinquency (spray painting gang symbols, taking part in a gang fight, and selling drugs for a gang). Still others measured the levels of parental involvement or what researcher Walker-Barnes calls behavioral control.

"Behavioral control, as I defined it, consisted in measuring the parents' involvement in decision making," says Walker-Barnes. "I asked a series of questions and the answers were based on a five-point scale, where the low end was, 'I decide on my own,' the middle was 'my parents and I discuss it and we make the decision together,' and [the] high end was 'my parents tell me what to do and do not discuss it with me.'" Walker-Barnes found that higher levels of the high-end authoritarian kind of parenting with African American kids resulted in lower levels of gang involvement and delinquency. Most surprisingly, it was among black youth, as compared with the Latino or white participants, that parenting behavior showed the strongest, most clearly measurable impact.[13]

I too have found that strong, no-nonsense parenting can shape the way kids view and use violence. To raise nonviolent kids, we need to set limits, be firm, offer alternatives, state consequences, follow through, and never be afraid to be a parent. Lay down the law at age-appropriate levels and make sure your kids know you mean it: "No, you can't kick the dog like that; let me show you how to make her obey." "No, you cannot have that violent video game, but I will buy you other ones." "No, you cannot hang out on the street corner with those kids, but you can have your friends over to the house for pizza, my treat." "No, you cannot come home anytime you want to, but I'm willing to talk about a reasonable curfew."

Then follow it up. "If you do not do as I say, this will be your punishment: you will not be allowed to have friends over or to visit their homes for whatever time I decide." As parents we have to decide which controls we want to use and how we wish to implement them. The key thing to remember is that we have the power to keep our kids in line if we choose to use it.

Predisposition to Violence

Do your children have trouble controlling their anger? Are they drawn to kids who are prone to rough play or even to violent gangs? Sometimes from an early age we can see signs of an aggressive personality in our child. In fact, according to *Reason to Hope*, the 1994 report by the American Psychological Association Commission on Violence and Youth, it is possible to predict from an eight-year-old's aggressive behavior in school how aggressive that child will be in adolescence and adulthood, including whether he or she will exhibit criminal and antisocial behavior. This is why prevention experiences that start early in childhood and continue throughout adolescence have the best chance for success.[14]

Teach Nonviolence

Social and behavioral scientists agree that violence is not innate but is a learned behavior. Given the amount of violent behavior our children see in the media and the world around them, it will take a conscious effort on our part to balance those lessons with ones that promote nonviolence or nonphysical ways to solve problems and handle stressful and conflict-laden situations. The most effective lessons are built by the examples children observe and from the development of a positive self-identity.

By Setting an Example

If we want our kids to believe that violence is not an acceptable solution to life's problems, we need to take a close look at how we resolve our own conflicts. Kids should grow up seeing people deal constructively with their anger. They need to learn that although anger is natural, it can and must be controlled.

How do you deal with your anger? If someone cuts you off while driving, do you yell obscenities or make obscene gestures? If you are tired or frustrated after work, do you act short-tempered and pick on the kids or your spouse? When you are angry with your children for breaking the rules, do you scream or hit? Every one of these actions teaches kids that violence is the best way to handle feelings of anger.

Instead, let your children see you using nonviolent coping skills. Count out loud to ten before saying anything in anger. Walk away until you have calmed down. Explain that you are very angry and will talk about the problem when you feel more in control of your actions. In other words: practice what you preach.

The way you resolve problems with your children and your spouse or significant other also has a major influence on how your children will resolve interpersonal problems. Domestic violence is traumatic for a child because it involves people the child loves and depends on for care. Children exposed to this violence are likely to suffer severe emotional and psychological damage. They may come to see the world as dangerous and unpredictable. They may lose trust and repress feelings, which can directly affect their emotional development. This can create intergenerational cycles of domestic abuse, because beating our children or our spouse gives the children permission to use this form of problem solving themselves. Thus, they repeat in adulthood the lessons they learned while young.

In this violent world, we have an obligation to give our children refuge. Our home must be a place where strong and angry feelings are handled without cruelty or brutality. Give your child armor against the world's violence by being a positive role model yourself.

By Building a Positive Self-Identity

Individuals who feel confident, proud, and valued are unlikely to go looking for trouble. Research from the American Psychological Association suggests that positive early experiences, relationships, and abilities that build self-esteem can counter the negative effects of violence:[15]

- Positive role models, exposure to a greater number of positive than negative behaviors

- Development of self-esteem and self-efficacy

- Supportive relationships, including those with teachers and friends

- A sense of hope about the future

- Belief in oneself

- Strong social skills

- Good peer relationships

- A close, trusting bond with a nurturing adult outside the family

- Great empathy and support from the mother or mother figure

- The ability to find refuge and a sense of self-esteem in hobbies and creative pursuits, useful work, and assigned chores

- The sense that one is in control of one's life and can cope with whatever happens

As discussed more fully in Chapter Three, if you teach your children to feel good about themselves, they are more likely to feel good about other people as well. Mutual respect is the basis of nonviolent existence.

Teach Kids to Avoid Violence

Teaching our kids how to solve their problems nonviolently and how to grow up with confidence and pride is the first and very important step in fighting back against this culture of violence. However, we also need to teach our kids how to protect themselves from the violent actions of others.

Part of being safe in a violent society is being aware of the dangers and knowing how to avoid them. Go over the following list with your kids to make sure they know how to stay away from danger.

- Do not take shortcuts through deserted places.

- Do not wander into isolated areas.

- Do not be out alone after dark.

- Do not look like a victim with your head down and shoulders slumped.

- Always walk with confidence at a quick pace.

- If attacked, fight back. Go for vulnerable areas such as eyes, groin, and throat, and use any "weapons," such as keys or fingernails, within reach.

- If you think you are being followed, go to the nearest house with a light on or go into an open place of business.

- Check inside and under your car before getting in after it has been parked.

- If you are followed when driving, do not go home. Drive to the nearest police station.

- If threatened for your money, jewelry, clothing, car, and so on, do not resist. Hand it over.

It is hard to make your kids proactive without perhaps scaring them a bit. But the reality of the world we live in makes it important that they are aware of the violent intentions of others and know how to keep their eyes and ears open.

Being Black in a White World

Although all are supposed to be equal in the eyes of the law that protects us from violence, blacks historically have found the equality to exist more in theory than in reality. Immediately after the Civil War, every Southern state enacted black codes to keep the former slaves under tight control. After the Union voided these, white Southerners began exploring other means to maintain their supremacy over blacks. Southern legislatures enacted criminal statutes that invariably prescribed harsher penalties for blacks than for whites convicted of the same crimes, and they erected a system of peonage that survived into the early twentieth century.

Through the generations, black parents taught their children how to avoid the wrath of white people by looking down and averting their eyes. They taught their children not to speak first and to be very circumspect when dealing with white people. Whites insisted that blacks say "yes, sir" and "yes, ma'am" to them but degraded blacks by calling them boy and girl if they were young and auntie and uncle if they were older. In Mississippi, where I grew up, I witnessed the daily humiliation of black men and women at the hands of white people. Black men were especially vulnerable to these rules. I can recall that a black man in Arkansas was charged with "eyeball rape" of a white woman. This is an example of how insidious these informal codes were. To fail to adhere to them was to risk death. These survival tactics were passed down through the generations until the passage of federal civil rights statutes. Fortunately, today these lessons are no longer as necessary as we gain economic, social, and political equality.

Sadly, there are still circumstances where our children (especially our sons) need to know how to stay alive when interacting with white people in authority. In today's criminal justice system, the inequities are more subtle, but they still exist. More blacks than whites are incarcerated. Blacks receive more severe prison sentences, and more blacks than whites sit on death row. Blacks are more likely to be sentenced to death for killing a white person than a black person. This situation makes it vital that we help our children stay on the right side of the law, even one that is unequally applied. They must try to avoid those situations where they may be brutalized as in the now-infamous 1992 beating of Rodney King by four white Los Angeles police officers and the 2002 case in which Inglewood, California, police officer Jeremy Morse slammed sixteen-year-old Donovan Jackson onto the trunk of a squad car and then punched him in the face.

I can well remember how my parents always taught us to keep our hands in clear view when we went to white-owned department stores, lest white salespeople accuse us of stealing merchandise. I taught my growing son survival strategies that my parents taught me. When stopped by the police, do not talk back; do not act hostile; keep your hands in clear view so that they cannot accuse you of reaching in your pocket for a gun; and do whatever else is necessary in order to stay alive. There are too many trigger-happy cops who appear to be waiting to ambush a young black man. I taught my son to swallow his pride and let out his anger after he got out of the situation with a policeman who stopped him for no reason other than harassment.

Our children should have the right to grow up and experience an adolescence that is protected and secure. It is unfair for our sons to go through life looking through a rearview mirror for the danger that lurks in the background. We must empower them to stand up for their rights. We must also be strong advocates on their behalf. If the police in your precinct are given to arresting black teenage males for no good reason, organize the other parents and protest this situation with the mayor and chief of police. File a lawsuit against them if they continue to practice this shameless form of discrimination.

We do play an important role in keeping our kids safe, but it is not an easy one. As black parents we must find a way to walk this line between teaching our children respect for the law and teaching them that they may not always reap its benefits. We must instill mainstream values in our children, make sure they are street-smart, and at the same time help them understand the ways in which racism affects their status in our justice system.

A DIFFICULT TASK

The task is difficult. But by talking with our children about the negative impact of drug abuse and violence, we take a first and most important step. The world is telling them that drug abuse and violence are fun and normal; children need to hear their parents' assurances that they are not. The world is telling them that drug use makes them feel good and there are no consequences to bear; they need to hear about the reality of drug abuse from you. Tell them, "You create the kind of world you will live in every time you make a decision about drug use or violence. Decide carefully." Make sure they know that their future success and happiness depend on the decisions they make today. They will not be able to reach high and feel the pride of accomplishment once they fall down into the world of drugs and violence.

We take a second important step every time we talk to our kids with respect. Say things that convey acceptance, appreciation, approval, admiration, and affection. Kids who get these things from their parents are not filled with the kind of despair or anger that lead them to drugs and violence. As we'll see in the following chapter, we can also meet their specific needs by understanding the way their gender affects their place in the world.

9

Raising Sons and Daughters

Gender Differences

Low self-esteem, negative peer influence, lack of self-discipline, poor education, drugs, and incarceration all have the potential to keep our children from reaching their career goals. Now, we must consider another obstacle that can be more insidious and unavoidable than these others: black gender bias. The negative stereotypes that plague the young black male and the young black female are less obvious today than they were throughout history (especially for the middle class), but they certainly still exist.

It is our job as parents to help our children recognize, face, fight against, and overcome the negative stereotypes that can keep them down.

RAISING SONS

There is a strong cry in the black community today for parents to raise responsible, high-achieving black males. Our sons need to finish high school, go on to college, and join the world of successful workers, whether professional or blue collar, that is now open to those who rise above the race-gender bias of the society.

The awareness of stereotypes often begins early for our sons. In first grade Andrew knew he was treated differently than his white male classmates. When the boys would engage in horseplay or tussle on the playground at recess, only he would be reprimanded for being too rough. Soon his teacher labeled Andrew as hyperactive. By first grade, before he was even taught to read and write, he was assigned to special education classes. In his young psyche, Andrew was being taught to see himself as an overly aggressive and slow-to-learn black boy.

As Andrew grew, the low expectations and stereotypical comments and behaviors by his teachers and classmates continued. When he reached adolescence, he noticed that white women would cross the street to avoid him. When he got his driver's license, he quickly learned that driving while black (or DWB, as it is known) requires exceptional diligence and attention to the rules of the road. In his senior year of high school, Andrew felt the sting of possible job discrimination when he went on an interview for an after-school job at a local medical-supply company. The interview ended abruptly when the office manager dismissed him, saying, "We have no office job for you, but if something comes up in our stockroom, we'll call you." Yet Andrew saw a white boy his age working in the office.

Andrew wonders why he did not get the job. Is it because he is a six-foot-three-inch-tall muscular black man whom the interviewer saw as imposing, threatening, and potentially violent? Or was the white teenager doing office work the son of the owner, for whom the personnel director made an exception because he had an inside track? Andrew would never know, but he would always wonder. When black males like Andrew do not get a job, a promotion, an apartment, or even common courtesies of everyday interactions, they cannot help but wonder if these things happen because of the color of their skin.

A New Form of Lynching

Today black men are no longer being lynched and castrated under Jim Crow laws, but one might argue that the disproportionate number of black men in the criminal justice system is a modern form of lynching. The Bureau of Justice Statistics notes that blacks are five times more likely to be in jail than are whites.[1]

Male Stereotypes

In the South after slavery, there was an expression that the only truly free people were white men and black women. This was true for white men for obvious reasons. It was partially true for black women. Although black women were not truly free because they were subject to exploitation in employment, matters of sex, and other areas, they were not perceived as a threat to society; they were neither the white women who were regarded by white men as goddesses sitting on pedestals nor the black men who were considered brutish subhumans.

Black males were a threat to white men in the competitive marketplace, and so they were denied jobs, loans, and most career opportunities. In addition, they were a threat to the society that feared their supposedly violent nature, and so they were arrested, jailed, and sometimes lynched for the slightest offense or no offense at all. These fears were fed by scholars of the day. In 1896 Dr. Frank Hoffman declared that there was such an "immense amount of immorality and crime" among black men that it had to be part of their "race traits and tendencies." In 1900 Charles Carroll took Hoffman's theory a step further, arguing in the very popular book *The Negro a Beast or in the Image of God* that the black man was left out of human creation and was a subspecies of the animal world.[2]

The media throughout the 1900s picked up these portrayals and fed them to the public as fact. In his book, *The Assassination of the*

Black Male Image, Earl Ofari Hutchinson recounts that in the years before World War I, the press milked the "black beast" angle for all it was worth. "The *New York Times, Chicago Tribune, Boston Evening Transcript, San Francisco Examiner, Atlantic Monthly* and *Harpers* had great fun ridiculing, lampooning, butchering and assailing black men in articles and cartoons," he says. "They were 'brutes,' 'savages,' 'imbeciles,' 'moral degenerates,' and always 'lazy, lazy, lazy.' "[3]

As the century progressed and members of the press supposedly became more racially enlightened, the direct insults and ridicule ceased. Instead, the black male became the target of negative news reporting. If a black man was involved in a crime, newspapers usually mentioned his race and plastered a picture of his face across the page. Front-page stories focused on black male dropouts, dope dealers, and violent gang members. These stereotypes permeated the white general public, giving rise to a negative impression of all black males. For many whites, the only exposure to black men was what they read in the paper and saw on the TV news. They saw few if any images of the many successful and prosperous black businesspersons, dedicated and compassionate civic leaders, or even the average family man, working hard to earn a living and raise his family.

Because the public image of the black male was so poisoned by the media, black parents traditionally taught their children that they had to work harder, be better at whatever they did to achieve, and always be on their best behavior just to get on the playing field. My parents taught all their children this lesson, and my grandparents taught them the same. They knew there was no such thing as a level playing field. No easy breaks were going to come our way.

The black male stereotypes that fuel the fears of some people continue today to keep many of our sons from reaching their full career potential. On the one hand, if a black male does not work hard and outdo his white peers, he is perceived as lazy or without ambition. If, on the other hand, he is aggressive and driven, he is perceived as pushy and hostile. Either way, he loses.

A Mother's Love

There is some concern among parents and others that some black mothers are unintentionally sabotaging their sons' success. The black sociologist Robert Staples published an article in which he reported that black mothers are less likely to discipline or to teach independence and responsibility to their sons than their daughters.[4] His findings are reminiscent of an old saying in the black community: "Mothers love their sons and raise their daughters."

One possible reason for Staples's findings is the mothers' desire to protect sons out of fear for their safety. Mothers might cater to their boys and keep them close to protect them from a world that still too quickly judges a black male as aggressive and dangerous and that is quick to impose on him the modern-day version of lynching, in which the police profile black males for suspicious activity or are quick to think they are guilty of any alleged illegal activity solely because they are black and male. Therefore, mothers are frightened for their sons and so may tend to be overprotective and less demanding. Unfortunately, this can deprive those sons of the sense of responsibility they need to survive in the work world. The challenge for parents is to find a healthy balance between protecting their sons and instilling the values of responsibility, hard work, and the desire to achieve an education.

Corporate Racism

Many corporate executive offices are filled with members of the old-boys' club. These are white men whose fathers played golf with the previous owners and CEOs and who today themselves play golf with the next generation of executives—who are certainly not black men. Some white males at high levels of business still feel that the up-and-coming black male threatens to surpass him not only on the job but in life. Therefore, some corporate executives have a tendency to keep a foot on the rising black male.

Fortunately, life in the corporate world has improved for our sons over the last twenty years. Affirmative action guidelines have eased race discrimination in the business place, and the increasing number of black male college graduates in areas such as engineering, law, business, and medicine has helped swell the ranks of high-achieving black males.

Men such as Frank Raines, chairman of Fannie Mae; Ken Chenault, head of American Express; and Richard Parsons, chairman and CEO of AOL Time Warner, are excellent role models for young black men to follow because they broke the color barrier in the top of the nation's major corporations. These men show our sons that there is no reason to back away from high career goals. They confirm that a black man can make it in any area of business if he is determined. They are proof that our sons need not see themselves as hapless victims of racism who will never be allowed by whites to reach the top; they can be triumphant survivors.

Although only a very small number of black men have broken the color barrier to head Fortune 500 companies, an increasing number of black men and women are in high-level management positions. Black parents must encourage their children to believe that through hard work, patience, survival skills, and a bit of luck—like Raines, Chenault, and Parsons—they too can reach the top.

Male Athletes

Athletics are a positive influence on most children, male or female. Their goals require commitment, dedication, teamwork, and an understanding that one must work hard now for later rewards. These are all lessons that contribute to later career success. However, athletics have a downside for our young black boys that can steer them away from positive career goals.

Our sons should not be encouraged to pursue sports to the exclusion of all other interests solely because it is a way to become a millionaire. Although some professional male athletes make millions of dollars, the odds for a high school basketball player making it to the pros are ten thousand to one. The odds of a high school football player making it—let alone having a career—are about six thousand to one; even for those talented and fortunate enough to play at the professional level, the average tenure in the National Football League is 3.2 years, yet a player must be in the league for 4.5 years to qualify for a pension and be fifty-five years old to draw on it.[5]

These numbers illustrate why the push to be the best athlete must be balanced with a push to be the best student. Parents and coaches do not do our boys a favor when they let them slide by school requirements and get passing grades for classes they have actually failed just so they can continue to be eligible for athletics. We do not help our sons find future security and success when we send them to college on athletic scholarships and then allow them to be pushed through the system with easy courses without any hope of getting a degree. We do not need to play into the stereotype of the strong black man who is aggressive on the playing field and stupid in the classroom and the world at large. We need to stand up and let the world know that black men can be both athletic, highly intelligent, and academically accomplished individuals.

Right from the start, teach your son to balance his responsibilities. Sports cannot interfere with schoolwork, and participating in sports should be contingent upon good grades. College sports must come second to a college education. Even the best of the best who make it to the big leagues have a relatively short athletic career. Make sure your son has a college degree that will prepare him to compete not only on the athletic playing field but also in the real world once he is no longer in professional sports. If your son is offered an athletic sports scholarship, check out the program to see what the graduation rates are for athletes in his sport. If it is very low, this will tell you a lot about whether the athletic program at the college or university is interested only in using your kid to further its aims or if staff members are truly interested in the development of the total person.

The Antidote to Discrimination

It would be wonderful if, as parents, we could protect our sons from racial and gender discrimination. But we can't. Instead, we can equip them with the personal characteristics that they will need to move toward their career goals—no matter what anyone else thinks or says.

Self-Confidence and Self-Esteem

Males who know they are just as capable of career success as their white peers will not be sidetracked by the way others define who they are, nor will they care about what others say about their efforts. They will not back away from their goals when someone says, "Who do you think you are to be competing with white people for this job? Don't you know that this is a white man's job?" They will know exactly who they are and where they are going. Such hostile verbal challenges are not likely to bother them because they will be focused on their goals and will have been socialized by their family and others to be single-minded in the pursuit of their careers. They will know that they do not need to fight their peers verbally or physically, peers who are carrying out their own modern-day form of racism in the professional marketplace. They will win the contest by earning good jobs and secure and fulfilling lives.

Resilience and Persistence

Our sons need to know that career doors still close on black men because of their color. Just because antidiscrimination laws are in place does not mean that discrimination does not exist. However, today they have legal recourse. They can file discrimination complaints whenever necessary. We must teach our children never to fear doing that. Most of all, our sons need to know that when one door is closed, they must keep pushing on other doors until one opens. They cannot give up or give in. Struggling to get what one wants is part of the game. But the rewards are great.

Focus

Our sons must focus on their goals and do what is necessary to reach those goals. They must be completely deaf to the racial put-downs and slurs meant to weaken their resolve to be accomplished individuals and productive members of the workforce.

The attributes that will propel our sons through the work world are learned while they are young. Every experience in school, in the home, on the playground, in the church, and in the athletic arena is preparing our sons for this challenge. We cannot let our boys give up on their schoolwork when they overhear a teacher say, "These black kids are just too stupid to learn." We cannot let them hide from peers who call them names. We cannot stand by and let others define who they are and what they are capable of.

From the moment our sons are born, we must be their strongest advocates and supporters. We must make sure that we react quickly and purposefully to incidents of racial bias and let them see that discrimination is not a reason for giving up; it is not an excuse for not succeeding; it is not insurmountable.

My mother gave me my key to survival through tough racial times when she taught me to develop "tough skin to take all the licks." She also said, "No matter how many times you are pushed down or fall down, you must keep getting up. Pretty soon those who push you down will stop because they will know it's a waste of time because you are tougher than they are." That alone is a measure of success.

Men Helping Men

Racial discrimination is a fact all black males live with, and yet many very successful and productive black men in this country give our sons reason to set their goals high and work hard to achieve them. The 1995 Million Man March in Washington, D.C., for example, was a powerful demonstration of black men helping, supporting, and encouraging other black men. (I went there myself to see this absolutely wondrous example of positive black power.)

Many doctors, lawyers, investment bankers, entertainers, judges, college students, university professors, and politicians marched alongside civil servants, salesclerks, and laborers who brought their sons. This was a self-affirming activity that gave these black men the opportunity to see themselves as a positive force. They looked around and saw other men who looked just like them and who were strong, peaceful, courteous, and caring. Men walked with their toddler sons aloft on their shoulders, alongside a father or grandfather in a wheelchair. Many men came with their wives and children. This was the black world as most black people know it to be, devoid of the stereotypes and typecasting in the wider society. It was uplifting and affirming. If only the spirit of that day could be captured to last forever.

Our sons need to be involved in many activities that build and sustain self-esteem, teach responsibility, and teach them how to achieve by opening their own doors. We must also teach them how to network with others who can help them. Countless organizations across the country have male support groups, manhood initiation rites, and mentoring programs aimed toward black boys and young men. The following organizations can get you started and support your efforts to encourage your sons to reach high and achieve more (see Helpful Resources for more information):

> *100 Black Men of America, Inc.* Since 1963, 100 Black Men chapters across the nation have touched the lives of more than sixty thousand young people. Through mentoring, educational, health and wellness, and economic development programs, young people are gaining the competitive edge. With a mission to improve the quality of life and enhance educational opportunities for African Americans, members serve as a strong force for overcoming the cultural and financial obstacles that have limited the achievements of African American youth, with a particular emphasis on young African American males. Although initially begun by a group of one hundred, membership now is unlimited.

The Urban League The nation's oldest and largest community-based movement is devoted to empowering African Americans to enter the economic and social mainstream. Its mission is to enable African Americans to secure economic self-reliance, parity, power, and civil rights.

RAISING DAUGHTERS

In 1972 Frances Beale, civil rights activist and writer, introduced the term "double jeopardy" to describe the dual discriminations of racism and sexism facing black women. She explained that, as blacks, women suffer all the burdens of prejudice and mistreatment that fall on anyone with dark skin. In addition, as women, they bear the additional burden of having to cope with the obstacles of sexism.[6] As all black women learn, each type of discrimination has a direct and independent effect on the attainment of career goals.

The effects of both racism and sexism have a profound effect on socioeconomic and educational status. Put them together and our daughters face a formidable challenge. White males earn the highest median incomes ($29,696), followed in decreasing order by black males ($21,659), white females ($16,216), and then black females ($16,084).[7] In educational rankings, both white males and females have more years of schooling than do black males and females. Black females have the least.[8] The black woman faces triple jeopardy if she is also poor. Scholars use the phrase "feminization of poverty" to highlight the harsh effects poverty has on women, especially those who are black heads of households.

Given their present position at the bottom of the hierarchy of success, our daughters need our help to dream bigger, reach higher, and climb out from under these statistics. Young women like Tamara show us that it can happen. Tamara was raised in a housing project in the Bronx in New York City. As a junior in high school, she was thinking seriously of dropping out of school. Many of her friends had already left. Some got jobs; some had babies.

School was boring. Besides, she knew that even her teachers felt that she would not succeed in life.

One morning she overheard her homeroom teacher tell another teacher, "All Tamara Jones is good for is to have a baby and go on welfare." In other words, her teacher did not expect her to be successful and as a result did not invest time and energy to help Tamara.

However, Tamara's mother had other plans. When her daughter mentioned wanting to drop out of school, Mrs. Jones made it clear to Tamara that she was going to get her high school diploma and make something of herself—whether she thought it was a good idea right now or not. To renew Tamara's interest in education, she enrolled her in a summer program called BizCamp. This is a nationwide program sponsored by the National Foundation for the Teaching of Entrepreneurship that seeks to teach entrepreneurship to lower-income children (see Helpful Resources for more information).

"My whole life changed because my mother made me go to Biz-Camp," says Tamara, laughing. "I learned that I have a talent for being my own boss, for buying and selling. I have a good head for numbers, and I love the freedom of working for myself with nobody to hold me back or say I can't."

Tamara is now applying to college as a business major. She has direction, passion, and high hopes. That is what all our daughters need in order to overcome the double bias of racism and sexism that they all will face. And that is particularly important for those facing the additional burden of poverty.

A History of Strength

Throughout history, necessity has made black women redefine the notion of womanhood to include the concepts of work, achievement, and independence. Before emancipation, enslaved black women and men could not legally marry; their children were ripped from their arms, and they were sold to distant plantations, never to be reunited. White men sexually abused and beat women. These hardships taught them to be tough, autonomous, responsible, and self-reliant. However, it also left them without the most basic form of support of a husband, father, and helpful companion. Women were viewed as breeders of other slaves to be sold, and their men fared even worse as beasts of burden, defined by the U.S. Constitution as three-fifths of a man.

As slaves and then later as sharecroppers, black women were hard workers. As an example, in the Cotton Belt, women spent approximately thirteen hours a day in fieldwork, engaged in such diverse and traditionally masculine tasks as plowing fields, dropping seeds, hoeing, picking, ginning, sorting, and moting cotton.[9] They also had to look after their own children as well as raise the children and clean the homes of the white slaveholders or plantation owners.

Interestingly, these positive characteristics of our strong, hardworking female ancestors did not first show themselves during the time of slavery. Early West African cultural values encouraged and even expected women to be independent-minded and economically productive.[10] We need to pass on to our daughters the legacy of independence and self-reliance, but without the historic burdens of broken families and backbreaking labor.

Female Stereotypes

Despite their obvious strength in the face of personal and economic difficulties, the stereotype of black women at the turn of the twentieth century was that of promiscuous low achievers. This negative image was given prominence in a number of publications, including newspapers, periodicals, philanthropic foundation reports, and popular literature.[11] Moreover, even today aspects of contemporary life keep these stereotypes alive.

It is true that marriage rates are lower and divorce rates are higher for black females than for their white peers. Moreover, according to the U.S. census, 64.8 percent of black households are run by never-married females with children under age eighteen, as compared to 32.8 percent of white households.[12] Despite popular belief, this has less to do with morality and more to do with the small pool of eligible black men available for black women to marry. The plight of black men in education and the marketplace is so dire that they have little to provide a wife and children. With few marketable skills, racial discrimination, and the increasing frequency of involvement with the criminal justice system, the pool of eligible men for black women to marry is very small.

This problem is not confined solely to poor black women. The very small number of black men available to marry also victimizes high-achieving professional black women. The decline of the number of black men who are entering college has a devastating effect on professional black women, who have always turned to this population for their marital partners.

This situation pushes more black than white women into either the labor market (and more often than not into jobs with low status and low pay) or the welfare system. Either way, the black woman is attacked for her choice. If she works toward self-efficiency, she is often in low-paying jobs where she struggles to meet her financial obligations and barely gets by. She is also labeled by bigots as incapable of higher employment, and she is blamed for not being at home to raise her children.

If she chooses welfare, recent Republican bills passed into law have made working long hours (usually for little pay) a requirement but without providing for affordable childcare, which makes it extremely difficult for single mothers on welfare either to be with their kids or survive financially. Yet these same bigots view her as a drain on working taxpayers who resent what they consider handouts to a lazy, undeserving poor woman whom they stereotype as promiscuous and a bad role model for her children. Either way, she cannot escape society's negative view of her lifestyle or the economic, personal, and social hardships that go with it.

Black women have long struggled against the economic difficulties caused by these stereotypes. At the turn of the twentieth century, the white community wanted black women out of the economic picture and preferably out of sight. In 1908 Daniel Webster Davis and Giles Jackson published *The Industrial History of the Negro Race of the United States*, which became a textbook for black children throughout the state of Virginia. The chapter on women concluded that the Negro race needed housekeepers and wives who would stay at home, supported by their husbands, so they could spend time training their children.[13] Some learned the lesson well. In 1975 researchers Gurin and Epps studied black college students and found that black females, more than white females, displayed lower mobility aspirations and aspired to stereotypic occupations with lower prestige, ability demand, and financial compensation.[14] This study examined the students' dreams and hopes and found them conforming to societal expectations and the stereotype of the low achiever. That is the danger of stereotypes; young black women too often come to believe that they have no choice but to remain society's underclass.

Today our daughters have reason to be more hopeful and ambitious. They have a record number of role models who are graduating college and moving into exciting and fulfilling high-level careers. They have loving parents behind them encouraging them to reach higher. They do not have to be nurses and elementary school teachers if they would rather be doctors, college professors, and business executives. They do not have to be bank tellers; they can be financial investors. They do not have to be satisfied with a college degree if they would like to go to graduate school. Indeed, they can become the national security advisor to the president of the United States; Condoleezza Rice has broken that barrier. They can become president of an elite Ivy League university as Ruth Simmons showed us when she was named president of Brown University. (Simmons is an especially good role model for overcoming adversity because she was one of a dozen children born into poverty.) Prize-winning author Alice Walker, who wrote *The Color Purple*, overcame poverty in rural Georgia to reach the highest levels of literary achievement. I am the third oldest of nine children from the rural South who fought for opportunities to achieve. Fortunately, the doors to career options are now open to all our daughters. Perhaps they will be the generation to smash the negative stereotypes and to break down the doors and glass ceilings.

Sexism

The nation's feminist movement has never really tried to relate to most black women. From the earliest women's rights movements at the turn of the twentieth century, few materials, information, speeches, readings, or persons have represented black women. Most black women rejected the contemporary women's liberation movement because the idea of liberation had little meaning to women who had the historical burden of carrying their own heavy load. Today many feel that groups like the National Organization for Women is partial to the so-called liberation of middle-class white women and insensitive to issues important to black women, such as poverty, lack of educational opportunities, welfare, hunger, poor housing, and limited health care. The economic concerns of women from lower-income backgrounds are relatively ignored in the contemporary women's movement. (The women's movement does appeal to some educated professional black women for whom poverty is not an issue.) Moreover, women of color know that the obstacles of racism and class discrimination that keep black women down have long overshadowed the issue of sexism.

Can-Do Female Power

A female's aspirations are limited only when caring adults do not nurture her dreams. Our daughters need to hear that they can be anything they would like. They need to know that their goals are never too high to achieve. They need to learn that they are just as capable and valuable and have as much to contribute to the professional world as do their white peers.

As their parents, you must pass on these messages. You must find the ways and the means to make these dreams a reality. However, you do not have to do it alone. The following organizations can support black females and help them overcome gender bias (see Helpful Resources at the back of the book for more information).

YWCA of the USA The YWCA hosts sports, physical fitness, and many other programs for girls. The 313 chapters across the country also support leadership, education, and activism activities.

Girls' Pipeline to Power This group teaches girls about politics by introducing them to state legislators, informing them about issues, and helping them become active in their schools and communities.

Ms. Foundation for Women The foundation creates opportunities for girls to develop the skills and tools necessary to make positive change in their communities. Its programs help girls lead the way in issues like environmental justice, sexual harassment, civil rights, and educational reform.

Independent Means This organization teaches girls how to start a business and how to use business strategies such as networking. The organization provides seminars, workshops, books, games, and other activities.

Association for Women in Computing Girls can learn about women who have careers in computers and information technology through this organization that explores the options available in computer science.

As black parents, we need to work hard to prepare our daughters for an independent and productive lifestyle. I can still hear the encouraging words of my own mother: "You go out there and show them a thing or two."

MALE AND FEMALE SEXUALITY

A chapter on the influence of gender on future success would not be complete without mention of pregnancy rates among black teens. In 2001 the Centers for Disease Control and Prevention found that African American high school students were significantly more likely than white students to report that they had initiated sexual intercourse before age thirteen, that they had sexual relations with four or more partners, and that they were currently sexually active.[15]

The actual numbers are high and disturbing. About two-thirds of black females report engaging in intercourse between the ages of fifteen and nineteen (compared to half of white females). Thirty-nine percent of black females report having sex before age fifteen (compared to 25 percent of white females).[16] In 2000 the birth rate for black females ages fifteen to nineteen was 73.1 per one thousand, as compared to 30.2 for white teens. Seventy-seven percent of the black teen births were out of wedlock compared to 24.5 percent for unmarried white females.[17] Because teen pregnancy can instantly dash the most well-thought-out career plans of our children, it is something we all need to address in our homes.

It is very helpful to have early and thorough talks with our teens about sexuality. Their world is filled with sexual messages in movies, TV, music, and print, but rarely do these messages include a word about the effect of teen pregnancy on life goals. We must give our teens a balanced view based on family values so that they are aware that premarital sex has serious consequences that include pregnancy and single parenthood, sexually transmitted diseases (including HIV-AIDS), and the possible destruction of life goals.

But talking alone will not keep your kids from being sexually active. Sexual activity among teens is not so much about having sex as it is about not having positive options. Kids need strong support networks of family, mentors, and teachers, as well as extracurricular activities. They need to feel valued, loved, and respected. They also need to be kept busy with positive activities that leave little time for sex. Teens who have this support are less likely to become teen parents and more likely to reach their life goals.

The organizations mentioned earlier in this chapter offer the kind of positive support that keep kids focused on their goals. There are countless organizations in your home area as well. Be proactive and seek them out. The activities and information they offer show kids the exciting range of life options available to them. They also boost self-esteem, which is so critical to keeping children on the path to achievement and away from problem areas that produce life-long consequences.

If your teenager should become pregnant or an expectant father, your parenting role does not end. It becomes more vital. Your son or daughter will need strong and supportive adult guidance to make the major decisions that follow.

If your son should impregnate a girl, you must also make sure that he acknowledges his responsibilities toward the girl and the child if she should decide to keep the baby. Do not let your young black father leave the female and the child behind as a mistake of youth. This is the time for all your family values and beliefs to surround the couple and support their struggle to grow up quickly. At the same time, you can encourage your son to continue reaching for his career goals. Teen parenting does not have to be the end to all his aspirations—*if* he has family and community support.

If your daughter becomes pregnant, she has life-altering decisions to make. She may choose abortion, adoption, or parenthood. In any case, she will need sound adult support and guidance. With family backing, she too must be supported to continue her education and stay on the path to achieve her professional goals. Studies show that if the teen mother can postpone her second child until she is in her early twenties, she will have more than an even chance to succeed. Again, the old saying would advise our daughters who have become teen mothers to get up off the ground, dust themselves off, and keep on achieving.

REACHING OUT

Our sons and our daughters may have different career desires, needs, dreams, and aspirations. However, they all face the challenge of overcoming gender bias in order to fulfill their potential. This is something they cannot do alone. In addition to your support, a black person's survival depends on his or her ability to use all the social, political, economic, and community resources available. In the next chapter, we will see how positive role models and community support can give kids the inner strength they need to stand up and be counted.

10

Role Models

How to Find and Use Them

No child is without a role model. All children from at least the toddler stage imitate and absorb the behavior, attitudes, and values of the people closest to them, whether these are positive or negative. And children have their closest contact with parents or their surrogates. That's why it's so critical that we make conscious efforts to be good role models and to surround our children with other positive models and influences that will inspire them to make good use of their talents and strengths. We parents and the people we choose to surround our children with are the yardsticks against which our children will measure their own behavior and goals. Without positive role models, far too many of our young black men and women lose their way.

WITH AND WITHOUT ROLE MODELS

The influence of role models on young people cannot be understated. They offer example, motivation, realistic expectations, and often a helping hand in difficult times. The following two stories illustrate how a child's probability of success can be tightly tied to the presence or lack of role models.

Jasmine: Cast Adrift in a White World

Jasmine's family moved from the inner city to the suburbs to give their daughter better educational opportunities.

As a child in her old neighborhood, Jasmine always said she wanted to be a teacher like her third-grade teacher, Mrs. Roberts, an African American woman who was especially encouraging and supportive. Even after the move, Jasmine and Mrs. Roberts kept in touch for a while through occasional phone calls. Eventually, however, they lost contact.

Now Jasmine goes to a school with mostly white children; she has access to the best computers, science labs, and advanced courses. But despite these advantages, her parents began to notice subtle changes in their daughter since she entered high school and started hanging out with children that her parents label losers. They are worried because now she seems to have no ambitions or career goals. When they try to discuss the problem with her, she accuses them of "trying to make [her] into a white girl."

Where would she get the idea, her parents wonder, *that being successful is for white people only?* There may be many reasons Jasmine feels this way, but one reason certainly arises from her immediate environment. All of Jasmine's teachers are white; her doctor, her family's lawyer, her father's accountant, and the owners of the local businesses are all white. In her supposedly advantaged environment, Jasmine has no role models like Mrs. Roberts to inspire her. None of the white teachers has reached out to her, nor has she tried to get to know any of them in a personal way. She hasn't learned how to cope with the barriers of race.

This is especially difficult for Jasmine to discuss with her parents because deep down she genuinely appreciates what they have done for her. She knows they moved to this neighborhood so that she and her younger brother and sister could have the services and facilities her old neighborhood and school did not have. She knows they work long hours to pay for the more expensive home. But still she feels isolated and alone.

Although Jasmine's parents worry about her, they don't realize that they are partly to blame for their daughter's lack of ambition. Although they've worked hard to earn money, they did not work at all to keep the values and traditions of their old neighborhood. They did not keep their church membership in the old community, nor did they keep ties with their many friends intact. Now Jasmine misses all those things, which were a security blanket, and she is rebelling because of the void in her life, one to which her parents appear to be oblivious.

Malcolm: Sticking Close to His Mentors

Back at her old school in a black neighborhood, Jasmine's friend Malcolm has a career goal. He wants to be a professional football player. He is influenced heavily by his black coach, who believes that Malcolm can get into college if he keeps his grades up. He is also close to his homeroom teacher, Mrs. Young, who has taken a special liking to Malcolm because of his gentle nature and her belief that he has what it takes to succeed. Mrs. Young and Coach Jefferson have warned Malcolm to stay clear of the neighborhood guys who join gangs and make fast money by selling drugs. Malcolm watches the news and sees black faces in the majority of criminal reports. He knows some of the guys shown on television because they come from his neighborhood. But he is determined that he will not be one of them.

Malcolm's parents are struggling to make ends meet in their blue-collar jobs; still, they are deeply involved in their son's life, always encouraging him to stay on the straight path. Knowing how many temptations are out there, they watch his choice of friends very carefully. His dad, who did not finish high school, has told him that the way out of poverty is to get an education. He lives for the day when his firstborn becomes the first in his family to get a college degree. If he gets a football scholarship, that will be fine. If he doesn't get a scholarship, they will send him to the local community college or the state university.

Both of Malcolm's parents keep in close contact with his teachers. His father shows up unannounced at football practice to talk to the coach, not about football but about his son's academic work. "We do not miss a single PTA meeting or class advisory," says his dad. Malcolm's mother has frequent conversations with his teachers just to stay in touch. The family does not have the money to move to a suburban neighborhood, so they try to make the best of their neighborhood by being involved in school, civic, and church activities. They are also adept at identifying affordable summer enrichment programs. If they have problems with Malcolm's school that they can't handle, they know they can go to the pastor of their church, the head of the Masons, the Elks, or the Eastern Star in their community to ask for help. What is most important is that they seek out and use all the resources available to them.

Malcolm is Jasmine's lifeline to the place and the people that gave her a sense of security. He has noticed the changes in her since the family moved to the suburbs, and he doesn't like what he sees and hears. She is no longer the effervescent, spirited girl who wanted to be a teacher. Now cynical and distrustful, she is no longer close to her parents as she once was because, she complains to Malcolm, they just want her to be like some of the high-achieving white kids in her school.

Malcolm tries to reason with Jasmine during their phone conversations and occasional meetings at the mall near the old neighborhood. "Being white is not all that it's made out to be," he tells her. "Just because your parents want you to be somebody doesn't mean they want you to be white. Besides, there are a lot of white students at your school who are struggling just to get by because they aren't 'all that.'"

Malcolm also encourages her to reach out to some of the white teachers that she admitted to liking. "Don't turn your back on them because of their race," he says, "because you've got to use what you've got. If all the teachers are white, try to find some that you like and see if they will help you out." Malcolm should know because one of his role models, Mrs. Young, is a white woman.

No matter where they live or what schools they attend, our children all need positive role models. The opportunities for hooking up with these role models are all around us, but we must be aware of the need and then become proactive to find and use them. Admittedly, in some ways this task is much harder today than in generations past because of mobility, working parents, and the breakdown of the extended family.

FINDING REALISTIC ROLE MODELS

In the late 1960s, I surveyed one hundred teenage girls in St. Louis about their role models. When asked, "Who would you most like to pattern your life after?" all but two chose a woman in their immediate environment: their mother, aunt, grandmother, or teacher. They said they admired character strengths that included kindness, responsibility, integrity, determination, and personal pride. If I conducted that same survey today, I am sure the results would be different.

Too many wholesome family role models might be overlooked. Today children are just as likely to choose a role model in the media (especially athletes and entertainers whom they will never meet or talk to) based on money, cars, clothes, and mansions, as they are to choose a relative whose character traits they respect. TV programming has brought our children into the homes of black entertainers and athletes; it has given them glimpses of the lifestyles of the rich and famous; it has indoctrinated them to equate success with fame, wealth, and extravagance. This dramatic change—choosing strangers as their primary role models—is caused by our failure as parents to purposefully create and teach our children high moral values and strong character. We must all work to replace these fantasy idols with real-life people with strong character, work ethics, and a belief in the value of education.

On the other hand, our children's image of realistic role models in the black community also suffers when they are bombarded with negative images of black people (especially young men) as thugs and muggers that saturate the mass media. As one of my son's friends said, "I feel like I was born with the word *suspicious* on my forehead because of the way white people look at me. The teachers are sometimes as bad as the cops are. They act like they are waiting and expecting me to do something wrong. They really act like they like seeing me mess up."

As discussed in previous chapters, this is played out by the police pulling our sons over for no good reason and some of their teachers always turning to them when someone else does something wrong in class. Our children must prove their innocence time and time again, and this wears them down. Without vigilant and supportive parents, they have a harder time staying the course. Children need help to balance these images with more positive mental pictures of black adults. They need to see blacks contributing to society and accomplishing positive goals. It is our task to make sure this happens.

We have many opportunities to expose our children to positive role models. In this chapter we will explore the possibilities of models found in ourselves, our extended families, the business environment, and our communities.

YOU AS A ROLE MODEL

Whether you are aware of it or not, you are your child's first and often most important role model. You are the one he or she sees daily from the moment of birth onward. You are the first person your child looks up to. You have a longer and more influential role in your child's life than anyone else.

The Perry Preschool Study in Ypsilanti, Michigan, supports this statement. This is the only study to follow African American children over an extended period, from preschool to age twenty-seven. Although all the children in this study lived in low income families during early childhood, the number of years of education achieved ranged widely from 6.5 to 18 (master's degree).[1]

The central question in this study was: What factors contributed to such diverse outcomes in the educational realm? The hypothesis was that the children who turn out to be most successful in the educational realm would identify one or both of their parents as their most significant role models. Researchers found that the results at age twenty-seven proved the hypothesis to be true. Those who finished high school or enrolled in courses beyond high school were much more likely than those who dropped out to identify their parents as role models.[2] At age twenty-seven, will your children look back and name *you* as their most influential role model? The answer to this question depends on the kind of behavior and attitudes you model now and every day of your life.

A strong work ethic is taught almost entirely through example. Regardless of your job, career, or lifestyle, your child should see that you get up each day and follow a structured daily routine. This is how the world in which our children will function as adults works. They should know early in life that the world would expect them to be prepared, be on time, dress properly, do a good job, and take the initiative to get things done. The easiest way for your children to learn this is by watching you as a positive lifelong example.

But going to work every day is not enough. Your child should also have a tangible sense of what you do in the work world. This too occurs through modeling. No matter what your occupation, let your child see you at work. Whether you like your job or not, tell your children why and let them watch you in action. If your place of business will not admit children during the week, take them for a visit on the weekend. Even if you don't like your job, say so and let your children see firsthand why you do not like it. Emphasize that you still do your best work even if you dislike your job, and then, if appropriate, share your plans for finding a different job. (Keep in mind that it is not a good thing to constantly criticize your job unless you also demonstrate that you intend to do something about it.) In this way your children will understand what it means to solve problems, have options, know how to make something happen, and move on to more satisfying work.

You should also talk openly about problems and obstacles you face in the work world. At age-appropriate levels talk to your children about the insufficient funding for your department or about your disappointment that your supervisor does not give you the recognition for a job well done. Then talk about how you plan to handle these or any other job-related problems. Talking about problem solving in these real-life situations can help your children develop critical thinking and problem-solving skills of their own.

Even parents who do not work or do not want their children to follow in their footsteps can still have a strong influence on their child's career success. When I look at my own life, I can see that I learned much from my mother that helped me achieve success even though she had no advanced education or high-powered career. She taught me vital lessons by the way she lived her life each day, lessons such as these: never give up; work hard no matter what your job; stand up for your beliefs; have a strong sense of independence; use critical thinking skills; do not go along to get along with the crowd; do not compromise your values. If I did not have these lessons behind me, I would not have found my highly satisfying career or life success, despite my advanced levels of education.

At every opportunity help your child to learn life and work lessons from your experiences or from those of others. Both the positive and the negative can be powerful examples that steer them onto the right path.

EXTENDED FAMILY

Your extended family can reinforce your efforts to raise your child by providing a broader source of role models. In generations past, grandparents, aunts, and uncles lived nearby, so it was quite natural for children to imitate the behavior of family members. My own grandparents lived on the street behind my house, and my great-aunt and -uncle lived next to them. They were all in agreement about how to raise the children. They all offered encouragement and support; they all had high expectations; and they all enforced strict rules of conduct. They also all modeled for me through their own daily lives positive values and work ethics. I was surrounded by good examples that had a definite impact on my life.

I realize that today the world is very different. Nowadays our children do not often have the immediate access to grandparents and other extended kin. Moving away from the homestead in search of better opportunities causes our kids to grow up in environments that are far more mobile. Even though things are often quite different now, with some effort the ties with family can still be strengthened and used to support our children's struggle to find the right road in life.

Keeping in Touch

Even though our extended families are often spread out across the country, that doesn't mean we can't stay connected so that our children have a broader base of successful examples to turn to. Family reunions are one popular way to bring everyone together so that children can make at least brief contact with their relatives. Spending holidays with grandparents is another way to keep the ties strong. In addition to learning the importance of kinship, our children can also find out all the different avenues of success their own family members have gone down. They can hear stories of struggles and triumphs. They can gain a sense of belonging to a large support group. They can own a sense of historical roots, learn their places in the family's genealogy, and gain an understanding of what the family has achieved and stood for over the generations.

My son, Thomas, still remembers the four silver dollars he received at a family reunion in North Carolina for being the youngest person present. He also got a chance to meet his great-great uncle from Chicago, who received the prize for being the eldest. This is the kind of connection across the generations that gives our children a shared sense of their roots, how far they've come, and how far they can grow.

Even though our families may be far apart, we should bridge that gap so that our children have contact with more people who can support our efforts to lead our children to success. If, for example, your child says he thinks he'd like to be a teacher, use your family as mentors. Put your child in touch with Cousin Harriet, who teaches in a nearby city. (If you haven't spoken to Harriet yourself in years, this is a good time for you to reconnect.) Use phone, mail, or e-mail to communicate with your parents, siblings, and cousins, as well as to help your children keep in touch with Grandpa, Aunt Mary, or Cousin Kojo.

At each family reunion I attend, I am delighted to reconnect with my cousins, to learn about their careers, the paths they have taken, and especially to see the cousins of my son's generation interact as young adults. Thomas and I attended my niece's wedding recently, and he was so happy to be in the midst of the cousins (as they call themselves).

At the end of our visit, he said something that was heartwarming and revealing: "Mom, you and my aunts and uncles did a very good job in raising the cousins because we are all very close to each other." That was, of course, quite wonderful for me to hear because I did not raise him in an area near most of the family. As they marry and have children, I am happy to know that they are interested in forging strong family ties among themselves and their children. In observing how supportive they are to each other, I feel it is important for all of us to invite the extended family to our home for a visit. If they live nearby, take your child to their place of business for a chat and brief tour. Let your children see the many career paths other people in their family have chosen. This expands their horizons.

From Underachiever to College Graduate

This is the route that brought young LaTasha from being an underachiever to being a college graduate. At age sixteen she was a good kid with an eye for fashion and a part-time job on Saturdays at the nearby clothing store. The owner recognized that LaTasha was a talented, honest, and hardworking girl; he often commented that someday he would like to make her manager. This became LaTasha's career goal, and she abandoned all thoughts of college. LaTasha figured, *Why study so hard in school when I already have a good job waiting for me after high school?*

LaTasha's parents, however, wanted more for their daughter. Neither had a college education, and they wanted LaTasha to achieve a level of education that would permit her to explore career options they had been denied. Although LaTasha had her heart set on managing this store, her mom, Gloria, knew her daughter needed to see that there was more out there for her. She remembered that her cousin, Sharmaine, had gone to college to study fashion design and wondered what had happened to her. She called her Aunt Hazel and learned that Sharmaine had become a manager of Bloomingdale's in a large city. *Perfect!* thought Gloria.

Gloria called her cousin to ask a favor: Could LaTasha visit her home and accompany her for a few days on the job? Sharmaine was delighted to welcome LaTasha into her home during the summer vacation and bring her to work so that she could see for herself all the many jobs in retail clothing that were open to those with training and education. LaTasha returned home with a completely different outlook. Thanks to Cousin Sharmaine, she now had not only new career goals but a new positive role model and friend in her cousin. And although she continued to work part-time at the clothing store, she began to see it as a temporary job, not the kind of fulfilling career she would get in the fashion industry after she completed college.

Sharmaine and LaTasha kept in close touch. When the time came, Sharmaine guided LaTasha through the college application process. She took her to visit various colleges that had good fashion programs. She even helped pay her tuition because she felt the need to give something back. What better way to do this than to help a cousin in need? On her visits home from college, LaTasha looks back now at that little corner store where she had once planned to spend her life, and she is very grateful to her parents and to Sharmaine for not letting her settle for less than she was capable of.

As parents we must avail our children of as much information on careers as possible. If LaTasha's mother had not done some networking with her cousin, LaTasha might still be working at the corner store. The extended family is a wonderful resource that can motivate, inspire, and support your children in their life journey. Don't let this mine of gold go untapped.

Historic Role Models

Our extended families contain many ancestral role models. These are the black people throughout American history who endured hardships and fought against all odds to succeed. Our children should know about this ancestry and add these heroic figures to their collection of positive role models.

Through bedtime stories and books, they can admire the courage of Harriet Tubman, who went into the South during times of slavery to bring slaves to the north on the underground railway. They can marvel at the conviction of Martin Luther King Jr. and Rosa Parks, who both stood tall in the face of discrimination. They can enjoy the discoveries of the scientist George Washington Carver who developed numerous products from the peanut. They can share in the triumphs of Sojourner Truth, Malcolm X, and Marcus Garvey, who fought for the liberation of black people. In recent years many wonderful books have been written for young children to demonstrate that black people have always been more than the negative depictions on television and the ignorant slaves of inaccurate history books.

Evoking the memories of our ancestors as positive role models reminds our children that if these people could overcome the odds under trying circumstances, we can do no less.

PROFESSIONALS ALL AROUND US

Use the successful role models who are all around you to show your children the many career options open to them. If possible, choose black professionals (such as doctors, dentists, nurses, lawyers, pharmacists, and accountants) for your family needs. Let your child see successful black people in action. Show them that career possibilities are not limited by color and are not the domain of white people alone. Give them an up close look at a person with dark skin who is working in the professional world.

But whether that person is black, white, Asian, or Latino, give your child insight into the lives of successful professionals. When you take your child to the pediatrician, for example, start a brief conversation with the doctor. Ask when he or she decided to become a doctor. Ask about the training required. Ask about the opportunities in the field for newcomers today. Engage your child in the conversation. And make sure your child knows that if she wants to, she too can be a doctor or any other professional she chooses.

And don't overlook your child's teachers as professional role models. Teachers and other school staff have achieved the kind of success we want our children to achieve: they have gone to college, stuck it out, and earned their degrees. They are examples of economic success because they are self-supporting. They also model the admirable traits of someone who chooses to give back to others. Today's college graduates are lured into many higher paying professions, but our teachers model the life of caring, giving individuals. These are the kind of people in our children's day-to-day world who can have a powerfully positive influence on their prospects for success.

As your child gets older and begins to think more seriously about a career, look around in your environment to find a mentor. If, for example, your sixteen-year-old thinks he might like to be a lawyer, give him the opportunity to find out more about this career through actual experience. Call on lawyers you know, or find them in the local phone book. Ask if they would consider spending some time with your son, who is interested in the field of law. Most are quite glad to give their time and share their experiences with young people.

You'll also find influential role models in the business news. More and more black professionals are making their way to the top of large corporations and paving a path for our children behind them. The Executive Leadership Council (a networking organization for senior black executives in Fortune 500 companies) today boasts 275 members; it was founded in 1986 with nineteen members.[3] Admittedly, we are still at the stage where almost every one is the first or the only black in his or her position, but our children can be right behind them. They know about Oprah Winfrey and Magic Johnson; now tell them about Cal Darden, the head of operations at United Parcel Service, and Cathy Hughes, founder of Radio One and the first black woman to head a publicly traded company. You can also point to several black role models in government and politics: Alexis Herman, the former U.S. secretary of labor; Hazel O'Leary, former U.S. secretary of energy; Condoleezza Rice, the national security advisor; Michael Powell, chairman of the Federal Communications Commission; and Roger Ferguson, vice chairman of the Federal Reserve.

Turn the Tables

Your children can gain a sense of pride in their own accomplishments by sharing their time and skill with younger children. If your child is a good student, you might arrange for her to tutor a family friend who is struggling in school. If your child has mastered a musical instrument, he might help a younger cousin learn how to play. If she is a good soccer player, encourage her to teach the skills to the neighborhood kids. When others look up to your children, they will feel a sense of obligation to be the best they can be. That is the flip side of modeling. Both the role model and the younger child gain the benefits.

REACH OUT TO THE COMMUNITY

The people, organizations, associations, and churches in your community offer an untapped wealth of role models. Some take pride in helping young people find their way in this world. One such person is the internationally renowned black male role model, Benjamin Carson.

Dr. Carson is director of pediatric neurosurgery at Johns Hopkins University Medical Center in Baltimore, Maryland. The son of a working single mother in Detroit, Dr. Carson's uplifting story of going from being on the brink of failure to Yale University is chronicled in his books, *Gifted Hands* and *Think Big*.[4]

"I did not like school very much and there was no reason why I should," recalls Carson. "Inasmuch as I was the dumbest kid in the class, what did I have to look forward to? The others laughed at me and made jokes about me every day. I really felt I was the stupidest kid in the fifth grade."[5]

His mother's love, devotion, and unwavering belief that education was the only way he was ever going to escape poverty led him to be so successful. She started by limiting the amount of television he and his brother watched and insisted that they read several books each week. Not only did he fall in love with reading, but he thrived on the world that reading opened up to him. His love of reading and his mother's constant mentoring and monitoring transformed him from failure to success. Dr. Carson is regarded by many parents as one of the best possible role models because of the adversity he has overcome, as well as his present status as a healer who takes on the most difficult brain surgeries that other doctors will not touch. These kinds of community role models are wonderful but far too uncommon.

Be Proactive

As parents we must be proactive and aggressively seek out role models in our communities. They're out there, but we have to find them. If your schools or local church or youth organizations (such as the Boys & Girls Clubs, the YMCA, or the YWCA) are not sponsoring mentorships or career-day programs, get one going. Work with these organizations to find area professionals who will come in (for free) and talk to your kids as a group. You might request that members of your local service organizations (black fraternities and sororities, Shriners, Masons, Elks, Eastern Star, local medical and legal associations, teachers' organizations, allied health sciences groups, engineers' groups, chamber of commerce, and others) to give their time to talk to the children in the community about what they do, how they trained, and what opportunities await young people. Get to know the people in your place of worship, because they most likely represent a wealth of occupations and resources. Network with them to get the kind of information you need in order to help your child. People from the community are real and accessible; our kids can see them, feel their passion, and admire their accomplishments up close. They make a far greater impression on our children than do those they simply read about or watch on television and in movies.

Use every opportunity available to you to give your children tangible evidence of what becoming a high-status professional involves. And do it today. We cannot abdicate the responsibility for finding role models, letting the schools and churches take care of it. We must be their partners in giving our kids what they need to see how far they can go.

Big Brothers Big Sisters of America

Do you think you cannot find a strong role model for your child? Call the Big Brothers Big Sisters of America and ask them how to contact the local affiliate in your town. Their mission is to make a positive difference in the lives of children, primarily through a one-to-one relationship with a caring adult. By providing committed volunteers, national leadership, and standards of excellence, this organization assists children in achieving their highest potential, as they grow to become competent, confident, and caring individuals. See Helpful Resources at the back of the book for more details.

Networking

We can also guide our children to successful futures by learning how to network. The white community knows very well how to use this career tool to full advantage, but black people traditionally have not had as many friends in high places to call on to help their children. We did not participate in the social circles and civic clubs where one hand helped the other. As we grew up, we were told that we had to struggle to achieve on our own merits. This attitude leaves our children on their own, even when people are available who are willing to help—*if* we ask them.

The most successful networkers put themselves in places where they meet people in high places. To do this, join some of the influential organizations such as the National Association of Negro

Business and Professional Women's Club, Inc.; the National Council of Negro Women; the Coalition of 100 Black Women; Black Women's Agenda; or your college alumni organization (if you went to college). Hundreds of organizations exist. Find those in your area and make use of them. Try this link to find a list of many organizations: http://www.littleafrica.com/resources/organizations.htm.

You should also forge as many community ties as possible by joining a place of worship, your school's parent-teacher association, or the local sports booster club. Look into business-affiliated groups. You never know where you'll meet someone who knows someone who can help your children move forward and up.

A Checklist for Finding and Using Positive Role Models

Use this checklist to remind yourself how to find and use positive role models to help your children be the best that they can be.

Role Model Number One: You

✓ Remember that you are your child's first and most influential role model.
✓ Make sure your words and actions support your efforts to guide your children to a successful future.
✓ Talk about your own work-related problems and their solutions.

Role Model Number Two: Extended Family

✓ Reconnect with your extended family so that your children have a broader base of successful examples to turn to.
✓ Celebrate the lives of your ancestors who struggled and overcame obstacles.

Role Model Number Three: Professionals in Your Environment

✓ Let your child see successful black people in action.
✓ Show them that career possibilities are not limited
   by color.
✓ Find a mentor for your child. Give your child the opportunity to find out more about a career of interest through
   actual experience.
✓ Celebrate the lives of contemporary achievers in science,
   education, technology, medicine, law, diplomacy, social
   work, and so on.

Role Model Number Four: Professionals in the Community

✓ Be proactive and aggressively seek out role models in your
   community.
✓ Use your influence through networking to give your child
   the advantage, especially when looking for a good job.

Good role models can mold our children into successful young
men and women who will lead the next generation. To achieve this
goal, many of our children will need to attain college degrees. The
next chapter will give you a helping hand through the college selection and application process.

College Preparation, Application, and Selection

A college education is a passport to a better life; it is a must for the majority of our black children. No other measurable method open to the vast majority of our children (excluding professional athletes and entertainers) guarantees a better life in the same way that a college degree does. The U.S. Census Bureau keeps track of income by levels of education, and the facts are startling: American males who have only a high school education have a median income of $27,669; females have $15,120. In stark comparison, males with a college degree have a median income of $49,180; females have $30,489.[1] Given the undeniable connection between future income and a college education, we owe it to our children to help them attain a college degree.

COLLEGE VERSUS JAIL: WHO'S WINNING?

Children in recent years have had greater educational opportunities available to them than have previous generations. The high school dropout rate for blacks from ages sixteen to twenty-four has dropped from 22 percent in 1970 to 12.6 percent in 1999.[2] By 2000, 78.5 percent of all African Americans had completed high school, and 16.5 percent had completed college or graduate school.[3] But along with this good news comes a 2002 study that has sounded the alarm alerting all black parents that much remains to be done.

The Justice Policy Institute, a Washington-based research and advocacy group, reported statistics showing that more black men are behind bars than enrolled in colleges or universities. Referring to this study, Todd Clear, a professor at John Jay College of Criminal Justice in Manhattan, said, "It tells you that the life chances of a black male going to prison is greater today than the chances of a black male going to college, and it wasn't always this way." In 1980, by contrast, three times more black men were enrolled in institutions of higher learning than were behind bars.[4] This is a trend that we as parents cannot ignore, especially at a time when the future of our children is so clearly tied to a college education.

A FAMILY EXPECTATION

Betty and James knew on the day of their son's birth that their boy would go to college. Betty earned her nursing degree from a local university and worked until her first child was born, when she became a stay-at-home mom. James began to work at his father's hardware store immediately after high school. Although he could have gone to college, he always understood that his father expected him to come to work as soon as he finished high school. Life had been good for both of them, but they wanted more for their son. So before little Henry's first birthday, James and Betty met with a financial advisor at their bank and set up an investment plan. They wanted to make sure that nothing interfered with their plans for their son's future.

With their money growing securely in their investments, Betty and James turned to the task of raising their son. They were very involved in his sports and scouting activities. They went to the parent-teacher association (PTA) meetings and monitored his homework. Betty was a parent volunteer in the classroom twice a week. However, as Henry moved into high school, Betty and James felt that the hands-on involvement was not as necessary because Henry was a good boy who worked weekends with his dad at the store. He was also a good student who had never gotten in trouble.

By then life was also more hectic with two younger children, so the parents had less time to volunteer at Henry's school or invest the amount of time in him as they had when he was an only child. Henry was left on his own to navigate his way through the high school years, and in the bustle of family life, no one thought to talk about postsecondary education until it was almost too late. In the summer prior to his senior year, Betty and James sat Henry down and asked him about his college plans. They suggested that the family's annual vacation be built around college visits. "You know your dad and I expect you to get a college degree," Betty said. "We started putting money away for your education when you were born. So which colleges are you interested in?"

Henry hedged a bit by saying, "I'd really like to keep working with Dad. I don't think I would like college as much as I like working in the business."

"That's not what you're going to do," said his mother with alarm. "Your dad and I have always expected you to go to college. Then you can come back to the store if you want to, but we want you to have all the opportunities that only a college diploma can give to you."

"Well, forget it," said Henry, laughing. "I didn't get very good grades in the college prep classes, and I know I won't do well on the SATs. You should use your money to send Jeffrey [his 14-year-old brother] to college."

Unfortunately, too many parents like Betty and James are less vigilant when they think their children are doing all right. What they don't understand is that older children oftentimes need more guidance than young kids do. Somewhere along the way, they stopped communicating their expectations to Henry, and he assumed that since he spent a lot of time working at the store, they would be pleased to have him follow in his dad's footsteps. Moreover, they made the mistake of thinking that their major responsibility for their child's higher education was investing and saving money to fund the expense. Then they waited until their child was entering his senior year of high school to bring up the subject. When this happens, many parents find that it is too late because their child has little to no interest in college or does not meet the academic qualifications necessary to enroll.

Don't let this happen in your family. Begin during your child's early years to build a family culture around the idea of a college education. In your home college should be a spoken expectation. Through conversation over the years, talk about career options and the required college training. Talk about different colleges and which ones your little ones would like to go to. Take your children to visit your college or wherever you received your training after high school. Even if you didn't finish high school, take them to visit your old elementary and high schools. Talk to them about your experiences and the things you did. These are the kinds of things that make your educational expectations real and tangible.

Your kids should never be uncertain about your educational expectations. Always encourage good grades "so that you can get into a good college." Monitor their classes from prekindergarten until they graduate from high school. Challenge the teachers and speak up for your child. Tell them that *you* expect them to help your kids get the kind of education that will prepare them for college. Also, remember that stating this once is not enough. You have to reinforce it as you act as your child's advocate throughout his or her precollege education. Over the years your children will grow to assume that the question is not "Will I go to college?" but rather, "Which college will I attend?"

The Value of a Home Computer

When you begin the college selection and application process, you will find that access to a computer becomes indispensable. As you'll see in this chapter, many resources and much valuable information are offered on the Internet. The computer is a helpful tool that you shouldn't overlook.

If you don't have a home computer, you can use one at your local library, but you should think seriously about investing in one for your home. New models are no longer very expensive, and you can find good used ones in the classified ads. Not only will a computer help you and your child in the college search, it will help your child do research and prepare papers for his or her classes. Kids of all ages use computers for many types of exploration and communication. There are many computer learning games that even your preschooler can use. A friend who is an engineering professor taught his two-year-old daughter to boot up the computer and play her educational games. A home computer is a tool that helps our kids stay competitive. (And the access to e-mail is a great way to keep in touch when your child goes off to college!)

Although owning a computer has a positive influence, it also has some major drawbacks. First, teenagers can become addicted to the Internet, using e-mail and chatting online with friends, or they may spend excessive time playing computer games. Second, they have access to Web sites with content that is inappropriate for their age. Because these activities reduce time spent on homework and study, parents need to monitor computer use carefully.

THE MOST IMPORTANT
HIGH SCHOOL YEARS

If you want your child to go to college, don't wait until the junior or senior year to set the plan into action. You can give your child a great advantage by becoming involved in the specifics of the college preparation process in the freshman year.

In the beginning of the freshman year, sit down and talk face-to-face with your child's guidance counselor. Make it very clear that your child plans to go to college. Explain that you would like to work with the counselor to make sure that your child has all the necessary college preparatory classes. Tell the counselor that you do not want your child to get lost in the system and then find out in the senior year that he or she does not have the educational background to go to college.

In many schools this meeting is especially important for black families. Far too many teachers and administrators have some very out-of-date or prejudiced ideas and still assume that black students are all headed for vocational and technical (or vo-tech) courses and therefore will not guide them along the path to higher education. Do not allow this to happen to your child. Stand up right in the beginning and make sure that your child is marked as a college prep student.

Continue to monitor classes in the sophomore year and begin preparing for the standardized college entrance exams. Unfortunately, too many black children do not take the college entrance exams such as the Preliminary Scholastic Assessment Test (PSAT), the Scholastic Assessment Test (SAT), or the American College Test (ACT). Don't let the testing dates slip by. If your child will be the first in the family to go to college and you feel uncertain as to which steps to take, talk to other parents at church and PTA meetings. Many black parents turn to college-educated relatives, colleagues, and club and church members if they are unsure about what to do. There are also many good books on the subject that can coach you through the process, which begins long before the senior year of high school. (See Further Reading at the back of the book.)

Sophomores should sign up through the school's guidance department for the preliminary test given in the fall. Taking this practice test is a good idea for all students so that they don't face the actual exam for the first time when it really counts. The results of this test can also help you map out a plan for getting ready for the actual SAT or ACT the following year. You'll find out if your child is stronger in math or verbal skills. You'll know if you should buy some of the prep materials (like workbooks or computer disks) that offer sample practice tests to work on at home. You'll also find out if your child has unacceptably low scores and needs personal tutoring.

Many tutoring programs for the college entrance exams exist. Some high schools offer a class in exam prep as an elective; find out if your child's school offers this, and if so make sure he or she takes it. You can also find commercial programs that have a sound record of raising scores, but they can be expensive (up to $1,000 for some programs). Churches, YMCAs, Boys & Girls Clubs, and some civic organizations offer other courses. You can also hire a private tutor. Your child's guidance counselor should have information on the availability of these options. Be sure to ask for it.

In descriptions of the steps that parents need to take to prepare their high-school kids for application to and acceptance at college, the bulk of the advice focuses on preparing students for the PSAT, SAT, and ACT exams. However, some top colleges do not weigh SAT scores as heavily as before, and some have dropped these scores entirely from the admission process. For some colleges, grades and extracurricular activities are more important than standardized exam scores.

In the junior and senior years, your involvement continues to pave that path to college. Although the school may have guidance counselors, these individuals usually have huge numbers of other students on their list and may have very little time to spend on your child. So remember: you are the one primarily responsible for getting your kids into college. You must sign them up for the SAT or ACT exams by the deadline and be sure they know the ropes and are prepared to do their best. You must make sure they take the required high school courses. You must make sure they fill out their college applications early in the senior year and gather on time all the necessary paperwork such as personal essays, letters of recommendation, and financial aid forms. (Read more about financing college later in this chapter.) Our high school kids are now maturing, but the college entrance process can be very complex, so they still need our help.

College or Trade School?

If your children want to go to a trade school after high school graduation, that may very well lead to a successful and happy life. But they should not make that decision early in their high school careers. They should not avoid college prep classes or pass up the college entrance exams, because doing so prematurely closes the door to college. Keep them on track to go to college so that they have choices and options when they graduate. If teens eventually change their mind about going to a trade school and *do* want a college education, they are prepared to take that next step.

If in their senior year, they still choose not to attend college, then you can support that decision and find the trade school that fits their needs. Each child is unique, and each child has different needs. One size does not fit all. If you recognize that your child is not cut out for the straight path to college, then find the best type of education that fits his or her needs.

For example, David, one of the young men I have mentored, decided that college was not for him. At the end of his sophomore year, he dropped out of the university and entered a technical school that offered training in computer technology. He finished the program and is now moving up the ladder in the company. I think he made the right decision.

Another young man I know opened his own landscaping business after high school graduation. Two years later he realized that he did not want to do manual labor for the rest of his life and wanted instead to get a college degree to be a teacher. Because his parents had made him take a college prep program and the college entrance exams in high school, he was able to change career direction easily.

Because we don't know what life holds for our children down the road, it's best to be prepared and give them options.

CHOOSING THE RIGHT COLLEGE

Today our children have the choice of attending thousands of colleges. To find the best match between your child's needs and the college he or she attends, take time to think carefully about which ones have the facilities, opportunities, and philosophy that your child is looking for.

College Fairs

Tell your child's guidance counselor that you want to know about college fairs in your area. These events gather together in one place representatives from many colleges. They offer literature, advice, and often information on scholarships, minority student programs, and the application process. Some fairs are geared especially toward black and minority students. These fairs feature black alumni who can share personal experiences and advice. And they emphasize the support and social organizations the schools have specifically for black students.

In addition to the many small, localized college fairs sponsored by high schools and civic organizations, the National Association for College Admission Counseling sponsors very large fairs around the country each year. You can find a list of their fairs at http://www.nacac.com/fairs.html. College fairs are a great way to help your child make an educated choice, so look for them and attend with your child.

Narrowing Down by Likes and Dislikes

Getting into college is the first major step your child will make toward a successful future, but staying in college is the real goal. To make sure that your child has a good college experience and earns a diploma, take some time to evaluate the kind of environment where he or she will be most comfortable.

As you gather together information about colleges and begin to evaluate each one, carefully consider these seven factors: type of institution, academic suitability, location, size, cost, racial makeup, and attitudes toward blacks.

Type of Institution

Before your child begins the college search, you both will need to consider the choice between a two-year community college and a four-year college. This decision is often based on your child's needs, academic record, and your financial situation. In the two-year college, your child will live at home, where you can monitor his development. Many students find careers in the allied health services and a host of other areas for which the associate's degree prepares them, or upon completion of the two-year associate degree they can transfer to a four-year school to earn a bachelor's degree. For many students not quite ready to take the academic or emotional leap to a four-year college, community colleges offer the perfect starting place.

On the other hand, if your child is academically and emotionally ready for a four-year college, this is the better choice. It is not unusual for community college graduates to take their associate's degree in a vocational area and move into the work world without ever going on for the bachelor's degree that opens more opportunities in the world of business. If your child is eligible for acceptance into a four-year college, keep that option open as well.

Academic Suitability

Academic level is an important consideration when choosing a school. Various college guide books give standard information about schools all over the country. You'll see that each school lists the entrance level of difficulty; this is based on several factors including the percentage of accepted students who rank in the top 10 percent and top half of the class, the percentage of students who scored above five hundred in the math and verbal sections of the SAT, and the number of students who applied versus the number accepted.

As you begin the search for a college that matches your child's academic strengths and weaknesses, you'll need an objective evaluation. Start with your school's guidance department. At the beginning of the junior year, make an appointment for you and your child to meet with a guidance counselor. Explain your child's goal of finding a school where he or she can achieve academically. Get a written record of three things: grade point average (known as the GPA), PSAT or ACT scores, and class rank (if an exact number is not available, ask for a percentile estimate such as "top 25 percent"). Use these numbers to match your child's academic level to colleges where similar academic performance is the norm.

You'll find a wide spread on the upper and lower ends of entrance difficulty. In the most selective colleges, more than 75 percent of the current freshmen were in the top 10 percent of their high school class and scored above 1310 out of a possible combined score of 1600 on the SAT or above twenty-nine on the ACT. These more selective colleges accept about 30 percent or fewer of applicants. In the minimally difficult entrance-level colleges, however, most current freshmen were not in the top half of their high school class and scored somewhat below 1010 on the SAT or below eighteen on the ACT; these colleges accept up to 95 percent of applicants. There are also noncompetitive colleges where virtually all applicants are accepted; this is especially so in public institutions that are required to admit all state residents.[5]

It is important for your child to apply to several colleges and also to include on your list what some call safety schools. These are colleges where your children are fully qualified and acceptance is highly likely. They may not be a student's first choice, but they offer a fall-back plan if the first picks fall through.

You should also include some "stretch" schools on your list. These are colleges that have admission standards that may be above your child's qualifications, at least on paper, but may consider other factors that put your child in the running. Through extracurricular activities, your children may show a strong sense of commitment and purpose, unusual and valuable experiences, or special interests and talents that can outweigh numbers that are weaker than average. Give these schools a try, but put the bulk of your efforts into gaining admission to colleges where your children have realistic chances for admission and success.

Location

Many high school students say they don't care where they go to college. This isn't a realistic view of college life for many reasons. Applying at random to several schools scattered around the country is not likely to bring a student success. When asked to be more thoughtful, most will admit that they do have preferences. Help your child consider the following when evaluating the location of colleges.

Distance If the school your child attends is very far away, he or she will probably not be able to come home very often, perhaps only on major holidays and during the summer. If the college is closer, the student can come home for a dose of security more often. The distance from home also affects the total cost of college because airfares add up quickly.

Climate Your child needs to consider honestly if he or she can bear the long, cold winters of Minnesota, the unceasing heat of Arizona, or the special climate of Florida. Does he want to be near the ocean? Does she like the change of seasons? Would he miss snowboarding? Will she miss the beach? These things matter when it comes to picking a spot to spend four years of one's life (especially such a young life!).

Geographic type When looking over the various colleges your child might attend, you will notice that they are spread out over three different geographic types: urban, suburban, and rural. Talk to your child about the differences in each type. Life in the city is not the same as life in the country or in town. This is something your child needs to think about. If you currently live in an urban area, could your child comfortably adjust to the slower country pace with no real nightlife or weekend activities? If you now live in a country area, your child might enjoy a visit to a noisy, hectic, and large city, but could she live there happily day after day? If you live in the suburbs now, could your child give up shopping malls and car rides everywhere? Talk about these differences and keep them in mind when you visit the campus. (Read more about campus visits later in this chapter.)

Size

The number of undergraduate students determines college size. Although your child might at first say, "I don't care about size," the size of the institution can have a dramatic impact on the learning environment. As a general rule, size classifications follow these guidelines.

Small A small college has fewer than three thousand students. In general, small colleges tend to give students more personalized attention; more access to library, computer, and laboratory resources; and fewer registration and housing hassles. On the other hand, students may have little privacy, and some schools may have a limited range of social activities and less exposure to state-of-the-art technological resources.

Medium A medium-sized school has between three thousand and twelve thousand students. The medium-sized schools often offer a sampling of the good and bad qualities of both the larger and smaller schools. These schools offer a wide diversity of students but not so many that you never see the same face twice. Students are not closely supervised, but professors are reasonably accessible.

Large A large school has more than twelve thousand students. At most large universities, students experience a more diverse student body and roster of social activities and often have access to highly specialized and up-to-date laboratory, computer, and library resources. However, in large universities classes run on the crowded side (lecture classes may hold three hundred to one thousand students); personal attention may be scarce; and graduate student assistants and fellows often instruct freshman and sophomore students.

Cost

This is a time of soaring tuition costs. This fact can certainly influence the colleges your children choose to apply to. Although almost all families apply for financial aid to pay college bills (see Financing a College Education later in this chapter), you should sit down as a family and determine how much you are able and willing to pay for college education. Can you afford the higher prices of private schools, or should your child apply only to the more affordable state schools? Can you afford to have your child live away at school, or will he or she commute to a local school? These decisions will certainly affect which schools your child applies to.

You should be realistic in your college evaluations, but it's also a good idea to apply to a few financial "reach" schools. These are schools that you could not afford to send your child to on your own but could afford if your child received a strong financial aid package from the institution or the federal government. As explained later in this chapter, the college application deadline comes before you are notified of your financial aid eligibility. So go ahead and apply to pricey schools that interest your child, knowing he or she will attend only if hoped-for grants, loans, or scholarships come through.

Racial Makeup

One aspect of colleges that you and your child should consider is the composition of the student population. Some students want a more diverse population that includes international (or foreign) students, an equal number of males and females, and a good combination of urban and small-town classmates. And a very important issue black students and their parents deal with is the racial makeup of the student body. There are pros and cons of going to both predominantly white and predominantly black colleges. You should weigh them both and choose what's best for your child.

If you haven't yet explored historically black colleges and universities (HBCUs), you should take some time to consider if they might be a good fit for your child. As we discussed in Chapter Seven, HBCUs were founded for black students during the era of racial segregation. Fisk University in Nashville, Tennessee, for example, was founded in 1866 and claims among its alumni the historian and prolific writer W.E.B. DuBois. These largely private schools that later became universities were founded to educate the children of ex-slaves. The private colleges continue to thrive even now when black students can attend the nations' top universities, which historically had few if any black students. In fact, many of the country's stellar black leaders have come from these schools. These include Thurgood Marshall, Supreme Court justice; Toni Morrison, novelist and Nobel Laureate; Debbie Allen, actress and dancer; her sister, Phylicia Rashad, of the *Cosby Show*; Andrew Young, former U.S. ambassador, U.S. congressman, and Atlanta mayor; Jessye Norman and Leontyne Price, opera singers; Douglas Wilder, former governor of Virginia. Howard University in Washington, D.C., and Meharry Medical College in Nashville, Tennessee, trained most of the black doctors and dentists prior to desegregation.

HBCUs offer quality education in a comfortable environment where black students do not have to add the race issue to their list of challenges in higher education. In these schools students gain a strong sense of self and the survival skills they will need to be effective in the mainstream. These colleges offer students a place where they feel validated and valued based on their accomplishments and merits. They learn to compete based on their skills and talents without the influence of color tainting the outcome. Here being black isn't an excuse or an advantage. It means nothing, and that may be its greatest asset.

As a graduate of Tougaloo College in Mississippi, founded in 1869, I am probably a bit partial to HBCUs. But my feelings are supported by interesting research. A widely cited study by Jacqueline Fleming indicates that black students, especially black men, do better on predominantly black college campuses than in predominantly white university settings. Fleming selected subjects from both black and white colleges and university campuses in Georgia, Mississippi, Ohio, and Texas. With regard to one set of Southern campuses she concluded: "[Black] students exhibit stronger personal attachments to faculty, enhanced involvement in the career process, greater satisfaction with their academic lives, improvement on measures of academic performance, more enterprising vocational interest patterns, and maintenance of higher occupational aspirations. Black students in white schools, however, show quite the opposite, with increasing dissatisfaction with academic life, negative attitudes to teachers who use unfair grading practices, little return on time and effort invested in schoolwork, and no net improvement in academic performance."[6]

One of the guiding ideas in Fleming's project was her belief that the college years are a time when all young people are working to solidify a sense of identity. This includes combining emotional and interpersonal growth with the intellectual development that will be the basis for a rewarding career. Though the white campus setting provides rich educational resources for academic development, black students do comparatively less well on those campuses because they do not experience the socioemotional context as nurturing.[7]

As you investigate HBCUs, you'll find that they are predominantly located in the Southern states. The most notable HBCUs include Howard University in Washington, D.C.; Hampton University in Virginia; Spelman and Morehouse Colleges and Clark-Atlanta University in Atlanta, Georgia; Tougaloo College in Mississippi; Fisk University in Nashville, Tennessee; and Talladega College in Alabama.

You can find out more about HBCUs from the National Association for Equal Opportunity in Higher Education, Educational On-Line's Listing of Historically Black Colleges and Universities, or Black Excel. You can also find information on the scholarships that the United Negro College Fund offers to private HBCUs. (See Helpful Resources at the back of this book for contact information.)

I don't believe, however, that all black kids should go to black colleges. It is not always a good fit, or these schools may not offer the major a student wants. But for my son, Thomas (who tried a large northeastern university and a small liberal arts college in the Midwest before transferring to Howard University), and for me, it was a good choice and gave both of us quality education and lifelong friendships and business connections. My son found it gave him a chance to find himself in an environment that immersed him in black culture and experiences. One of the most compelling reasons many parents send their children to black colleges is because they value the experiences and education they were offered when they attended one. As a very well-known parent of a Howard University student told me when he brought his daughter for a campus visit, "This is my daughter's last chance to experience what it means to be a black person in America in a very positive way. This is where she will firm up her identity." It is an option that you might consider.

Attitudes Toward Blacks

When applying to some colleges and universities, being black can be an advantage. Many colleges try to recruit blacks because they seek diversity in their student population. Even elite institutions such as Harvard, Columbia, Yale, Princeton, Brown, and others compete for black students and often stretch their requirements, not to take someone who's unqualified but to fulfill their own diversity goals. In a pinch, therefore, a black kid with the same marginal academic achievement as a white kid may often have the advantage.

If these opportunities are open to your child, don't hesitate to take them—without feeling in any way shamed by the experience. Tell your children that they do not need to be any more defensive about the situation than does the quarterback who is admitted for his athletic skills or the legacy student whose father and grandfather are alumni. Colleges make exceptions to admission standards for many reasons; improved diversity is just one of them.

The downside of this advantage is the fact that not all of these schools know how to create a welcoming atmosphere or are able to retain the black students they recruit. Campuses vary in culture depending on how seriously they take their diversity goals. Are they simply trying to get their minority numbers up? Or do they truly value diversity for its intrinsic worth, its ability to expose students to the realities of the real world? When considering a college or university that may admit your child because of his or her race, try to make sure that the campus has an accepting and welcoming atmosphere to back up the offer.

When you visit a school and meet with an admissions officer, don't be shy about asking direct questions about black student issues. You'll want to know the following:

- How many black students attend the college?

- Are the black students active in the major campus organizations?

- Does the school have a Black Student Union?

- Do black students sponsor events?

- Does the school have any black sororities and fraternities?

- How does the school handle student grievances over
  racist remarks or acts?

Ask to meet black students and ask them candid questions about their experiences such as these: Why did you choose this college? How have you been accepted by nonblack students? Have there been any major racial incidents on campus? If so, how did the administration handle them? Other black students are often the best source of inside information.

TAKING A CAMPUS TOUR

Once you have narrowed down your college choices based on the criteria previously discussed, it's time to get serious about choosing one. An important way to evaluate the colleges your child is interested in is to visit them. This is the best way to evaluate the school on the criteria of distance, climate, location, size, and student body discussed earlier.

In the early stages of college selection, you can begin your college visitations on-line. All colleges now have Web sites full of information about the school, the curriculum, student activities, athletics, and the application process. Many also have what they call a virtual campus tour. These allow you to tour the campus without ever leaving home. It's a good place to start, but once you get serious about a school, nothing takes the place of an actual visit.

When planning a campus visit, you can go to the school on your own, unannounced, and take a look around, but you'll make better use of your time if you call ahead, arrange to join a guided tour, and attend one of the many formal information sessions presented by the admissions office; you can also arrange an overnight stay for your child. Student tour guides can show you the ins and outs of the campus in places that are not open to the general public, such as dormitory rooms. (Do remember, however, that the personality and experience of the individual student tour guide may have a big impact on your impression of the school. So factor that in to your deliberations as well and watch out for either cheerleading, chips on the shoulder, or other potential bias that may skew the information and attitudes that you receive.) You might also organize your summer family vacations around college visits, but it's often better to go while the college classes are in full session so that your child can get a feel for campus life and activity.

Black College Tours

You should ask your child's guidance counselor to find out if there are any group tours in your area. Some schools, churches, and civic organizations take busloads of kids on tours, especially to a number of historically black colleges. For example, Black Excel's Web site listed the following college tours for 2002 (see Helpful Resources at the back of this book):

- Nashville's Sixth Annual Black College Tour (Nashville, Tenn.)

- Ninth Annual Black College Spring Tour (San Jose, Calif.)

- Historical Black College Tour (Houston, Tex.)

- AYA (African Youth in Action) Tour of Historical Black Colleges and Universities (Bronx, New York City)

- Historical Black College Tour of the BAI Mentor Program (Harlem, New York City)

- Black College Tour 2002, Omega Psi Phi Fraternity (New York City)

- Los Angeles Black College Tour (Los Angeles, Calif.)

- Historically Black College Tour, Delta Sigma Theta Sorority, Inc. (Pontiac, Mich.)

- National Black College Alliance Black College Tours (Boston, Mass.)

- Black College Tour, Alpha Kappa Alpha (Wichita, Kans.)

- LAAPS Black College Bus Tour (St. Louis, Mo.)

Many communities feel a sense of social responsibility to help and encourage their children to attend college. Take advantage of these opportunities.

Talking to Admissions Officers

To make the most out of your campus visit, plan ahead to talk with an admissions officer at the college. Every college employs admissions officers to help pave the way into college for high school students. They are trained to grab your interest, answer your questions, and if the students meet their eligibility requirements, convince them to come to their school. They'll usually tell you only the good, positive, and attractive information about their college, but they do have some facts your child will need before making a final college selection.

Before sitting down with an admissions officer, make sure that both you and your child have gathered information by reading the college catalog and taking the tour. Many admissions officers are put off by prospective students who come in and waste their time by asking questions such as "Do you offer a major in business?" You should know this before scheduling a visit. Instead, read the college's catalog and Web site and listen during your large group information session and tour; that way, you and your child can ask intelligent questions that go beyond the obvious.

During your visit with an admissions officer, you or your child might ask, for example: Do the courses have to be taken in a required order? What happens if the class is closed when I register? Can I take summer classes at a college near my home and transfer the credits here? Do graduate assistants or professors teach the freshman and sophomore classes? These kinds of questions show you've taken the time to find out about the institution and are interested in learning more than the catalog already explains. Remember to write down the answers to your questions so that you'll be able to compare schools when it's time to make the final choice.

FINANCING A COLLEGE EDUCATION

Many families start early to save for their children's college education, and many students work summer jobs to contribute their share. But whether they have been saving for eighteen years or not, most families look for some financial aid to help pay the bill. The source and amount of money you receive is usually dependent on your child's academic qualifications, his or her area of prospective study, and your family's financial situation.

Three kinds of financial aid can help you afford your child's college education:

> *Grants or scholarships* These sources of aid have no strings attached; you do not have to pay them back.
>
> *Loans* This money must be repaid after graduation or departure from school. Student loans have lower interest rates than do commercial loans.
>
> *Work-study awards* The college can arrange on- or off-campus employment to help students meet their financial obligations.

Money is available, but it doesn't knock on your door. Early in the senior year, go after it from the following three sources.

Scholarships from Private Organizations

Lots of scholarship money is out there just waiting for you. Some funds are earmarked for minority students, and others are available to all interested students. The trick is to find them! Did you know, for example, about the McDonald's Golden Arches Scholarships, which offer $1,000 to winners entering their first year of college, $5,000 to the student displaying outstanding academic achievement, and $5,000 to the student who best demonstrates a commitment to community service? Also, the National Academy of Television Arts and Sciences offers $7,500 for each year of college study to exceptional students who intend to major in television, telecommunications, or a similar communications-related field. Pilot International Foundation offers a $1,000 scholarship to students enrolled in physical therapy, occupational therapy, speech or hearing therapy, mental health, or rehabilitation courses.

You can find these scholarships by browsing through the college scholarship books in the reference section of your library and in local bookstores. But the best source for finding potential scholarships is the Internet. When I put in the search term "college scholarship," I found 1,950,000 matches. Of course, looking at every one of these would be overwhelming, but once you start to dig, you'll find a few sites that will lead you to everything you need. Try these to get you started:

- http://www.findaid.org

- http://www.fastweb.com

- http://www.freschinfo.com

- http://www.embark.com

- http://www.srnexpress.com

- http://www.gocollege.com

These sites can lead you to customized searches for scholarships from individual schools, private organizations, corporations, religious groups, the government, military, and many special interest groups.

Many scholarships are specifically for black students. You can get a good start on your search by logging on to the Black Excel Web site. You'll find listings like these two that will direct you to valuable information.

Herbert Lehman Scholarships
Contact: Scholarship Program
99 Hudson Street
New York, New York 10013
Telephone: (212) 965-2200
Fax: (212) 219-1595
Award amount: $2,000
Number given: 20
Eligibility criteria: Each year the Herbert Lehman Fund offers a limited number of scholarships to highly qualified African American high school graduates who are beginning their studies at colleges and universities.

Ron Brown Scholar Program
Contact: Executive Director/Ron Brown Scholar Program
1160 Pepsi Place, Suite 306-B
Charlottesville, Virginia 22901
Telephone: (804) 964-1588
Fax: (804) 964-1589
E-mail: mmallory@ronbrown.org
Web site: http://www.ronbrown.org
Award amount: $10,000
Number given: At least ten
Eligibility criteria: The Ron Brown Scholar Program is a national program that awards scholarships to academically talented, highly motivated African American high school seniors who intend to pursue undergraduate degrees full-time. The program honors the late Ronald H. Brown, secretary of commerce during the Clinton administration.

Institutional Scholarships

The colleges your child applies to will offer financial aid in many forms. Beyond the typical funding through government loans, grants, and work-study awards (explained later in this chapter), ask about scholarships specific to that school. Find out if the school offers, for example, athletic, academic, merit, service, or minority scholarships. Remember, however, that students who receive scholarship funds from outside sources may see proportionately reduced aid from institutional scholarships. You can call the institution's financial aid office directly or go to college fairs to get this information. Some schools also list their scholarship opportunities on the school's Web site, but don't rely solely on that; ask someone in the know. Be sure to ask the black college students you know about possible scholarship possibilities they may have explored.

Government Grants and Loans

In January of your child's senior year, you can apply for federal and state loans, grants, and work-study money through the U.S. Department of Education. You must fill out a form called the Free Application for Federal Student Aid (FAFSA) to determine your eligibility for aid from various federal Student Financial Assistance (SFA) programs. These programs provide over $33 billion a year to students attending colleges and universities. Most colleges around the country participate in the SFA programs. You can obtain the form from your child's guidance counselor, from the college your child is applying to, by calling the Federal Student Aid Information Center at the number shown in Helpful Resources, or by downloading it from the Internet at http://www.fafsa.ed.gov.

The most common SFA programs include the following:

> *Federal Pell Grants* These are available to undergraduate students only. (Remember, grants do not have to be repaid.) Federal Pell Grant awards commonly range from $400 to $3,000.

Perkins Loans These loans are for students with great financial need. Students can borrow up to $4,000 a year with a $20,000 limit. Interest rates are low, and the federal government pays interest on the loan while the student remains in school. Repayment begins nine months after the student graduates or drops below half-time status.

Federal Stafford Loans These student loans are available to both undergraduate and graduate students. Dependent students can borrow $23,000 over a four-year period. The family must demonstrate financial need (as determined by FAFSA guidelines) to receive a subsidized Stafford Loan. The government pays the interest on the loan while the student is in school. Any student can receive an unsubsidized Stafford Loan and is responsible for all interest payments. The interest rate is variable but never exceeds 8.25 percent. Repayment begins six months after the student graduates or drops below half-time status.

Federal PLUS Loans These are loans to parents whose federal financial aid package (as determined by the FAFSA form) does not meet the cost of the child's college education. PLUS loans can be taken up to the cost of education minus the financial aid awarded. Rates are lower than bank loan rates, and repayment begins sixty days after disbursement.

You can get an estimate of how much federal financial aid your child might be eligible for by going on-line. The Web site http://collegeboard.com offers a financial calculator that helps you get your money facts together and see how much in loans or grants your child may receive. If the FAFSA application determines that the student is eligible to receive financial aid, the award will be paid directly to the college your child attends. The school will notify your son or daughter of the aid package by sending an award letter. The aid award will likely be disbursed each semester, quarter, or other payment period.

A great deal of information about federal and state college aid is available on the Internet. A good source to get you started is http://www.ed.gov/studentaid. Also try the site sponsored by Student Loan Funding at http://www.studentloanfunding.com, which offers a free service called "Ask a Counselor" to answer general questions about financial aid and student loans.

The early expectation that your children will go to college is one of the most important gifts you can pass on to them. A college degree is the fuel that will power their launch into the real world. Along with your teen should go a trunk full of coping skills. The following chapter will give you a few to pack along when your child leaves home to make his or her own way in the world.

12

Coping Skills
The Key to Survival

Black children begin to learn coping skills at a very early age as we teach them through example how to interact with their world. As they grow, through discussion and experience, we give them the background and knowledge they need to survive the destructive effects our racist society can have on their development. These coping lessons are important because they help our children accept the duality of existence they must live with: the fact that they are wonderful human beings surrounded by a loving family, while at the same time they will inevitably face discriminatory insults from the larger world because of their color.

Throughout this book we have explored the many ways that you can proactively help your children develop the know-how to succeed in this world. These discussions are the foundation for the coping skills offered in this final chapter. A combination of strong parenting skills and our own coping skills equip our children with all they need to live secure, happy, and productive lives.

TALK ABOUT RACISM

Hammering children over the head with the horrors of racism does not help them cope, yet hiding the facts of racism does not help them either. I believe the best approach is somewhere in the middle. Without a chip on your shoulder, you should talk to your children in age-appropriate ways about the obstacles your ancestors faced because of skin color. Talk about your own experiences with racism too—not just to complain or rant and rave, but to discuss the lessons you learned.

Stories of racism are not shameful pieces of family history to hide; they are facts of the past that have brought you to where you are today. They are also not indictments of the entire white world. Share them without conveying any sense of hopelessness or help-lessness. Be positive and optimistic about the opportunities the world now offers your children, but caution them too about the obstacles they may face.

These stories give children a coping mechanism of experience so that they will not be surprised or devastated when they too face a prej-udicial or discriminatory act. Being forewarned gives children a sense of reality along with feelings of control and power, both of which are tools they will reach for many times in the coping-skills toolbox.

Sustained Self-Empowerment

A child who feels in control and strong, rather than helpless or hopeless, is a child who will grow to be successful; it's as simple and as difficult as that. Feeling empowered builds an affirmative framework in which to live a resilient life. This framework supports an individual who doesn't despair when knocked down, doesn't take on the victim role, and doesn't blame others for all failures. This is a person who stands up to be counted among those who will not let racism get in the way of goals and aspirations.

BE PROACTIVE

Racism is a frustrating foe that is often invisible. Your children can better cope with the feelings of helplessness it can cause if they have the opportunity to do something about it. Working for social change is a time-honored way to deal with the menacing nature of racism.

My own involvement in the civil rights movement of the 1960s gave me a sense of purpose and empowerment. I worked alongside civil rights martyrs Vernon Dahmer, Clyde Kennard, and Medgar Evers. They all died because of their determination to eliminate racism in this country. Their dedication to this goal inspired me to go beyond complaining into action. Their determination motivated me to fight for change rather than wait for others to bring it to me. Even as a young child, I had family members and friends of my parents who told me that people of my generation would have to dedicate themselves to getting rid of racial discrimination. They impressed upon me that it was my generation's responsibility to take the political struggle for equality to the next level.

Although today there are fewer events to protest than there were when I was growing up because legalized segregation and discrimination have been abolished, we can pass on this proactive attitude by showing our children through example how to use social activism as a powerful coping skill. You might run for a seat on the school board or city council. You might organize petitions for a referendum; join a political action, educational, or legal defense group like the National Association for the Advancement of Colored People (NAACP) Youth Council, the National Urban League, or one of countless local groups. You might also take an active part in your local political parties (Democratic, Republican, the Green Party, Independent, and so forth) if you think they have the potential for progressive change.

As your children grow into their teens, they too can become socially or politically active. You can suggest that they run for a class office or become active in a safe and meritorious local political action like picketing a store that discriminates in its hiring practices. Your children might write letters to politicians to protest conditions of inequality affecting others. They might help obtain signatures for a local petition or whatever would be appropriate in your community.

Children whose parents are engaged as activists for change are more likely to do the same. Remember that you are their models. If you do not show your children this critical link, they will not be able to carry the struggle with them as they mature. Moreover, many of the changes won by previous generations may well evaporate. Doing something to cause change fosters that sense of control and power that helps all black people stand tall and be counted.

TEACH THE IMPORTANCE OF DIVERSITY

Black children cope better with their minority status when they learn to see themselves not solely as America's oppressed minority group but as members of the broader society that is not just black and white anymore. The reality of the American culture today is one of great diversity. We must encourage our children to befriend children of many races without prejudice in order to thrive in this environment. This helps them expand their understanding of the different cultures that will be part of their lives in the larger world.

My niece, who graduated from the International School in Washington, D.C., is a good example of the benefits of early exposure to a diverse population. Because she went to school with children from families who came to this country from around the world, she learned early in life to understand and appreciate cultural diversity. This did not diminish her sense of pride in her own Ethiopian–African American culture, but rather it enhanced it, allowing her to place her culture in a global context.

My son, too, learned to enjoy diversity at an early age when he began his education in the United Nations preschool in New York City. His classmates from around the world did not interfere with his identity as a black person. We lived in Dakar, Senegal (West Africa), where he attended first grade. By the time he reached college, his father lived in Lagos, Nigeria, for four years. He visited his father each summer and during the Christmas holidays. These were invaluable personal experiences in understanding and accepting himself as an African American within the context of a global community. He has carried that acceptance of others and pride in self with him into adulthood. I am sure that those early experiences help him to function very well today in our diverse society. I recognize that most parents cannot move to an African country or place their children in schools that have tremendous diversity. However, there are things you *can* do.

When your children are young, create play groups that include children of varied races whenever possible. Together, read storybooks and watch television programs about children from other cultures. As your children grow, seek out diverse cultural activities for them to participate in. Encourage them to join organizations and activities that put them in contact with children of other races. Encourage your child's school to add a multicultural focus to the curriculum if none exists. And all the while, make your home a prejudice-free environment. Avoid making negative comments about people of other races that teach your children to become racist themselves. We will all best cope with being different when we can celebrate and appreciate differences. Teach your children to enjoy diversity.

CHOOSE AN ASSERTIVE RESPONSE OVER A PASSIVE OR AGGRESSIVE ONE

Even accomplished and empowered black people live in a world that will sometimes insult them. The way they respond to these insults strongly influences their ability to move ahead in life. So it is important to teach our children how to react to hurtful comments and actions. You can use hypothetical situations from your own life and from theirs at any age to role-play appropriate reactions. In this way you can teach your children to consider the consequences of the three most common responses: ignore it; react with aggression or violence; or be calm, firm, and assertive.

You might, for example, imagine with your children that your supervisor at work says to you, "You're doing very well . . . for a black woman [man]." Talk about how that would make you feel and then together explore these three responses:

Ignore it This is a passive behavior that implies the acceptance of an inferior status and teaches your child to be silent in the face of racism.

React with aggression or violence If you start yelling, "You racist bigot, I'll have your job for that remark!" you teach your child to have no impulse control and to react to racism with hostility.

Be calm, firm, and assertive Confronting the insult with dignity, you might say, "I find that racist remark insulting. Please evaluate my performance, not the color of my skin." This teaches your child to stand tall and address the insult without becoming confrontational.

Now try it with an example from your child's life. You might imagine that a classmate calls him or her "nigger." Ask your child to consider each of the three responses with these questions:

- What would happen if you ignored the comment?

- What would happen if you reacted with violence or aggression?

- What would happen if you responded with a firm and assertive statement?

Then ask your child which consequence he or she thinks best resolves the situation. Talk about the choice and encourage your child to be firmly assertive whenever possible. Give your children the words to say. You might practice responses such as these: "I don't like that word because it is insulting. Don't say it to me again, or I will tell my parents [or teacher]."

In addition to this kind of role playing, you can practice this coping skill over the years whenever you read or hear about an act of prejudice or discrimination. If your child tells you that classmates got into a fistfight on the playground because one of the kids said that black kids are dumb, talk about the three possible responses the black children could have used and the consequence of each. If you read in the newspaper about a prejudiced remark made by a public figure, talk to your kids about how they think the black community should respond. Keep these conversations going through the years so that when your children are faced with racist situations, they will know how to react.

Above all, you can teach your children to be calm, firm, and assertive through your own daily example. Don't take slights and insults in silence; don't respond with violent outbursts. Instead, practice taking a stand with dignity and strength. Show your children how to apply the role-playing game to real life whenever you find yourself in a racist situation. When faced with a bigoted salesperson, real estate agent, school official, or employer, for example, think before you respond and then stand tall and show your children what integrity looks like.

MANAGE ANGER

For your children, knowing how to respond to racist situations does not mean that they will not get angry over the way they are treated. In these situations they should know that anger is perfectly normal, that they have a right to be angry, but that they also need to know how to handle that anger so that they can respond appropriately. It's no secret that for black people the difference between being aggressive and being assertive can often determine if they succeed or fail in life and even if they live or die a violent death.

While teaching your children how to cope by being firmly assertive, also teach them how to cope with their anger. Anger management skills give them the ability to stay calm and use their heads, not their fists. There are many types of anger management you can teach your children. The school or community may offer your children a program on conflict resolution. Find out the details so that you can use the program as a springboard for your family discussions. If the school does not offer such a program, encourage the parent-teacher association to develop one to help all the children learn to cope with their anger while standing up for their rights.

You can teach your children of any age the five most basic forms of anger management: breathe deeply; think happy thoughts; count to ten; test reality; and ask for help. Give them a try; it's good for the whole family.

Breathe Deeply

Anger is a very stressful emotion. The heart beats faster. The blood rushes through the body. Adrenaline is pumped up. Breathing becomes fast and shallow. Help your children learn proper breathing from the diaphragm so that when faced with conflict, they can more readily maintain their cool. Try it out right before bedtime; it makes a nice way to relax before falling off to sleep at night. It will be a good way for both of you to unwind at the end of the day. Demonstrate to your children:

1. Place one hand on your chest and one on your upper stomach.

2. As you inhale to take a deep breath, feel the hand on your stomach rise. The hand on your chest should not rise.

3. Let the air go. Don't push it out; let it go gently. Feel the hand on your stomach go down.

4. As you release the breath, repeat a calming word or phrase to yourself like "relax" or "take it easy." And let go of muscle tension you may feel in your shoulders or jaw.

As you practice this technique together, keep the pace of the breathing slow and steady. Take in a slow easy breath to the count of four. Then release the breath to the count of four.

Once your body is familiar with this relaxing type of breathing, you can use it calm the body down when anger begins to rise. When you see your children getting wound up about something, remind them to breathe deeply. Eventually, they will use this technique out of habit when tensions rise, and it will help them keep calm in even the most stressful situations.

Think Happy Thoughts

This technique is also one to use to calm the tensions of each day as well as to manage anger when necessary. The technique, also called guided imagery, takes your mind off the tense situation and focuses it on something positive, fun, or funny, causing the brain to release chemicals that diminish stress. You can actually trick your brain into thinking that you're having fun, rather than having a fit of anger.

Sit down with your children and take turns thinking of places that make you both feel safe and happy: a certain birthday party, a family trip to the beach, or simply a moment when you laughed yourself silly with a good friend. Each of you should choose one enjoyable event to use as your anger antidote. When you feel yourself getting upset, go to that moment in your mind and relive it. Feel the joy, the security, and the fun. Let your mind think that you are having a good time. This little mind trick won't make the reason for your anger go away, but it will calm the body down long enough so that you can respond more productively to the angry feelings. This is another exercise that you and your child should practice often so that you can use it easily.

Count to Ten

This anger management technique has been around a long time, and it works. By your example, teach your kids to count to ten before they say or do anything in anger. When your child spills his drink on the floor for the second time in five minutes, count out loud before you say anything. This ten-second pause gives you time to calm down and rethink your impulse to scream. When you see your child is about to explode in anger, jump in and tell her to count to ten before she says or does anything. Your child can use these strategies anytime, at home, school, play, or anywhere else. Even the youngest child can learn to manage anger better with this simple strategy.

Test Reality

When we are angry, our thinking can get very exaggerated and overly dramatic. This causes the situation to appear far worse than it really is. We can teach our children to test the reality of their thoughts before letting them get out of control. This is easy to do if you stay alert for words like *always* and *never*. Let's say, for example, that your child says to you, "My teacher always picks on me." Ask him to replace that thought with a more rational one (assuming you have determined there is no truth to the allegation).

For instance, instead of saying "always," try "sometimes." The situation looks better already. If your child says, "I'll never get the job I want," help her to think about the obstacles she faces more realistically. "Never" is a very long time and is probably far from the truth. If your child says, "Everything's ruined," you can encourage him or her to consider saying something like, "It's frustrating and I'm upset, but it's not the end of the world."

Reality testing is a good way to stop the generalizations that turn anger into personal defeat.

Ask for Help

Coping does not necessarily mean handling hurtful situations without help. Children should be taught to tell the teacher or parent about what happened. These children may feel hurt and defenseless and need to have an adult reassure them of their positive worth and intervene on their behalf. It does not make kids tough when we tell them, "Don't tell me about it; stand up for yourself." After all, as adults we are not expected to handle discrimination alone. When faced with housing discrimination, harassment, or bias crimes, we seek out the lawyers and law enforcement personnel who can best help us. Give your children the same freedom of redress. Make sure they know they can tell you or an adult in authority when they feel they are being treated unfairly.

Of course, our children are human, and there will probably be times when they get into fights. You can use this too as a teaching device. Engage your child in a discussion about how and why she resorted to a physical altercation. Then use the experience to remind her how to be calm but firm and assertive and how to manage her anger in the future.

VOTE FOR PROGRESS

One of the most concrete things we can do to cope with discrimination and prejudice is to be proactive in selecting our elected officials. Through your own example, raise your children to understand the value of their vote when they come of age. Make sure they know that past generations of black people fought very hard for this right.

As mentioned earlier, getting the legal right to vote was not the end of black voter discrimination. I remember being very disappointed in the 1960s that even though the law gave black people the right to vote, obstacles were placed in our way. Only black people, for example, failed the literacy test that asked them to do things like interpret sections of the Constitution and note the number of bubbles in a bar of soap. I could not pass the voter registration test, even though I was a college senior when I took it. My failure to pass the test had nothing to do with my literacy. It was the result of a strong, bigoted, and prejudiced county voting registrar who did not feel that any blacks should vote. Ultimately, I gained the right to vote through a federal court order that prevented the voting registrar from practicing racial discrimination.

Also at that time, all people had to pay a poll tax and keep the receipt for several years and present it when they wanted to vote. Each voter's name was printed in the local newspaper, so any other registered voter could challenge a person's moral fitness to vote. The real reason for this was to inform white employers that they had some "uppity" Negroes working for them who expected to vote. Sometimes this led to violence and termination of employment. The black employee was told to take his or her name off the voter registration file or be fired.

Obviously, the white people knew how powerful the black vote could be. Make sure your children know it too. Read books to them about the courage of civil rights leaders who fought for the right to vote, such as Fannie Lou Hamer, Bob Moses, Medgar Evers, and Martin Luther King Jr. Make sure they grow up with a consciousness of the importance of the right to vote. When they reach voting age, make sure they register and vote. It is one of the most important rites of passage in their continuing empowerment. Having the right to elect representatives who will work for civil rights for all people gives a feeling of control and power. Encourage your children to use this right wisely.

Lifelong Coping Skills

Use the coping skills discussed in this chapter to help your children stand up tall every day of their lives:

- Talk about racism.
- Be proactive.
- Teach the importance of diversity.
- Choose an assertive response over a passive or aggressive one.
- Manage anger.
- Vote for progress.

GIVE THEM DIGNITY, STRENGTH, AND JOY

Thankfully, fewer overt acts stigmatize and demean children because of their blackness today than when I was growing up. But no matter how protective an environment you create for your children, there is no control over the single mean-spirited child who may use a racial epithet against your child on the playground. We need to prepare our children to handle that, without teaching them to hate others. Yes, racism is a part of American society, so deal with it. Let's raise our children to grow up without a lot of animosity and without inflicting on others the same stereotypes that were applied to us, but at the same time let's teach our children the skills they need to defend themselves.

We do this each time we contribute to the development of their positive self-image and pass on family values, every time we use positive discipline and monitor their education, every time we talk to them about the danger of drugs and violence and surround them with supportive black role models, every time we use positive coping skills and talk to them honestly about the world we live in. When we have done these things, we have given our children a priceless gift that will guide them with dignity, strength, and joy through all the days of their lives.

Helpful Resources

Throughout this book I have recommended organizations and various resources that can help you raise your children to be self-confident and successful. For convenient use here is a list of those organizations, presented in the order they appear in the book.

Chapter Six

Jack & Jill
P.O. Box 70635
Pasadena, California 91117
(626) 584-6410
http://www.jack-and-jill.org

Boys & Girls Clubs of America
1230 W. Peachtree Street NW
Atlanta, Georgia 30309
(800) 854-CLUB
http://www.bgca.org

YMCA of the USA
101 North Wacker Drive
Chicago, Illinois 60606
(312) 977-0031
http://www.ymca.net

Chapter Eight

National Foundation for Depressive Illness
P.O. Box 2257
New York, New York 10116
(800) 239-1265
http://www.depression.org.

National PTA
330 N. Wabash Avenue
Suite 2100
Chicago, Illinois 60611
(312) 670-6782; toll-free (800) 307-4782
http://www.pta.org

Quick Contacts

TheAntiDrug.com
http://www.antidrug.com

Parents' Resource Institute for Drug Education (PRIDE)
http://www.prideusa.org

The National Council on Alcoholism and Drug
Dependence
http://www.ncadd.org

Drug Abuse Resistance Education (DARE)
(800) 223-3273
http://www.dare-america.com

National Clearinghouse for Alcohol and Drug
Information (NCADI)
(800) 662-HELP
http://www. health.org

Chapter Nine

100 Black Men of America, Inc.
141 Auburn Avenue
Atlanta, Georgia 30303
(800) 598-3411 or (404) 688-5100
http://www.100blackmen.org
e-mail: 100blackmen@100bmoa.org

The Urban League
120 Wall Street, 8th floor
New York, New York 10005
(212) 558-5300
http://www.nul.org

National Foundation for the Teaching of Entrepreneurship
(NFTE)
120 Wall Street, 29th floor
New York, New York 10005
(800) FOR-NFTE
http://www.nfte.com

YWCA of the USA
Empire State Building
350 Fifth Avenue, Suite 301
New York, New York 10118
(212) 273-7800
http://www.ywca.org

Girls' Pipeline to Power
95 Berkeley Street
Boston, Massachusetts 02116
(617) 482-1078
http://www.girlspipeline.org

Ms. Foundation for Women
120 Wall Street, 33rd floor
New York, New York 10005
(212) 742-2300
http://www.ms.foundation.org

Independent Means Inc.
126 Powers Avenue
Santa Barbara, California 93103
(805) 965-0475
http://www.anincomeofherown.com

Association for Women in Computing
41 Sutter Street, Suite 1006
San Francisco, California 94104
(415) 905-4663
http://www.awc-hq.org

Chapter Ten

Big Brothers Big Sisters of America
(215) 567-7000
http://www.bigbrothersbigsisters.org

Little Africa
http://www.littleafrica.com/resources/organizations.htm

Chapter Eleven

National Association for Equal Opportunity in Higher
Education
8701 Georgia Avenue, Suite 200
Silver Spring, Maryland 20910
(301) 650-2440
http://www.nafeo.org

United Negro College Fund
8260 Willow Oaks Corporate Drive
Fairfax, Virginia 22031
(800) 331-2244
http://www.uncf.org

Black Excel: The College Help Network
PMB H281
New York, New York 10001
(212) 591-1936

U.S. Department of Education
400 Maryland Avenue SW
Washington, D.C. 20202
(800) USA-LEARN or (800) 872-5327
http://www.ed.gov

National Association for College Admission Counseling
1631 Prince Street
Alexandria, Virginia 22314
(703) 836-2222
http://www.nacac.com/fairs.html

Quick Contacts

Educational On-Line Listing of Historically Black Colleges and
Universities
http://www.edonline.com/cq/hbcu/

U.S. Department of Education Student Guide
http://www.ed.gov/prog_info/SFA/StudentGuide/2002-3/

Federal Student Aid Information Center
(800) 4-FED-AID or (800) 433-3243
http://www.fafsa.ed.gov

The College Board
http://www.collegeboard.com

Federal Student Aid
http://www.ed.gov/studentaid

Student Loan Funding
http://www.studentloanfunding.com

Notes

Chapter Three

1. W.E.B. DuBois, *The Souls of Black Folk* (New York: Fawcett, 1968), 16.

2. E. G. Graves, "The Difference Between Yes and No," *Black Enterprise*, 30, no. 7 (February 2000): 18.

3. J. Brown, "Black Intellectual Development," *National Black Child Development Institute* [http://www.nbcdi.org/_disc2/00000041.htm], February 3, 2002.

4. Brown, "Black Intellectual Development."

Chapter Four

1. F. Douglass, *Narrative of the Life of Frederick Douglass, An American Slave: Written by Himself*, ed. Benjamin Quarles (Boston: Harvard University Press, 1960), 35–36.

2. My Family Café, "Integrity on the Net" [http://myfamilycafe.topcities.com/Quotations/integrity.html].

Chapter Five

1. I. Tofler and T. DiGeronimo, *Keeping Your Kids Out Front Without Kicking Them from Behind* (San Francisco: Jossey-Bass, 2000).

2. S. Hill, *African American Children: Socialization and Development in Families* (Thousand Oaks, Calif.: Sage, 1999).

Chapter Six

1. D. Century, "Rap's Fighting Words," *New York Times*, 25 February 2002.

2. T. Martinez, "Popular Culture as Oppositional Culture: Rap as Resistance," *Sociological Perspectives*, 40, no. 2 (1997): 265–286.

3. R. Baraka, "Rap & Hip-Hop," *Billboard*, 114, no. 14 (April 6, 2002): 23.

4. F. Lee, "Hip-Hop Is Enlisted in Social Causes," *New York Times*, 22 June 2002.

Chapter Seven

1. S. Hill, *African American Children: Socialization and Development in Families* (Thousand Oaks, Calif.: Sage, 1999).

2. *Encyclopaedia Britannica*, s.v. "American Missionary Association" [http://search.eb.com/blackhistory/micro/19/50.html].

3. H. Morgan, *Historical Perspectives on the Education of Black Children* (Westport, Conn.: Praeger, 1995).

4. "Introduction to the Court Opinion on the Plessy v. Ferguson Case" [http://usinfo.state.gov/usa/infousa/facts/democrac/33.html], n.d.

5. K. Bauman, "Schools, Markets, and Family in the History of African-American Education," *American Journal of Education*, 106 (August 1998), 500–529.

6. R. Moses and C. Cobb, *Radical Equations* (Boston: Beacon Press, 2001).

7. A. John-Hall, "Rutgers President Tries to Soothe Students, Faculty Upset by Racial Remark," Knight-Ridder/Tribune News Service, 3 February 1995.

8. Hill, *African American Children*, 62.

9. H. McAdoo, *Black Children: Social, Educational, and Parental Environments* (2d ed.; Thousand Oaks, Calif.: Sage, 2002).

10. A. H. Jenkins, *Psychology and African Americans* (Needham Heights, Mass.: Allyn & Bacon, 1995).

11. J. Mercer, "What Is a Racially and Culturally Nondiscriminatory Test? A Sociological and Pluralistic Perspective," in *Perspectives on Bias in Mental Testing,* ed. C. R. Reynolds and R. T. Brown (New York: Plenum, 1984), 293–356.

12. Jenkins, *Psychology and African Americans.*

13. S. Fordham and J. Ogbu, "Black Students' School Successes: Coping with the 'Burden of Acting White,'" *Urban Review,* 18 (1986): 177.

14. R. Humphrey, "Voice Up! Black in White Schools: A Cautionary Tale," *Black Parenting Today,* 31 October 1998, 7.

15. D. Ford and J. Harris, "A Study of the Racial Identity and Achievement of Black Males and Females," *Roeper Review,* 20 (1997), 105.

Chapter Eight

1. American Psychological Association, "Is Youth Violence Just Another Fact of Life?" *APA On-Line* [http://www.apa.org/pi/pii/isyouthviolence.html], 2002.

2. "General Colin Powell Speaks at the GOP National Convention," Online Newshour: Convention Speeches, August 12, 1996. [http://www.pbs.org/newshour/convention96/floor_speeches/powell.html].

3. American Psychiatric Association, *Diagnostic and Statistical Manual of Mental Disorders* (4th ed.; Washington, D.C.: American Psychiatric Association, 1994).

4. U.S. Department of Education, *Growing Up Drug Free: A Parent's Guide to Prevention* (Washington, D.C.: U.S. Department of Education, n.d.).

5. C. Wren, "Drugs and Teenagers," *New York Times,* 26 April 1999.

6. C. Wren, "Drugs and Teenagers."

7. C. E. Schaefer and T. F. DiGeronimo, *How to Talk to Teens About Really Important Things: Specific Questions and Answers and Useful Things to Say* (San Francisco: Jossey-Bass, 1999).

8. National Institute on Drug Abuse, *Peer Pressure: It's OK to Say No,* DHHS publication no. AADM 83-1271 (Rockville, Md.: National Institute on Drug Abuse, 1983).

9. American Psychological Association, "Is Youth Violence Just Another Fact of Life?"

10. C. Perkins, "Age Patterns of Victims of Serious Violent Crime," Bureau of Justice Statistics, U.S. Department of Justice, publication no. NCJ-162031 [http://www.ojp.usdoj.gov/bjs/pub/ascii/apvsvc.txt], September 1997.

11. H. McAdoo, *Black Children: Social, Educational, and Parental Environments* (2d ed.; Thousand Oaks, Calif.: Sage, 2002).

12. K. Hamilton, "Gangbusters: Parents Still Play Key Role in Saving Kids from the Streets," *Black Issues in Higher Education* [http://www.blackissues.com], 2002.

13. Hamilton, "Gangbusters."

14. American Psychological Association, "Is Youth Violence Just Another Fact of Life?"

15. American Psychological Association, "Is Youth Violence Just Another Fact of Life?"

Chapter Nine

1. U.S. Department of Justice, Office of Justice Programs, Bureau of Justice Statistics, "Jail Statistics: Summary Findings" [http://www.ojp.usdoj.gov/bjs/jails.htm], 2002.

2. E. O. Hutchinson, *The Assassination of the Black Male Image* (Los Angeles, Calif.: Middle Passage Press, 1994).

3. Hutchinson, *Assassination of the Black Male Image*, 15.

4. S. Hill, *African American Children: Socialization and Development in Families* (Thousand Oaks, Calif.: Sage, 1999).

5. I. Tofler and T. DiGeronimo, *Keeping Your Kids Out Front Without Kicking Them from Behind* (San Francisco: Jossey-Bass, 2000).

6. F. Beale, "Double Jeopardy: To Be Black and Female," in *The Black Woman: An Anthology*, ed. T. Cade (New York: New American Library, 1979).

7. U.S. Bureau of the Census, *Median Income of People by Selected Characteristics, Table 7* [http://www.census.gov/prod/2001pubs/p60-213.pdf], 2000.

8. D. King, "Multiple Jeopardy, Multiple Consciousness," in *Black Women in America*, eds. M. Malson, E. Mudimbe-Boyi, J. O'Barr, and M. Wyer (Chicago: University of Chicago Press, 1988).

9. S. Mann, "Slavery, Sharecropping, and Sexual Inequality," in *Black Women in America*.

10. Hill, *African American Children*.

11. E. B. Brown, "Womanist Consciousness," in *Black Women in America*.

12. U.S. Bureau of the Census, *One-Parent Family Groups with Own Children Under 18, Table FG6* [http://www.census.gov/population/socdemo/hh-fam/p20-537/2000/tabFG6.txt], 2000.

13. Brown, "Womanist Consciousness," in *Black Women in America*.

14. W. Allen, "Family Roles, Occupational Statuses, and Achievement Orientations Among Black Women in the United States," in *Black Women in America*.

15. Centers for Disease Control and Prevention, "Youth Risk Behavior Surveillance—United States 2001," *Morbidity and Mortality Weekly Report*, 51, no. SS-4 (June 28, 2001).

16. F. Hrabowski, K. Maton, M. Greene, and G. Grief, *Overcoming the Odds: Raising Academically Successful African American Young Women* (New York: Oxford University Press, 2002).

17. National Center for Health Statistics, *Health, United States, 2000* (Hyattsville, Md.: Centers for Disease Control and Prevention, 2001).

Chapter Ten

1. H. McAdoo, *Black Children: Social, Educational, and Parental Environments* (2d ed.; Thousand Oaks, Calif.: Sage, 2002).

2. McAdoo, *Black Children*.

3. C. Daniels, "The Most Powerful Black Executives in America," *Fortune*, July 22, 2002, 60.

4. B. Carson, *Gifted Hands* (Grand Rapids, Mich.: Zondervan, 1990); *Think Big* (Grand Rapids, Mich.: Zondervan, 1996).

5. Quoted in "From Detroit Ghetto to Brilliant Brain Surgeon," American Dreams [http://www.usdreams.com/Carson.html], 2002.

Chapter Eleven

1. U.S. Census Bureau, *Median Income of People by Education* [http://www.census.gov/prod/2001pubs/p60-213.pdf], 2001.

2. U.S. Census Bureau, *Statistical Abstract of the United States: 2001* (21st ed.; Washington, D.C.: U.S. Department of Commerce, 2001).

3. National Center for Educational Statistics, *Educational Statistics Digest, 2000* (Washington, D.C.: U.S. Department of Education, 2001).

4. F. Butterfield, "Study Finds Big Increase in Black Men as Inmates Since 1980," *New York Times*, 28 August 2002.

5. *Peterson's Guide to Four-Year Colleges* (Lawrenceville, N.J.: Peterson's Thomson Learning, 2002).

6. J. Fleming, *Blacks in College: A Comparative Study of Students' Success in Black and White Institutions* (San Francisco: Jossey-Bass, 1984), 166.

7. A. H. Jenkins, *Psychology and African Americans* (Needham Heights, Mass.: Allyn & Bacon, 1995).

Further Reading

For further reading on the subject of parenting black children, I recommend the following.

Beal, A. C., Villarosa, L., and Abner, A. *The Black Parenting Book*. New York: Broadway Books, 1999.

Black, I. *Black Excel African American Student's College Guide: Your One-Stop Resource for Choosing the Right College, Getting In, and Paying the Bill*. New York: Wiley, 2000.

Boyd-Franklin, N., and Franklin, A. J., with Toussaint, P. A. *Boys into Men: Raising Our African American Teenage Sons*. New York: Plume, 2001.

Comer, J. P., and Poussaint, A. F. *Raising Black Children: Two Leading Psychiatrists Confront the Educational, Social, and Emotional Problems Facing Black Children*. New York: Plume, 1992.

Hale-Benson, J. E. *Black Children: Their Roots, Culture, and Learning Styles*. (Rev. ed.) Baltimore: Johns Hopkins University Press, 1986.

Hopson, D. P., and Hopson, D. S. *Different and Wonderful: Raising Black Children in a Race-Conscious Society*. New York: Simon & Schuster, 1992.

Hrabowski, F. A., Maton, K. I., Greene, M. L., and Greif, G. L. *Overcoming the Odds: Raising Academically Successful African American Young Women*. New York: Oxford University Press, 2002.

Hrabowski, F. A., Maton, K. I., Greif, G. L. *Beating the Odds: Raising Academically Successful African American Males*. New York: Oxford University Press, 1998.

Kunjufu, J. *Developing Positive Self-Images and Discipline in Black Children*. Chicago: African American Images, 1997.

Tatum, B. D. *Why Are All the Black Kids Sitting Together in the Cafeteria? And Other Conversations About Race: A Psychologist Explains the Development of Racial Identity*. (5th ed.) New York: Basic Books, 2003.

About the Authors

Joyce A. Ladner, Ph.D., is a senior fellow at the Brookings Institution in Washington, D.C., and the first woman to serve as president of Howard University, where she was also vice president for academic affairs and professor of social work. President Clinton appointed her to the Financial Control Board in the District of Columbia, where she is now chair of the Campaign to Prevent Teenage Pregnancy and a board member of the Maya Angelou Charter School.

Ladner has written for the *Washington Post, New York Times, Philadelphia Inquirer, Ebony, Essence,* and *Black Enterprise.* She has authored or coauthored several books, including *The Ties That Bind; Tomorrow's Tomorrow: The Black Woman, Adolescence, and Poverty; Mixed Families: Adopting Across Racial Boundaries;* and others. She has received many awards for her work in education and public service. A civil rights activist, she received an honorary doctorate from Howard University and the Washingtonian of the Year Award for her work in the D.C. public school system. Ms. Ladner has also appeared on *Nightline,* National Public Radio, and other major media.

Theresa Foy DiGeronimo, M.Ed., is the author of several successful Jossey-Bass publications, including *How to Talk to Your Kids About Really Important Things* and other titles in the How to Talk series.

Index

A

ABC, 115
Abdul-Jabbar, K., 139
Academic environment: and academic suitability, 225–226; and black children in black schools, 130–131; and black children in integrated schools, 129–130; and black children in white schools, 131–132; support for, 128–132
Accountability, 68–72
Achievement, value of, 54
ACT. *See* American College Test (ACT)
Acting black, 50–53
Acting white, 53–55; stigma of, 138–142
Admissions officers, 235–236
African Youth in Action (AYA) Tour of Historical Black Colleges and Universities (Bronx, New York), 234
Algebra Project, 128
Ali, M., 33, 109
Allen, D., 229
Amends, making, 101
American Association Commission on Violence and Youth, 167
American College Test (ACT), 135–138, 220–222, 225
American Express, 180

American Missionary Association (AMA), 125–126
And the Winner Is (LL Cool J), 112
Anger: managing, 249–253; and violence, 165
AOL Time Warner, 180
Arkansas, 172
Assassination of the Black Male Image (Hutchinson), 177–178
Assertiveness, *versus* passive or aggressive response, 243–244
Association for Women in Computing, 191
Athletics, discipline of, 96
Atlanta University, 126
Attention deficit disorder (ADD), 133
Attitude, developing, 81–82

B

Baby and Child Care (Spock), 3
Back to Africa movement, 44
Baker, E., 33
Banneker, B., 71
Baptist Church, 125
Beale, F., 185
"Been Down So Long, Seems Like Up To Me" (traditional spiritual), 80–81
BET. *See* Black Entertainment Television (BET)

Big Brothers Big Sisters of America, 211
BizCamp, 186
Black College Tour, Alpha Kappa Alpha (Wichita, Kansas), 235
Black college tours, 234–235
Black dress code, 52–53
Black English, 51–52
Black Enterprise magazine, 52–53
Black Entertainment Television (BET), 55, 110
Black Excel, 231, 234, 238
Black History Month, 142
Black identity: and black self in larger world, 49–55; building strong, 43–57; proud heritage of, 44–45; and root of negative black self, 45–46; and root of positive black self, 47–49; and steps toward developing positive self-image, 56–57
"Black Intellectual Development" (Brown), 53
Black Muslims, 44
Black Nationalism, 44
Black Panthers, 44
"Black Students' School Successes: Coping with the Burden of 'Acting White'" (Fordham and Ogbu), 139
Black Women's Agenda, 211–212
Blues, 109
Boys & Girls Clubs, 120, 210, 221
Brown, B. (Justice), 126
Brown, R. H., 238
Brown University, 189, 231
Brown v. Topeka Board of Education, 127
Bryant, C., 14–15
Bryant, R., 14–15
Bunker, Archie (television), 113
Bureau of Justice Statistics, 177
Bush, G. W., 161–162

C

Can-do spirit, 37–38
Career guidance, meaning of, 27
Carroll, C., 177
Carson, B., 209, 210

Carver, G. W., 71, 207
CBS, 115
Centers for Disease Control and Prevention, 192
Century, D., 109
Chenault, K., 180
Chicago, 14, 15
Child, evaluation of: and can-do spirit, 37–38; and child's difficulties, 38–39; and child's envisioning of future, 40–41; and child's friends, 34; and child's sense of racial identity, 39–40; and child's social skills, 33–34; and child's source of information about world, 35–36; and child's talents and interests, 30–32; and child's temperament, 29–30; and child's work habits, 36–37; and feeling safe, 38; honesty in, 28–29; as individual and ongoing process, 28; and schoolwork, 34–35; and valuing honesty and integrity, 33
Childhood, concept of, 89
Christian denominations, 89
Church of England, 125
Civil Rights Act of 1964, 11
Civil War, 126, 171
Clark-Atlanta University (Atlanta), 231
Clear, T., 216
Cleaver, Beaver (television), 113
Clinton, H., 12
Clinton, W. J., 161–162
Coalition of 100 Black Women, 211–212
College, financing: and government grants and loans, 239–241; and institutional scholarships, 239; and scholarships from private organizations, 236–238
College preparation: and choosing right college, 223–233; and college *versus* jail, 215–216; and college *versus* trade school, 222–223; and family expectation, 216–218; and high school years, 220–223; and value of home computer, 219

College selection: and academic suitability, 225–226; and attitude toward blacks, 231–233; and college fairs, 223–224; and cost, 228; and location, 226–227; and racial makeup, 229–231; and size, 227–228; and taking campus tour, 233–236; and talking to admissions officers, 235–236; and type of college, 224–225

Color Purple, The (Walker), 189

Columbia University, 231

Common Sense: Strategies for Raising Alcohol- and Drug-Free Children (National PTA), 160

Computer, value of home, 219

Consequences, negative. See Penalties

Coping skills: and being proactive, 244–246; and choosing assertive response over passive or aggressive one, 247–249; and managing anger, 249–253; and talking about racism, 243–244; and teaching importance of diversity, 246–247; and voting for progress, 253–254

Corporal punishment, 90; nonviolence versus, 91–92

Corporate racism, 179–180

Cosby Show, The (television), 114, 229

Cotton Belt, 187

D

Dahmer, V., 245

Dakar, Senegal, 39

Darden, C., 208

Daughters, raising: and can-do female power, 190–191; and female stereotypes, 187–190; and history of strength, 186–187; overview of, 185–186; and sexism, 190

Davis, D. W., 189

Democratic National Convention (1964), 79–80

Dependence, versus resiliency, 80–81

Depression, signs of, 153

Desegregation, struggle for, 126–128

"Difference Between Yes and No, The" (Graves), 52–53

Dillard University, 126

Discipline: of athletics, 96; checklist for positive, 104; goal of, 100; history of black, 89–92; how-to of, 94–105; punishment versus, 92–94; use and abuse of, 87–94

Discrimination, self-esteem as antidote to, 182–183

Diversity, teaching importance of, 246–247

Douglass, F., 71, 73, 142

Drew, C., 142

Drug abuse: and being good example, 161; and honesty about own past, 161–162; overview of, 147–150; signs of, 150–164; and support for school prevention programs, 160–161; and talk about future, 163–164; talking to children about, 156–157; use of media for, 158–160

Drug Abuse Resistance Education (DARE), 160

DuBois, W.E.B., 43, 229

DWB (driving while black), 176

E

Ebonics, 51–52

Education: early efforts at black, 125–126; overview of, 123–125; and raising educational expectations, 135–138; and stereotypes of black children, 132–134; and stigma of acting white, 138–142; struggle for desegregation in, 126–128; and support for good teachers, 142–145; to-do list, 145

Elders, respect for, 63–65

Emancipation Proclamation of 1863, 11, 125

Enforcing: with penalties, 100–102; with rewards, 102–105

English, black versus standard, 51–52

Evers, M., 245, 254

Example, teaching through, 94–96, 104; and drug abuse, 161; and violence, 168–169

Executive Leadership Council, 208
Eyeball rape, 172

F

Family: expectation concerning college, 216–218; extended, 203–207; and respect for family name, 65–67
Family values: and gift of love, 60–62; and love, 82–84; optimism, resiliency, and, 77–82; overview of, 59–60; and respect, 62–68; responsibility, accountability and, 68–72; and strong work ethic, 72–77
Fannie Mae, 180
Farleigh Dickinson University, 92
Federal Communication Commission, 208
Federal Pell Grants, 239
Federal PLUS Loans, 240
Federal Reserve, 208
Federal Stafford Loans, 240
Federal Student Aid Information Center, 239
Ferguson, Plessey v., 161
Ferguson, R., 208
Fisk University, 126, 229, 231
Fleming, J., 230
Focus, 183
Fordham, S., 139
Fortune 500, 180
FOX, 115
Free Application for Federal Student Aid (FAFSA), 239, 240
Friends, 34
Future, 40

G

Gangs, 120
"Gangsta" rap, 109, 111–112
Garvey, M., 44, 207
Gaye, M., 109
Gender differences: and raising daughters, 185–191; and raising sons, 175–176; and sexuality, 192–193
Gifted Hands (Carson), 209
Girls' Pipeline to Power, 191

Golden Rule, 93
Good Times (television), 113–114, 159
Grade point average (GPA), 225
Grandma's rule, 102
Graves, E. G., 52–53
Greenville, South Carolina, 54
Grounding, 101
Growing Up Drug Free: A Parent's Guide to Prevention (United States Department of Education), 155

H

Hamer, F. L., 33, 79, 80, 254
Hampton Institute, 126
Hampton University, 231
Harvard University, 111, 231
Hattiesburg, Mississippi, 127
HBCUs (historically black colleges and universities), 229–231, 234
Herbert Lehman Scholarships, 238
Heritage, 44–45
Herman, A., 208
High school years, 220–223
Hill, S. A., 91
Hip-hop, 108–111. *See also* Media
Hip-Hop Summit Action Network, 110
Historical Black College Tour (Houston, Texas), 234
Historical Black College Tour of the BAI Mentor Program (Harlem, New York), 234
Historically Black College Tour, Delta Sigma Theta Sorority, Inc. (Pontiac, Michigan), 234
HIV-AIDS, 2
Hoffman, F., 177
Holiday, B., 109
Honesty, 33
How to Talk to Teens About Really Important Things, 157
Howard University, 8, 126, 229–231
Hughes, C., 208
Humphrey, R., 140
Huston-Tillotson College, 126
Hutchinson, E. O., 178

I

In Living Color (television), 114
Independent Means, 191
Industrial History of the Negro Race in the United States, The (Davis and Jackson), 189
Information, sources of, 35–36
Inglewood, California, 172
Integrated schools, black children in, 129–130
Integrity, 33, 62
Intelligence quotient (IQ) test, 135–138
Interests, 30–23
International School (Washington, D.C.), 246
Invisible Child Syndrome, 134

J

Jack & Jill of America, Inc., 119
Jackson, D., 172
Jackson, G., 189
Jail, college *versus*, 215–216
Jasmine (case study), 195–197
Jay-Z (rapper), 109, 110
Jeffersons, The (television), 113–114
Jim Crow laws, 61, 177
John Jay College of Criminal Justice (Manhattan), 216
Johns Hopkins University Medical Center, 209
Johnson, E., 208
Johnson, R., 55
Jordan, M., 67, 124
Jumping the broom, 73
Juneteenth, 56
Juvenile Policy Institute, 216

K

Kennard, C., 245
King, M. L., Jr., 75, 206–207, 254
King, R., 15, 172
Ku Klux Klan, 2
Kwanzaa, 56

L

LAAPS Black College Bus Tour (St. Louis, Missouri), 235

Lawrence, F., 132
Le Moyne College, 126
Lear, N., 113–114
Limits, setting, 96–100, 104; in advance, 98; consistency in, 98–99; and making rules positive, 99–100
LL Cool J (rapper), 109, 112
Los Angeles, 172
Los Angeles Black College Tour, 234
Louisiana State University, 124
Lynching, new form of, 177

M

Magee, G., 134
Malcolm (case study), 197–198
Malcolm X, 44, 207
Male athletes, 180–181
Marshall, T., 142, 229
Martinez, T., 109
McDonald's Golden Arches Scholarships, 236–237
Media: checklist for countering, 121–122; countering negative, 107–122; impact of, 108–116; and influence of hip-hop and rap, 108–111
Meharry Medical College, 229
Mercer, J., 136
Methodist Church, 125
Miliam, J. W., 15
Million Man March, 183
Mississippi, 18, 79
Mississippi Delta, 109
Money, Mississippi, 14–15
Montgomery County Jail (Mississippi), 79
Morehouse College, 231
Morrison, T., 229
Morse, J., 172
Moses, B., 128, 254
Ms. Foundation for Women, 191
MTV (television), 110
Muhammed, B., 110

N

Narrative of the Life of Frederick Douglass, An American Slave (Douglass), 73

Nas (rapper), 109
Nashville's Sixth Annual Black College Tour, 234
National Academy of Television Arts and Sciences, 237
National Association for College Admission Counseling, 223–224
National Association for Equal Opportunity in Higher Education, 231
National Association for the Advancement of Colored People (NAACP), 110, 115, 245
National Association of Negro Business and Professional Women's Club, Inc., 211–212
National Basketball Association, 124
National Black College Alliance Black College Tours (Boston, Massachusetts), 235
National Clearinghouse for Alcohol and Drug Information, 156, 164
National Council of Negro Women, 211–212
National Crime Prevention Council, 120
National Football League, 181
National Foundation for Depressive Illness, 155
National Foundation for the Teaching of Entrepreneurship, 186
National Institute on Alcoholism and Drug Dependence (Web site), 156
National Institute on Drug Abuse, 163
National Organization for Women, 190
National Research Council, 166
National Urban League, 245
National Youth Anti-Drug Media Campaign, 155–156
NBC, 115
Negro a Beast or in the Image of God, The (Carroll), 177
Negro spirituals, 109
New Jersey, 126
New York City, 126
New York Times, 109, 149

Ninth Annual Black College Spring Tour (San Jose, California), 234
Nonviolence: versus corporal punishment, 91–92; teaching, 168–170
Norman, J., 229

O

Ogbu, J., 139
O'Leary, H., 208
100 Black Men of America, Inc., 184
O'Neal, S., 124
Optimism: and family values, 77–82; models of, 78–80
Original sin, 89

P

P. Diddy (rapper), 110
Parent power, 165–167
Parents' Resource Institute for Drug Education (PRIDE), 156
Parent-teacher association (PTA), 144, 160, 217, 220
Parent-teacher organization (PTO), 144
Parks, R., 206–207
Parsons, R., 180
Partnership for a Drug-Free America, 156
PBS, 159
Peer groups: checklist for countering, 121–122; countering, 107–122; and gang membership, 120; influence of, 116–120; and surviving rebellion, 120–122
Penalties: enforcing rules with, 100–102, 104; loss-of-privilege, 101; as negative consequences, 102–105
Pennsylvania, 126
Perkins Loans, 240
Perry Preschool Study (Ypsilanti, Michigan), 201
Persistence, 182
Pilot International Foundation, 237
Plessey v. Ferguson, 126
Powell, C., 150
Powell, M., 208

Praise, 103
Preliminary Scholastic Assessment Test (PSAT), 220, 221, 225
Prevention Online, 156
Price, L., 229
Princeton University, 111, 231
Privilege, loss of, 101
Progress, voting for, 253–254
Punishment: *versus* discipline, 92–94; history of black, 90–91

Q
Quakers, 126

R
Racism, talking about, 243–244
Radio One, 208
Raines, F., 180
Rap, 108–111; living with, 111–113. *See also* Media
Rashad, P., 229
Reality TV, 66
Reason to Hope (American Psychological Association Commission on Violence and Youth), 167
Reconstruction, 126
Reinforcement, positive, 103
Resilience, 77–78, 80–81, 182
Respect, 62–68; for elders, 63–65; for family name, 65–67; for self, 67–68
Responsibility, 68–72
Restorative justice, 101
Rewards: concrete, 102; enforcing rules with, 102–105; social, 103
Rice, C., 189, 208
Righting a wrong, 101
Ritalin, 133
Role models: and being proactive, 210–211; checklist for finding and using positive, 212–213; and community, 209–213; and extended family, 203–207; finding realistic, 199–200; historic, 206–207; and networking, 211–213; oneself as, 201–203; and professionals in community, 207–208; with and without, 195–199

Ron Brown Scholarship Program, 238
Rules: enforcing with penalties and rewards, 100–105; making positive, 99–100
Rutgers University, 132

S
Safety, 38
Sanford and Son (television), 113–114
Sanford, Fred (television), 113–114
SAT. *See* Scholastic Assessment Test (SAT)
Saturday Night Live (television), 114
Schaefer, C., 92, 93
Scholastic Assessment Test (SAT), 132, 135–138, 220–222, 225
Schoolwork, 34–35
SEG (segregation) academies, 127
Self-assessment: and bottom line, 20–24; as foundation for looking ahead, 24–26; overview of, 5–6; and past, 6–12; and personality assessment, 12–15; and reality check, 15–20
Self-confidence, 182
Self-control, 94, 100
Self-discipline, 94
Self-empowerment, sustained, 244
Self-esteem: as antidote to discrimination, 182; building positive, 43–57. *See also* Black identity
Self-identity, positive, 169–170. *See also* Black identity
Self-respect, 67–68
Senegal, 39
Sexism, 190
Sexuality, male and female, 192–193
Sharpton, A., 111
Simmons, R., 110, 189
Smith, D., 3
Smith, K., 162
Smith, W., 109
Social skills, 33–34
Society for the Prevention of Cruelty to Children, 90
Society for the Propagation of the Gospel in Foreign Parts, 125, 126

Sons, raising: and corporate racism, 179–180; and male athletes, 180–181; and male stereotypes, 177–179; and men helping men, 183–185; overview of, 175–176
Souls of Black Folk, The (DuBois), 43
Spelman College, 231
Spiritual backup, 84
Spock, B., 3
St. Louis, Missouri, 199
Standardized tests, 135–138
Staples, R., 179
Stillwell, S., 54
"Strange Fruit" (Holiday), 109
Student Financial Assistance (SFA) programs, 239
Student Loan Funding, 241
Styles P (rapper), 159
Summers, L., 111

T

Talents, 30–32
Talladega College, 126, 231
Teach Your Child to Behave (Schaefer), 92
Teaching, 94–96
Television, 108; blacks on, 113–114; living with, 115–116; rating, 113. *See also* Media
Temperament, 29–30
TheAntiDrug.com, 155–156
Think Big (Carson), 209
Till, E., 14–15
Time-out, 100–102
Topeka Board of Education, Brown v., 128
Tougaloo College, 126, 230, 231
Trade school, college *versus*, 222–223
Truth, S., 207
Tubman, H., 33, 71, 142, 206
Turner, N., 33

U

United Nations preschool, 246
United Negro College Fund, 231

United Parcel Service, 208
United States Census Bureau, 215
United States Department of Education, 123, 124, 155, 239
University of Kansas, 91
University of North Carolina, Chapel Hill, 124
University of Utah, 109
Urban League, 110, 184

V

Vietnam, 149
Violence: and anger, 165; and being black in white world, 171–173; and building positive self-identity, 169–170; overview of, 147–150, 164–165; and parent power, 165–167; predisposition to, 167; and teaching by example, 168–189; teaching kids to avoid, 170–171; and teaching nonviolence, 168–170
Virginia, 189
Voting, 253–254
Voting Rights Act of 1965, 18

W

Walker, A., 189
Walker-Barnes, C., 166
Wells, I. B., 33
West, C., 111
"What's Going On?" (Gaye), 109
White schools, black children in, 131–132
Wilder, D., 229
Winfrey, O., 208
Work ethic, 72–77
Work habits, 36–37

Y

Yale University, 209
YMCA, 120, 210, 220
Young, A., 229
YWCA, 120, 191, 210